Endorsements

In this book, David Fletcher provides numerous illustrations and examples that reflect many years of experience as an executive pastor in a large church environment. He offers both principles of good stewardship and practical solutions to the myriad of challenges inherent in addressing the staffing and related compensation realities of churches of any size.

Dr. Gene A. Getz
Professor, Pastor, Author

Smart Money for Church Salaries *is an excellent and practical book that combines both a massive amount of research inside an engaging format. David Fletcher has delivered a brilliant work in writing the story of WheatFields Good News Church, using a story format and compiled case study method. This book will help you pay church staff with confidence, wisdom and good biblical stewardship. From charts and graphs to lots of examples, this book is a must for senior staff and church financial leaders. Now you can't say, "I didn't know."*

Dan Reiland
Executive Pastor, 12Stone Church, Lawrenceville, Georgia

Unfortunately, most churches and church leaders have very little training or context to lean on when it comes to setting salaries. In Smart Money for Church Salaries, *David Fletcher has done the body of Christ a big favor by producing a book that covers both the mythological and philosophical issues that every church with a paid staff must deal with. You may or may not agree with everything he suggests. That's not the issue. Grappling with these real-life issues is the issue. I recommend it to you and your team.*

Larry Osborne
Pastor and Author, Vista, California

Everyone, and I mean literally everyone will learn new information communicated in such a refreshing format. David Fletcher has brought together his decades of church leadership into this wise book. Smart Money for Church Salaries *is a gift to the Church. This book will change how you do church governance and compensation. I would highly recommend this to all senior church leadership. With this book, ignorance is no excuse. Brilliant. Helpful. Blessing.*

Sam Chand
Leadership Consultant and author of *Bigger Faster Leadership*

Fletch's mastery of all things related to church administration permeates every page of his latest book, Smart Money for Church Salaries. *This "one stop shopping" not only provides the means to reliably, fairly, and appropriately set church staff salaries, it is a comprehensive primer to navigate the legal labyrinth of church salary regulations and policies. His story telling approach is legendary Lencioni-style ... I couldn't put the book down. This is a "must" desk reference volume for every XP.*

Tim Beltz
Former XP, Church consultant, and author of
Charting the Course: Navigating the Legal Side of a Church Plant

Working with Executive Pastors across the country, one constant refrain is better discernment and knowledge around staff compensation issues, levels and processes. This tool will provide you with a handbook and reference point to make you better at working with your staff, your pastor and your board. You can move on to other issues to worry about.

Brad Leeper
President and Principal of Generis

Establishing a fair and legally compliant compensation structure for your church is critical—and it won't happen by accident! This book is just what you need for an engaging, deep dive into the key areas of compensation that your church must have soundly addressed. Bravo, XPastor, for offering this much-needed resource!

Dan Busby
President of the Evangelical Council for Financial Accountability

Smart Money for Church Salaries *covers so many important areas for churches and their Executive Pastors. David's thoughtful case study should be carefully analyzed to make sure every compensation factor is considered by church leaders.*

David Middlebrook
Founding Attorney, The Church Lawyers

All I know is there's a problem and there's no other resource like this. The story format and characters with names helps digest the material. Church leaders at the board level need this.

Eddie Park
Founder of HUG Church, Fullerton, California

SMART MONEY

FOR CHURCH SALARIES

NAVIGATE MURKY TOPICS
FROM TOP-LEVEL MEETINGS TO PUBLIC DISCUSSIONS

DAVID R. FLETCHER

XPastor
PRESS

Smart Money for Church Salaries
Published by XPastor Press, Austin, Texas

Printed in the United States of America
ISBN 978-0-9855559-2-4
Library of Congress Control Number: 2018910487

Credits
- Cover design and chapter title artwork by Nuclear Sugar.
- Typesetting by the Herringbone Bindery.
- Artwork of U.S. Currency—Images courtesy of the National Numismatic Collection, National Museum of American History, Smithsonian Institution. Photography by Godot13.
- Charts from "12 Salary Trends Every Church Leader Should Know" courtesy of Leadership Network, http://leadnet. org/salary/

Scripture quoted by permission. All scripture quotations, unless otherwise indicated, are taken from the NET Bible® copyright ©1996-2017 by Biblical Studies Press, L.L.C.
All rights reserved.

A case study is used for teaching purposes. It does not contain legal or professional counsel. WheatFields is a representative scenario, to be used as a springboard for application to your church. The decisions made in the case may not be pertinent to your situation. Work through the issues and get professional counsel on your situation as needed.

Acknowledgements

Great appreciation goes to Dan Busby, President of the Evangelical Council for Financial Accountability, Vonna Laue, Executive Vice President and Michael Martin, Vice President. The detailed review by Dan, Vonna and Michael ensured financial accuracy and tax compliance. Thanks also to Warren Bird, Vice President of Research, for being a reader.

Enhancing Trust

Thanks to readers of the manuscript ...

National Leaders
- Jac LaTour, writer, editor, storyteller
- Brad Leeper, President and Principal, Generis
- David Middlebrook, Founding Shareholder, The Church Lawyers
- Rob Toal, Matthew Branaugh, Jim Bolton, and Louise Ferrebee from Christianity Today's Church Law & Tax Team, who provided encouragement and support regarding the vision, direction, and distribution of this book
- Wade Wilkerson, Regional Manager, Insurance Plans, GuideStone Financial Resources

Pastors
- Mike Gould, Grace Covenant Church, Texas
- John Austin Helm, Teaching Pastor, California
- Russ Jacobson, Executive Pastor, Shepherd's Grove and The Hour of Power with Bobby Schuller, California
- Gavin Kajikawa, Executive Pastor, Lighthouse Community Church, California
- Eddie Park, Church Planter, HUG Church, California
- Jon Platek, Senior Pastor, The Grove Church, Minnesota
- Daniel Rolfe, Senior Pastor, Mountain Springs Church, Colorado
- Tim Samuel, Chief Financial Officer, Bridgeway Community Church, Maryland
- Warren Schuh, Executive Pastor Consultant, California
- Pat Wester, Executive Pastor, Autumn Ridge Church, Minnesota
- Jon Wright, Executive Pastor and Consultant

Table of Contents

- 1 -

SALARY ISSUES
IN THE CHURCH

Setting the Stage for Compensation

WheatFields Good News Church could be across the street or a few miles down the road from your church. Attendance is increasing, worship is thriving and ministry is booming. WheatFields is a dynamic ministry. As good as things look on the outside, though, there are problems on the inside. The salary budgets are in chaos. Though no one is yet admitting wrongdoing or breaking the law, there are strong suspicions that things are amiss.

Journey with Dan Black, a leader at WheatFields. Walk through back-room meetings and staff discussions. Step through the thinking of how to solve the compensation problem at his church. With Dan, analyze salaries and learn a maze of state and federal regulations. Your goal with Dan is to gather comparative salaries and create a compensation guide ... if only the path were that easy.

When working in the business world, Dan often cited the words of Jesus, "The gate is wide and the way is spacious that leads to problems." As Dan admits, "Okay, Jesus said 'leads to destruction,' but in business I changed that to 'problems.' I didn't want to scare my employees to death. We're not on the road to destruction." If Dan only knew the level of problems that he was about to get into.

The story of WheatFields Good News Church is a compiled case study. Several churches are melded in the case. WheatFields is a fictitious name, so as to protect the guilty and the innocent. It is compiled from different churches, as no church wants to publicize their confidential salary information—nor air their dirty laundry. The stories, though, are real. The facts come from churches just like yours.

This book is an insider's reveal of how to pay church staff. This is a top to bottom, step-by-step guide to ensuring equitable salaries and benefits in your church. The case allows this to happen in real time with deadlines, dialogue and delivery. WheatFields couples employee names with complete salary information, so that a picture emerges of the entire church staff.

Walking through the case allows in-depth learning, just as Jesus used life examples:

> At that time Jesus went through the grain fields on a Sabbath. His disciples were hungry, and they began to pick heads of wheat and eat them. But when the Pharisees saw this they said to him, "Look, your disciples are doing what is against the law to do on the Sabbath." Matthew 12:1-2

As you walk through WheatFields, the chances are almost 100% that you will catch a glimpse of issues at your church.

Benefit for Your Church

This book will help you address fairness and generosity in compensating your staff. Pastors and church staff often ask three pivotal questions about compensation:

- Am I being paid fairly?
- Is our church staff being underpaid or overpaid?
- Do we have a compensation plan that reflects the values of God's Kingdom?

When it comes to compensation, consider three scenarios that you may face at your church. These and others like them play out thousands of times each year in churches around the world:

> "Joe Fantastic" is interviewing to be your next preaching pastor. His resume and videos demonstrate enormous experience and competency. Joe could take your ministry to the next level—he is as good as it gets. Joe currently earns twenty-five percent more than your former preaching pastor. Your church desperately needs this guy. How are you going to decide what salary to offer Joe?

> "Pastor Faithful" has been on your staff for thirty-five years. Every year he received a cost of living increase and often a raise. Now, it seems that he may be overpaid. You are not sure. What criteria will you use to evaluate the compensation for this longtime staff pastor?

> "Suzie Potential" is interviewing for an open position but she lacks paid ministry experience. Her interviewing pizzazz is amazingly bested by her spiritual and intellectual capabilities. Suzie exudes the culture and mission of your church. She is "wow" spelled in both directions. Without a benchmark of prior full-time work, how are you going to decide what salary to offer Suzie?

These inane names illustrate different kinds of staff. Your church has staff that are *fantastic, faithful* and of *great potential.* How will you answer the salary questions? The challenge is to determine equitable and generous compensation. The budget of your church is finite. You only have so many dollars to work with each year. When it comes to church staff, wisdom dictates that you invest that money well in hardworking people of proven character. How much should you pay the senior pastor, pastors and support staff?

WheatFields Good News Church has similar issues. Senior Pastor Wilson is retiring and Steve Borneo has been developed as his replacement. Dan Black left his thriving business to become the church's first executive pastor. Mission Pastor Ed Baker hired on as a senior leader at a salary that he made while serving in a less-developed country. Ed would say, "Overseas I could afford house help. Living back home, I need help with my house payments." Other staff seem to be overpaid ... and the list continues.

Whether at your church or at WheatFields, the goal is to attract and keep gifted staff. You want to pay your staff fairly and generously—yet not overpay them. What will you do?

A Parable from Jesus

Compensation is an intersection of the business marketplace and church. Jesus frequently incorporated marketplace principles in His teaching. He knew that where people did business, there should be the working out of the Kingdom of God. Jesus told the parable of an unfaithful, yet clever, steward. He began by saying:

> There was a rich man who was informed of accusations that his manager was wasting his assets. So he called the manager in and said to him, 'What is this I hear about you? Turn in the account of your administration, because you can no longer be my manager.' Then the manager said to himself, 'What should I do, since my master is taking my position away from me? I'm not strong enough to dig, and I'm too ashamed to beg. Luke 16:1-3

Jesus concluded the challenging story:

> The one who is faithful in a very little is also faithful in much, and the one who is dishonest in a very little is also dishonest in much. If then you haven't been trustworthy in handling worldly wealth, who will entrust you with the true riches? And if you haven't been trustworthy with someone else's property, who will give you your own? No servant can serve two masters, for either he will hate the one and love the other, or he will be devoted to the one and despise the other. You cannot serve God and money. Luke 16:10-13

A principle from the parable is that church leaders must be trustworthy in handling worldly wealth, using it to serve God. Handling money often makes church leaders feel uneasy, as leaders want to serve God and not money. The dishonest manager in the parable was shrewd; in contrast, the church leader is called to be trustworthy. Whether your church budget is $500,000 or $5 million, your calling is to skillfully invest those funds in God's Kingdom. If a church leader fails to excellently handle a church budget, then why would God trust them with spiritual riches? We need *smart money* principles to lead our churches.

Principles of Smart Money

WheatFields needs biblical principles for paying their staff. Jesus used a *smart money* illustration from the marketplace to demonstrate spiritual truth:

> There was a landowner who planted a vineyard. He put a fence around it, dug a pit for its winepress, and built a watchtower. Then he leased it to tenant farmers and went on a journey ... When the harvest time was near, he sent his slaves to the tenants to collect his portion of the crop. But the tenants seized his slaves, beat one, killed another, and stoned another.

> But when the tenants saw the son, they said to themselves, 'This is the heir. Come, let's kill him and get his inheritance!'

> For this reason I tell you that the kingdom of God will be taken from you and given to a people who will produce its fruit. Matthew 21:33-35, 38, 43

A principle from the parable is: if a leader is not faithful, then God will take away what they have. If we fail to follow the principles of Jesus, then we are in peril. Often church leaders see the congregational donations as a secure and fixed source of income. Jesus has another point of view: if a leader fails his financial responsibility, then God may take away those financial resources. If leaders underpay or overpay church staff, they are in danger of violating the principles of Jesus.

Just as Jesus used the marketplace to enrich His teaching, today we can do the same. Investopedia claims to be "the world's leading source of financial content on the web, with more than 30 million unique visitors and 90 million page views each month."[1] They are a proven leader in their field. In an online article, Investopedia provides a marketplace definition:

What is 'Smart Money'

Smart money is the capital that is being controlled by institutional investors, market mavens and other financial professionals. Smart money was originally a gambling term that referred to the wagers made by gamblers with a track record of success. Usually these gamblers had

---

[1] Investopedia, *About Investopedia* (New York: Investopedia, 2018) available from https://www.investopedia.com/corp/about.aspx.

deep knowledge of the sport they were betting on or insider knowledge that the public would be unable to tap into. In the investing world, the implications are the same. The smart money in the market is perceived as being invested by people who have a better understanding of the market or access to information channels that a regular investor can't easily access.[2]

Smart money in the business world is capital that is sagely invested. Those sage investors are people with a deep knowledge of the issues. That knowledge comes from the hard work of learning from others. *Smart money* gains wisdom from valuable information channels and insider knowledge.

In a similar way, best-selling author Dave Ramsey has a *Smart Money Tour* on his website.[3] The tour teaches the principles of "the basics of budgeting, dumping debt, planning for retirement … Stop wondering where your money went and start telling it where to go!" These are information channels and insider knowledge for personal finances. This is *smart money* at home.

A Wikipedia article says about Ramsey: He "advocates a fiscally disciplined approach to personal and household finances, including the strict management of debt, and often feature a Christian perspective that reflects Ramsey's religious beliefs."[4] The key words are "fiscally disciplined" and "Christian perspective." Churches need Christ and discipline in the areas of church finances and staff compensation. This is *smart money* in the church.

Ramsey says "I've paid the 'stupid tax' (mistakes with dollar signs on the end) so hopefully some of you won't have to." He adds, "We define our success by the number of lives changed."[5] Ramsey's "stupid tax" can be avoided by learning from others who have more experience. Ramsey's goal of "lives changed" is a gospel-centric view of helping others. That view should pervade our church and how we pay our staff. *Smart money* in the church means learning from the stupid tax paid by others.

---

[2] Investopedia, *Smart Money* (New York: Investopedia, 2018) available from https://www. investopedia.com/terms/s/smart-money.asp.

[3] Dave Ramsey, *Smart Money Tour* (Brentwood, Tennessee: Ramsey Solutions) available from https://www.daveramsey.com/store/smart-money-tour/cSmartMoney.html.

[4] Wikipedia, *Dave Ramsey* (San Francisco: Wikimedia Foundation, page last edited April 21, 2018) available from https://en.wikipedia.org/wiki/Dave_Ramsey.

[5] Dave Ramsey, *How It Started* (Brentwood, Tennessee: Ramsey Solutions) available from https://www.daveramsey.com/careers/about-dave?snid=footer.company.about.

The words from Ramsey and Investopedia help form a definition of *Smart Money for Church Salaries*. With the teachings of Jesus and modern day insights, there are seven principles:

Elements of Smart Money for Church Salaries

1. **Invest** in staff salaries with skill, towards fulfillment of the church's vision statement, so that God will entrust spiritual riches.
2. **Handle** worldly wealth with excellence and trustworthiness, using money to serve God ... and not the other way around.
3. **Implement** a fair and generous compensation guide that neither underpays nor overpays.
4. **Follow** federal or state regulations with integrity.
5. **Learn** from information channels of those with deep knowledge of church finances, avoiding the "stupid tax."
6. **Be fruitful** lest God gives resources to others who will produce fruit.
7. **Find success** in the wise use of the finances that God provided as measured by changed lives.

With the elements of *Smart Money for Church Salaries*, your church can set the compensation of Joe Fantastic as your next preaching pastor. The salary of Pastor Faithful can be evaluated. A fair starting salary for Suzie Potential can be offered.

WheatFields needs to learn and apply the biblical principles of *Smart Money for Church Salaries* to their compensation crisis.

A Confusing Maze at WheatFields

WheatFields is like your church. Compensation gets complex the minute you investigate the regulations of the Internal Revenue Service and the Fair Labor Standards Act (FLSA). Salaries for pastors have unique challenges, such as the ministerial housing allowance and the Self Employed Contributions Act (SECA). Churches have managers who are exempt from the FLSA and support staff who are non-exempt.

There is a dizzying complication of terms, acronyms, rules and regulations. To follow the law and help church staff, all must be complied with. There is no easy fix with the myriad of issues. Senior pastors must be aware of the principles. Other staff must become localized experts in implementing them.

A few months ago, WheatFields had 1,500 in worship. With Steve Borneo, the new senior pastor, attendance grew to 2,025. The church staff consists of 35 pastors, directors and administrative staff. The weekday preschool at WheatFields has 600 students and 93 staff. Including the preschool, the salary budget is $4.39 million. The church leaders want

Dan Black, their newly-minted executive pastor, to move the church beyond the family business model of Pastor Wilson. Like you, Dan must navigate the challenging waters of church compensation.

Dan needs to learn the total cost of each employee. He needs to compare salaries to other churches and non-profits. Staff need to be sorted into ministerial, exempt and non-exempt classes. Dan needs to understand the unique issues of pastoral wages. Non-exempt staff must adhere to the FLSA. A compensation guide needs to be created, one that presents equitable minimum and maximum salaries.

Why Case Study?

As WheatFields illustrates, there is nothing simple about compensation. Learning the abstract principles of compensation can be as dry as dust. To foster learning, Jesus used stories to convey spiritual truths. In the business and academic world, those stories are called *case studies*.

A case presents a pertinent story and walks through how problems are solved. A case is more than just an example. It has depth and gives perspective on a situation:

> In business education, the case method has been closely identified with the Harvard Business School. Though the approach was not invented on the banks of the Charles River—witness the long Talmudic tradition—the Business School is well known for its commitment to an active, discussion-oriented learning mode, disciplined by case problems drawn from the complexity of real life.[6]

The parables of Jesus are miniature case studies. For example, in 240 words the parable of the good Samaritan has depth and complexity.

In church and in business, the case study method provides a rich soil for learning:

> The case method enables students to discover and develop their own unique framework for approaching, understanding, and dealing with business problems. To the extent that one can learn business practice in a classroom, and the limits are substantial, it achieves its goal efficiently.[7]

---

[6] Louis B. Barnes, C. Roland Christensen and Abby J. Hansen, *Teaching and the Case Method: Text, Cases, and Readings* (Boston: Harvard Business Review Press, 1994) p. 34.

[7] Barnes, Christensen and Hansen, p. 42.

The case is drawn from the complexities of church life. Consider part of Dan Black's first conversation with the Compensation Team:

> Attorney: "Dan, what are your recommendations for raises?"
>
> Dan: "Our staff is working hard. Attendance is up 500 people, 25%. Giving is up 7.9%. We need to give our staff raises."
>
> Attorney: "So let me ask my question again. What are *your* recommendations for raises?"
>
> Dan: "In the sheet that I handed out, I put 4%. In that WheatFields has never done annual reviews, I am recommending 4% raises across-the-board."
>
> Attorney: "So you want to do a merit increase for all staff? That won't encourage your best performers to excel even more. We need people who can scale with the growth of our church. Is that the best way to invest a raise number that is closing in on $200,000?"
>
> Dan: "Um, er, well ... wow. Is it getting hot in here? I wouldn't have done across-the-board raises in my business. Yet, our church has been doing raises this way for its entire history."
>
> Entrepreneur: "We thought that you were going to bring something new to the table, not this same ol', same ol'."

The backroom discussion shows the conversation as it happened. It gives an opportunity to learn and interact with the issues as they are discussed.

A case study is used for teaching purposes. It does not contain legal or professional counsel. WheatFields is a representative scenario, to be used as a springboard for application to your church. The decisions made in the case may or may not be pertinent to your situation. As needed, work through the issues and get professional counsel on your situation as needed.

How to Solve the Puzzle

WheatFields was missing a system for understanding and working with their staff. Churches of all sizes need a compensation guide. It doesn't matter whether there are four staff members at your church, 128 at WheatFields or 400 at an über-church. All churches can use the principles of *Smart Money for Church Salaries*.

A compensation guide segments staff into various divisions according to their job description. The first division of staff is ministry staff, the second division is exempt staff and the third division is non-exempt support staff. An example looks like this:

Ministry Staff—senior leadership, core team, pastors, assistant pastors, ministry directors.

Exempt Staff—directors, executive assistants.

Support Staff—assistant directors, coordinators, administrative assistants, receptionists, facility workers.

A student in XPastor's course, *Ops 101—Staffing*, created a guide for one department of five people:[8]

Finance and Office Salary Guide

	Quad 1	Quad 2	Quad 3	Quad 4
Finance Director	$58,076	$61,132	$64,350	$67,568
Finance Support p/t	$18,720	$20,280	$21,060	$22,113
Office Manager p/t	$8,917	$9,386	$9,880	$10,374
Receptionist p/t	$6,336	$6,669	$7,020	$7,371
Staff Support p/t	$11,856	$12,480	$14,560	$15,288

In hiring a new finance director, the guide provides ranges. If the applicant has moderate experience, the salary could be between Quads 1 and 2, which is $58,076 to $61,132. If a new finance director has broad experience and specific education that would greatly benefit the church, that new employee may be offered a salary in Quad 2 or 3, which is $61,132 and $64,350.

Next Steps With Dan
Walk with Dan Black through the compensation crisis at WheatFields. He will wrestle with complex issues, such as:

- What happens when an employee reaches their maximum salary?
- What determines when an assistant pastor becomes a pastor?
- Can directors legally be ministerial employees?

At the core, your church needs a compensation guide that fits your church staff and community. Churches should not underpay staff for their hard work, nor should they

---

[8] XPastor, *Operations 101* (Austin, Texas: XPastor) available from https://www.xpastor.org/courses/ops-101-staffing/.

be giving money away. Solid data, research and a good-faith compensation guide gives confidence in the salaries that are paid.

Your church could be near WheatFields in geography, history or current challenges. The ministry at WheatFields looks solid on the surface but serious issues are smoldering. Insiders know that something is wrong but do not know the details ... yet.

Join Dan Black on his trek through the maze of compensation issues. From confidential discussions to staff meetings, get an insider's perspective on the process of solving the compensation problem at WheatFields. Slog with Dan in a mire of initials and acronyms—FICA, SECA, UBIT, COBRA. Arrive with him at sound decisions that treat well the staff of WheatFields.

Walk through the process of understanding the compensation problem. Analyze salaries, gather comparative salaries and create a compensation guide. Don't pay the stupid tax of ignoring federal and state rules and regulations. Follow solid principles of *Smart Money for Church Salaries*.

Toolbox

Principles

The Principles section distills the chapter into core ideas. The narrative of WheatFields provides a rich tapestry of inner thoughts, closed-door discussions and staff interaction. Without the narrative, the principles can be dry and lifeless. The compiled case study animates the principles, bringing them to life in real-time.

Elements of Smart Money for Church Salaries

1. **Invest** in staff salaries with skill, towards fulfillment of the church's vision statement, so that God will entrust spiritual riches.
2. **Handle** worldly wealth with excellence and trustworthiness, using money to serve God ... and not the other way around.
3. **Implement** a fair and generous compensation guide that neither underpays nor overpays.
4. **Follow** federal or state regulations with integrity.
5. **Learn** from information channels of those with deep knowledge of church finances, avoiding the "stupid tax."
6. **Be fruitful** lest God gives resources to others who will produce fruit.
7. **Find success** in the wise use of the finances that God provided as measured by changed lives.

Core Concepts

1. Jesus was *the* master teacher. Learn from His marketplace stories, parables and examples. Follow the example of Jesus and litter your teaching with marketplace stories. Your church members fill up their cars with gasoline, get their hair cut and go to the supermarket. Illustrate the principles of the Kingdom of Jesus from common places of business.
2. A budget ought to be the fleshing out of your church vision statement. In both organization and spending, your budget should point toward your vision and mission. Where you spend your cash signals your true values. The vision statement may be theory but where you spend your money is reality.
3. Your church has staff that are fantastic, faithful and of great potential. The goal is to determine equitable and generous compensation.
4. Churches often let issues smolder. Inequity in pay can smolder for years under the surface. Though the ill feelings may not often be seen, your staff may feel cheated and poorly used.

Steps

The Steps section is your recipe to create a compensation guide. The section will assist you by asking questions to solve the maze of compensation issues at your church.

❑ Address Common Salary Questions

Church staff often ask three questions about compensation:

- Am I being paid fairly?
- Is our church staff being underpaid or overpaid?
- Do we have a compensation plan that reflects the values of God's Kingdom?

You need cogent answers to these questions. Since you are reading *Smart Money for Church Salaries*, one answer is, "We're working on it right now."

❑ Evaluate Your Current Compensation System

Remember that *no method* is itself a method, albeit a bad one. *No method* means that you have stumbled backwards into paying staff. You may have adopted unhealthy cultural values.

- Do you pay well enough to keep fantastic staff?
- What is your process for evaluating longtime, faithful staff that may be earning too much?
- How do you set the salary for a person of great potential but who lacks full-time ministry experience?

❑ Consider Cultural and Biblical Values

- The Puritans are attributed to have said: "We keep our pastors poor and God keeps them humble." Have you equated poverty with spirituality? Some large churches subscribe to the adage: "We pay low salaries because it's a privilege to work here." Are these thoughts biblical or cultural?
- Some in church leadership reason: "The people in our congregation work fifty hours a week and their ministry is on top of that. Our staff should do the same." Is this biblical or cultural? Why do many in your church work fifty hours a week?
- Reflect on the teachings of Jesus about money. Add in thoughts from the apostle Paul. Do your values reflect generosity, shrewdness, good stewardship, wariness, fruitfulness, fairness and love?

Questions to Consider

The Questions section is ideal for group discussion on the concepts of *Smart Money for Church Salaries*.

One

Consider the parable of the landowner (Matthew 21), the pearl of great price (Matthew 13) or the phrase "good measure, pressed down ..." (Luke 6). Jesus often used marketplace examples in His teaching. What did Jesus accomplish by using such parables and examples? How often did Jesus talk about money and commerce business to demonstrate greed versus the values of His Kingdom?

_____
_____
_____
_____
_____
_____

Two

The seven elements of *Smart Money for Church Salaries* are: Investing, Handling Implementing, Following, Learning, Being Fruitful and Finding Success. Which one or two are most important for you?

_____
_____
_____
_____
_____
_____

Three

It was reported about WheatFields that, "No one is yet admitting wrongdoing or breaking the law ... there are strong suspicions that things are amiss." Why do you think that issues often smolder in churches? Why do some issues take so long to receive proper attention from church leaders?

_____
_____
_____
_____
_____

Tools

This section provides you with material that was introduced or finalized in this chapter. These items are also available at https://www.xpastor.org/smart. The password for this page is: smart money.

Example of Staff Classification

Ministry Staff—senior leadership, core team, pastors, assistant pastors, ministry directors

Exempt Staff—directors, executive assistants

Support Staff—assistant directors, coordinators, administrative assistants, receptionists, facility workers

Your Church Staff Classifications

List the people in each category:

Ministry Staff

_____
_____
_____
_____
_____
_____

Exempt Staff

_____
_____
_____
_____
_____
_____

Support Staff

_____
_____
_____
_____
_____
_____

Sample Salary Guide

By the end of *Smart Money for Church Salaries*, you will construct a table like this:

Finance and Office Salary Guide

	Quad 1	Quad 2	Quad 3	Quad 4
Finance Director	$58,076	$61,132	$64,350	$67,568
Finance Support p/t	$18,720	$20,280	$21,060	$22,113
Office Manager p/t	$8,917	$9,386	$9,880	$10,374
Receptionist p/t	$6,336	$6,669	$7,020	$7,371
Staff Support p/t	$11,856	$12,480	$14,560	$15,288

Terms

Become familiar with these significant acronyms used in church compensation:

- ACA—Affordable Care Act. The goal of this act is to "Make affordable health insurance available to more people; Expand the Medicaid program to cover all adults with income below 138% of the federal poverty level; Support innovative medical care delivery methods designed to lower the costs of health care generally."[9]
- COBRA—Consolidated Omnibus Budget Reconciliation Act for the continuation of health coverage. The Department of Labor defines COBRA further on their website.[10]
- DOL—Department of Labor. Their mission is "To foster, promote, and develop the welfare of the wage earners, job seekers, and retirees of the United States; improve working conditions; advance opportunities for profitable employment; and assure work-related benefits and rights."[11]
- ECFA—Evangelical Council for Financial Accountability. Their mission is to "Provide accreditation to leading Christian nonprofit organizations that faithfully demonstrate compliance with established standards for financial accountability, transparency, fundraising, and board governance."[12]
- ERISA—Employee Retirement Income Security Act of 1974. The Department of Labor says, "ERISA is a federal law that sets minimum standards for most voluntarily established pension and health plans in private industry to provide protection for individuals in these plans." They add, "In general, ERISA does not cover group

---

[9] U.S. Centers for Medicare & Medicaid Services, *Affordable Care Act (ACA)*, available from https://www.healthcare.gov/glossary/affordable-care-act/.

[10] U.S. Department of Labor, Employee Benefits Security Administration, *COBRA Continuation Health Coverage FAQs*, available from https://www.dol.gov/agencies/ebsa/about-ebsa/our-activities/resource-center/faqs/cobra-continuation-health-coverage-compliance.

[11] U.S. Department of Labor, *Our Mission*, available from https://www.dol.gov/general/about-dol/mission.

[12] Evangelical Council for Financial Accountability, *About ECFA*, available from http://www.ecfa.org/Content/About.

health plans established or maintained by governmental entities, churches for their employees, or plans which are maintained solely to comply with applicable Workers' Compensation, unemployment, or disability laws."[13]

- FICA—Federal Insurance Contributions Act. The Social Security Administration has an *Infographic* on FICA.[14]
- FLSA—Fair Labor Standards Act. The Department of Labor has a *Reference Guide*.[15]
- SECA—Self Employed Contributions Act. IRS *Publication 517* outlines Social Security for religious workers.[16]
- UBIT—Unrelated Business Income Tax. The IRS defines the role of UBIT.[17]

---

[13] U.S. Department of Labor, *Health Plans & Benefits: ERISA*, available from https://www.dol.gov/general/topic/health-plans/erisa.

[14] U.S. Social Security Administration, *What is FICA?* March, 2017, available from https://www.ssa.gov/thirdparty/materials/pdfs/educators/What-is-FICA-Infographic-EN-05-10297.pdf.

[15] U.S. Department of Labor, Wage and Hour Division, *Handy Reference Guide to the Fair Labor Standards Act*, revised September, 2017, available from https://www.dol.gov/whd/regs/compliance/hrg.htm.

[16] U.S. Department of Treasury, Internal Revenue Service, *Publication 517, Social Security and Other Information for Members of the Clergy and Religious Workers*, December 29, 2017, available from https://www.irs.gov/pub/irs-pdf/p517.pdf.

[17] U.S. Department of Treasury, Internal Revenue Service, *Unrelated Business Income Tax*," last reviewed or updated April 3, 2018, available from https://www.irs.gov/charities-non-profits/unrelated-business-income-tax.

- 2 -

THE COMPENSATION CRISIS

Color Commentary about WheatFields

WheatFields Good News Church of south Orange County, California, may have once been in actual wheat fields and whence its eponymous name. Thirty years ago, in a semi-rural area, Pastor Wilson began the church with five families. The church named itself *WheatFields* and the neighborhood around it adopted that name. As the city incorporated itself twenty years ago, it nearly took the name *WheatFields*. At a city council meeting, another city name was selected at the last moment.

In terms of demographics, the church is in an upscale neighborhood of an urbanized area. WheatFields is not in the big city but many of its members daily commute to it. The people of WheatFields have a variety of professions, from managers to graduate school professors to entrepreneurs. Its members come from many races and nationalities.

A "Family Business"

Pastor Wilson has run the church as preacher, chairman of the elders, executive pastor, hospital chaplain ... essentially chief cook and bottle washer. Pastor Wilson, as he likes to be called, is the go-to man for everything and every decision. The church's organization chart has a hierarchy of departmental leaders. Everyone knows, however, that all staff essentially report to the pastor.

As Pastor Wilson says, "I run our church like a family business." When Pastor Wilson says, *family business*, he emphasizes the word *family*.
Pastor Wilson likes to say:

> "Let me tell you about our *family* business. I created the logo of WheatFields on my first computer in 1988, when we had just five families. That's how we started our church vision, with *Family*. Then came *Mission* and *Worship*."

"In thirty years, the farmland has disappeared from around our church. Houses and businesses went from sparsely spaced to tightly packed. Schools and hospitals began as small, one-story buildings and morphed into tall landmarks for our region. We grew from five families to 1,500 adults in worship each Sunday."

"Now, our pastoral leadership has eleven pastors and nine directors with a salary budget of almost $1.2 million. 108 people are support staff and preschool teachers with a budget of over $2.5 million. Our huge weekday preschool gives Christian education to 600 children from ninety of the best full-time teachers in the region. And we treat our staff well; we spend $725,000 in benefits."

"All in all, we have 128 church and preschool employees, $4.44 million in salary and benefits, with total donations and tuition income of $8.5 million. That's some *family* business!"

During the week, the campus is flooded with preschoolers and parents. On Sundays, the grounds are awash in babies, toddlers, elementary age children and youth. There is no class space for adults on Sunday morning—just for kids and teens. Family for WheatFields means kids, and lots of them. WheatFields vibrantly lives out its vision of *Family, Mission and Worship*. This is an exciting place to be.

The family business has few rules and little policy. For a number of years, they did not use time cards for hourly workers. Fear of a payroll audit forced the church to start using time cards, among a few other HR practices. Pastor Wilson says that "they mostly follow or try to follow state and federal regulations." Some elders are concerned about the risks that the family business takes and possible violations of the law.

What Pastor Wilson lacks in sermonic excellence, he makes up for in personal warmth. His preaching tends to be shorter than his contemporaries with longer stories and anecdotes; the application is indirect. The key in the worship services is the music and liturgy. There is no church nearby that has as exciting and innovative worship as WheatFields.

Pastor Wilson's Retirement

At one elder meeting, seemingly out of thin air, Pastor Wilson floated an idea. With eyes a little more tired than usual, his face creased with stress lines, Pastor Wilson said:

"I may want to retire in a few years."

The room fell silent and no one moved. With a faltering voice, Pastor Wilson continued:

> "I thought that it was going to be easier than this but I'm finding it rather hard. Please bear with me."

A few nodded in nervous support. Pastor Wilson took a good two minutes to regain composure and continued:

> "Well, I was a little choked up there, but let me get to this. Soon, it will be time to turn over the leadership to a new senior pastor and then let him carry this enormous weight. Some of you have concerns over our leadership structure and the toll that it's taking on my health. I'm ready to see the finish line for my *paid* ministry role at WheatFields."

With words of thanks and appreciation, the stunned elders slowly began to respond to Pastor Wilson's monumental announcement. Unsaid was the subtext that Pastor Wilson appeared to recognize that WheatFields had outgrown the family business model.

The board began to discuss the future. With the blessing of Pastor Wilson, the elders organized a six-person Transition Planning Team. The team would report back in two months. The Chair began the first meeting:

> "Our transition team will meet every week and we'll do our best to have a plan ready in two months. We're pleased that Pastor Wilson is on this team and look forward to fruitful discussions with our founding pastor. We owe so much to our beloved pastor."

> "This team is comprised of elders and other congregational leaders. Men and women are around this table to work with Pastor Wilson to create an acceptable roadmap for the future. This will be challenging work and we all want to honor our founding pastor. Yes, we have some issues that need a solution, but those pale in comparison to our strengths."

> "Now, let me cast some vision and see if it connects with you. The next senior pastor of WheatFields needs to understand our culture and ethos. That's going to take time, probably a few years. We don't want to bring someone in who will change the spiritual DNA of our church."

> "I'm putting on the table that we need to hire an associate pastor of teaching in the next four months. Let's grow that new staff member into our next senior pastor. Then, at the right time, our next senior pastor will come from within our staff."

Over the next weeks, the first part of the transition plan was agreed upon. It called for immediately beginning a search for an associate pastor of teaching. The main qualification for the new role was excellence in biblical exposition. The new associate pastor would have four years to become equipped, ready to be WheatFields' next senior pastor.

The second part of the transition plan centered on the creation of a new church organizational model. The new structure would have the senior pastor as the directional leader and an executive pastor as the organizational leader. Pastor Wilson endorsed the new structure. "Yes, this is what we need ... and it will ease my transition. Let's do it," he said.

The team presented their *Four-Year Transition Plan* to the Elder Board. There was rapid consensus on hiring a teaching pastor. While some wanted a faster transition than four years, others saw the wisdom of training a new pastor in the culture of WheatFields.

Pastor Wilson Slows the Transition

Things changed when the Transition Team presented the new organizational structure to the elders. While the Chair was mid-stream explaining the envisioned organizational structure, Pastor Wilson interrupted in an uncharacteristic manner:

> "I do have a few comments."

> "I thoroughly endorse hiring an associate pastor of teaching to replace me in four years. But I've been doing some thinking about the executive pastor role ..."

Pastor Wilson went through the history of the church, beginning with the five families and recounting the name of every staff member over the years.

> "In summary, I'd like to suggest that the church wait to hire the executive pastor until I retire. I'd like to continue to run the church until then. You can't teach an old dog new tricks."

There was a sigh from two elders. They thought, "We can't say it, but we may be at risk in some of our practices. We need change, but it will have to wait four years. Who can oppose the founding pastor of WheatFields?" Pastor Wilson's motion carried.

It was four years ago that the church implemented the transition plan. WheatFields hired Steve Borneo as the Associate Pastor of Teaching. The congregation quickly fell in love with this young and talented communicator. Steve went from teaching twice a year, to once a quarter, to once a month. In the last year of Pastor Wilson's tenure, Steve was teaching two out of every four weeks.

It was true that Pastor Wilson did not want to work with an executive pastor. Yet, he was true to his word about having the position in the future. Pastor Wilson frequently spoke about the need for a future XP and put in motion the steps to make the position possible. He asked that the church constitution be amended, recommending that the future executive pastor be voted on by the congregation. When asked about that, Pastor Wilson said:

> "Not many churches vote in their XP, but I think it fits our church and community. After I retire, things need to be done differently. The future will be here and we'll need a new staff structure. That XP will need the full support of the congregation, so let's vote on him up front."

The constitutional change took six months to work its way through the needed steps. A year before Pastor Wilson's retirement, the congregation voted 99% in favor of the change.

End of the 4-Year Transition

Pastor Wilson retired on Sunday, January 7, 2018. On that day, the church held a grand celebration of his thirty years of ministry. Pastor Wilson gave a long retelling of the history of WheatFields and summarized his thoughts to the congregation:

> "Sally and I have been here for thirty good years. When we came, our community had just a few houses. We began the church with just five families. Now we're 1,500 in worship each week. You've been so kind in your words of appreciation for what God has done in the church through everyone's hard work."

> "When my friend Gene Getz retired as senior pastor at Fellowship Bible Church in Dallas, he stayed in the church. It worked because when someone would ask Gene about a leadership decision, he would say, "Go talk to the elders, don't talk to me." That's what I'm going to do. I want to stay and retire here. But my days of being the head of this family are over. Don't ask me about leadership issues!"

> "It is my final wish as senior pastor that the church vote on the new senior pastor and executive pastor today, the very day of my retirement party. Nothing could be better than for this church to have zero transition. As I retire, I want to give this church into capable hands."

Associate Pastor of Teaching Steve Borneo was voted in as the new senior pastor with 95% of the vote. Pastor Wilson complimented Steve on the vote, saying, "There will always be 5% who can't agree on what they ate for breakfast. Don't worry about it."

Steve Borneo wanted Dan Black to be the executive pastor of WheatFields. Having a friendship that went back fifteen years, there was a good history of communication and trust. When Steve was publicly named a candidate for the senior pastor role at WheatFields, he approached Dan:

> Steve: "What are you doing spinning your wheels in your family business? You're a builder, not a maintainer. Sell this shop to your brother and come work with me."

> Dan: "What? Me? A pastor? I never thought I'd do anything like that with my life. I'm not qualified!"

> Steve: "Your strong business skills are exactly what WheatFields needs in an executive pastor. You've been an elder for years and can do the ministry part of the job. Remember, it's because of you that I came to WheatFields four years ago! You owe me."

With these and other words, Steve lured Dan away from his prosperous business to become the first executive pastor at WheatFields.

There could not have been a more popular candidate for executive pastor than Dan Black. Everyone knew Dan from his role as an elder, Chair of the Search Team that brought Steve and his many other ministry activities. For most people, it seemed normal that Dan was elected with 99% of the vote. Pastor Wilson commented at his retirement party, saying, "I guess the congregation really wants things to be on a better organizational footing. Maybe I was wrong in not going with the position earlier ..."

From the first Sunday in January to Palm Sunday, church attendance grew by 525 people. The 1,100 seat worship center averaged 90% capacity and an overflow room began to show a video of the services. The crowds topped 3,500 people in four Easter services. The church had never seen such growth—Steve's preaching, coupled with outstanding worship, was a formula for growth.

This growth in attendance put pressure on the staff. Children's classrooms neared or exceeded maximum capacity. Discipleship groups filled with many new Christ followers. Welcoming and directing the visitors became a challenge. These issues fell to Dan, the newly-made executive pastor.

Steve avoided tactical discussions on the growth problems. Though retired, Pastor Wilson urged him: "Get involved in the details. You're the leader now." Steve thought otherwise. He wanted to preach and cast vision—he trusted Dan to lead the organization. The plan of the Transition Team called for a new organizational structure with a highly competent staff, one that would allow the church to double and triple in attendance. Steve wanted to stay at the visionary and strategic levels, not to micro-manage the staff as Pastor Wilson had. He was excited that the Transition Team had seen the need four years before for an executive pastor. Now, Dan Black was the man to handle the organizational challenges of church growth.

Compensation Team Meeting

Dan held Finance Team meetings in January and February. Each one was more exciting than the last. At the March meeting he said:

> "Attendance is up 525 people and each week it continues to increase. The video overflow is fine but we may add a third service soon. We might experiment with that this summer."

> "Donations are up 7.9% from our budgeted amounts. We currently have a cash surplus of $552,097. Next to no churches get such a bump in giving with a new senior pastor, but we have. This is one for the textbooks."

> "These are easy days on the Finance Team. If I can get a preliminary ministry budget drafted, we will be well on our way to final budget for the May elder meeting. I meet with the Compensation Team next week to work on the salary budget."

Dan thought, "This job has its challenges but it isn't that hard."

Dan's intuition, however, sensed that trouble was brewing before his first Compensation Team meeting in April. WheatFields Church had never done annual reviews, so there were no benchmarks for merit increases. He and Steve talked about the percentage of raises for various staff, but their discussion was fruitless. With ministry so busy, Dan failed to prepare well for the April Compensation Team meeting.

"From a financial capacity perspective, it looks like creating a salary budget will never be easier. With the staff working so hard, and with the church having the cash, I need to present a list of raises," Dan mused to himself. From a criteria-based quality perspective, Dan felt uneasy. "I'm not sure about the raises, it's all moving so fast. Perhaps we can get a raise pool approved this month and then could work out the details next month."

The Compensation Team was comprised of talented and opinionated leaders—an attorney, a certified public account, an entrepreneur and Dan. With all the ministry growth, Dan's preparation consisted of a lone sheet with a summary of church wages. Dan began the meeting by passing around printed copies:

4% Across-the-Board Raises

Area	$$
Pastors & Directors	$1,220,392
Support Staff	$2,471,357
Benefits Budget	$721,572
Total	**$4,413,321**
4% Raises	**$176,532**

Immediately after passing out copies to each member, Dan regretted putting down the words "across-the-board raises." The discussion was polite but simmering with anxiety:

Attorney: "Dan, what are your recommendations for raises?"

Dan: "Our staff is working hard. Attendance is up 500, or rather 525 people. Giving is up 7.9%. We need to give our staff raises."

Attorney: "So let me ask my question again. What are *your* recommendations for raises?"

Dan: "In the chart that I handed out, I put 4%. Since WheatFields has never done annual reviews, I'm recommending 4% across-the-board raises."

Entrepreneur: "Checking the math on my phone, I get the amount of $176,533 in raises. But we should take the benefits expense out of that. I mean, medical insurance isn't tied to raises but retirement benefits are. So that brings the number to, well, let's see here ... I brought my own recommendation and I labeled the increases as a raise pool. Here, let me pass this around."

Entrepreneur's Table of Raises

Area	$$
Pastors & Directors	$1,220,392
Support Staff	$2,471,357
FICA	$225,576
403B Retirement Plan	$77,543
Total	**$3,994,868**
4% Raise Pool	**$159,795**

Dan: "I like your format but our totals are within about $16k of each other. Let's remember too, that all these numbers are provisional. I really haven't examined the salaries yet."

CPA: "Do you know what inflation was last year? Have you factored that in?"

Dan: "Somewhere between 2% and 2.3%."

CPA: "Let's just call it 2%. You want to do a 2% inflation adjustment and that *may* make sense. You *also* want to do a 2% merit increase for *all* staff? That won't encourage your best performers to excel. We need people who can *scale* with the growth of our church. Is that the best way to invest a number that is *closing in* on $200,000?"

Dan rarely liked it when people emphasized certain words like that. It meant that he was in trouble.

Dan: "Um, er, well, wow ... it is getting hot in here? Our church has been doing raises this way for its entire history."

Entrepreneur: "We thought that you were going to bring something new to the table, not this same ol', same ol'."

At this point, Dan saw that the sharks had circled around him. These folks were old friends but they were not going to let him get by with shoddy thinking. Dan had trapped himself. He just admitted that he wanted to do something in the church that he never would have done in the business world.

It was time for Dan to be the shark and probe the Compensation Team:

Dan: "All right, you bring up a valid point. In my business experience for the last thirty years, I never gave across-the-board raises. I've been on the Elder Board for some time but never on the Compensation Team. I've been looking through what I could find of your records but I don't see any prior recommendations on the methodology of raises. What have you discussed?"

Entrepreneur: "Hmmm ... hmmm. That's a perceptive question. We never settled on a process."

CPA: "We were always fighting with the senior pastor who just wanted to give everybody big raises. Our job was to keep raises at a manageable level. We were too busy arm wrestling Pastor Wilson to do any real analysis of our compensation system."

Attorney: "We used to get all the proposed salary budgets just a week before the elder meeting. If truth be told, and I'm reticent to say so, we were a rubber stamp for Pastor Wilson. I mean, he was our founding pastor and all that. There wasn't any real interaction with each and every salary. We just did across-the-board raises. Now, your suggestion of doing the same ol', same ol' hit a sore spot for this team."

Entrepreneur: "I apologize for that verbal jab. I was feeling the sting of our own inactivity. I'm sorry ..."

Though the Compensation Team was on the defensive, they could respond to such questions with a few of their own:

Attorney: "Let's ask some conceptual questions. Are we even paying our staff a fair wage? What if we're paying some people too much? Could some of our low wages explain why a few key staff have left in the last four years?"

CPA: "What are fair wages for churches in our community? Or our state? Are we competitive with other non-profits?"

Entrepreneur: "I'm more concerned about attracting top talent and keeping them once they're here. Across-the-board raises just don't do that. Perhaps we should pay bonuses this year. A New York Times article in February, 2018 said that bonuses are becoming a common practice in business."[18]

CPA: "But we've never given bonuses before. Should a church really do that? Wouldn't that look corporate and too much like a business? And I hate using the word, *corporate*. It makes it seem like there's a disjuncture between good business practices and what we should do as a church."

---

[18] Patricia Cohen, *Where Did Your Pay Raise Go? It May Have Become a Bonus* (The New York Times, February 10, 2018) available from https://www.nytimes.com/2018/02/10/business/economy/bonus-pay.html.

Now Dan brought out the white flag and called a truce to the sparring:

> Dan: "Look, you guys got me when I recommended across-the-board raises. That was my bad. You're right, I would never have done across-the-board raises in my business. And $180,000 isn't chump change. We need to invest it well in our staff."

> CPA: "We're with you, and, to be fair, some for-profits do across-the-board raises and they seem to prosper."

> Dan: "But we, as the Compensation Team, need to up our game. We've never done a compensation survey. There needs to be a thorough analysis of our salaries, classifications and systems for raises."

> Attorney: "That's right, as a team we're in the mud. Let's move on from the past and do the right thing, beginning right now."

> Dan: "Great. Let's adjourn early and come back in three weeks. I'll create a draft compensation guide and we can review it then."

> Entrepreneur: "Three weeks! Really? Dan, are you sure? That's a lot of work ... but it does need to be done before we present the salary budget to the Elder Board."

Everyone was happy about adjourning early, except Dan. He wondered if he had made a mistake. He had three weeks to draft a compensation guide for all 128 staff! "I must be crazy," Dan concluded.

Debrief with the Coach

After the meeting, Dan called his coach. Being a new XP, he found someone outside of his church to be a sounding board. Dan needed someone with an objective perspective on strategic issues. His coach had been an executive pastor for many years and had a keen perspective on church ministry. Dan recounted the Compensation Team discussion to his coach.

The coach said, "The context for making a decision can be as important as the decision itself." He went on to explain that there are three contexts for a church compensation guide:

A New Church

"It might seem crazy to have a compensation guide for a three person staff—the pastor, bookkeeper and administrative assistant. While initially a short list, each new staff member easily can be added."

A Church with no Guide

"This is an enormous challenge. For years, staff may have been paid fairly or unfairly. There may be disparity in titles, roles and pay. The lines may be blurred between exempt and non-exempt staff. The church may be violating the Fair Labor Standards Act or other rules."

Church Revising Its Guide

"Revisions to existing guides are relatively easy if the categories of staff and pay scales are solid. New salary numbers can be researched and discussed. A church should review its guide every three years."

The coach concluded, "You have the hardest challenge. You are a large church with thirty years of history ... and no compensation guide. You need to bring a fair system without hurting good people along the way." Dan hung up the phone and thought, "Can it really be 'the hardest challenge?' Can it be that hard to create a church compensation guide for WheatFields?"

The more that Dan thought about it, the more he realized that it *was* a challenging scenario. "WheatFields has eleven pastors, nine directors, eighteen support staff and ninety staff in the preschool—$4.44 million in salaries and benefits. I have three weeks to sort out salaries, examine classifications of all employees and create a sane system for raises."

The staff at WheatFields was happy, enjoying the recent and rapid growth. They were working harder than ever. Raises were generally announced in the new budget year, which began on June 1. If Dan delayed raises, that would be a bad sign in his first year as executive pastor. Dan needed to create WheatFields' first compensation guide—and fast. Time was of the essence for this project.

"After just four months on the job, I may be having my first ministry crisis," Dan thought. "The salary issue will touch the Compensation Team and Elder Board. It will impact every staff member and their families. Everyone's perception of me in this new role hinges on this compensation study. The records are a mess and there is poor history. Yes, this is a crisis!"

New Executive Pastor Dan Black wondered if this compensation crisis was a harbinger of things to come. Would his church career be one of jumping from one impossible task to the next?

Toolbox

Principles

1. Let's review the first of seven elements of *Smart Money for Church Salaries*:

    > **Invest** in staff salaries with skill, towards fulfillment of the church's vision statement, so that God will entrust spiritual riches.

    Invest is the right verb. A church budget should not be unintentional. It takes skill to direct, and re-direct, money towards fulfilling a church vision.

2. God wants to entrust your church with spiritual riches, as seen in changed lives and impact in your community. Scripture poses the question: "Why should I entrust true spiritual riches if you are faithless in financial matters?"

3. The *Law of Unintended Effects* is outcomes not foreseen when you took action. This happens in churches, as it did at the WheatFields' Compensation Team meeting. While often the unintended effect is challenging or painful, a great deal of good can come when the effect is handled in an appropriate fashion.

4. A good coach or consultant can leverage leadership, a sounding board to challenging issues. We all need someone to give an objective perspective on strategic issues. Find a mentor who has broad knowledge and experience in leading the church.

Core Concepts

1. Few people are privy to Compensation Team discussions. Learn from the WheatFields' meeting. As salaries and benefits often comprise 50% of a church budget, those discussions can become rough and tumble. The stakes are high and the implications are significant.

2. A church is a family but not a family business. Most churches incorporate to protect liability, otherwise each member could be a party to a lawsuit against the church. As Peter Drucker said, "The function of management in a church is to make the church more churchlike, not more businesslike. It's to allow you to do what your mission is."[19] Churches often grow into large enterprises but need to keep the warmth of a family.

3. Each church has a unique history and spiritual DNA. Those are two key ingredients in culture. The gospel is enacted differently in every church. As Sam Chand wrote:

---

[19] Bob Buford, *Halftime: Changing Your Game Plan from Success to Significance* (Zondervan; revised and updated edition, 2011) p. 200.

"Culture—not vision or strategy—is the most powerful factor in any organization. It determines the receptivity of staff and volunteers to new ideas, unleashes or dampens creativity, builds or erodes enthusiasm, and creates a sense of pride or deep discouragement about working or being involved there."[20]

4. Church growth brings complexity in personnel, compensation and laws, rules and regulations. Preschools, day care facilities and schools can be an extension of your ministry but also bring complex issues. About 500 years before Jesus, Heraclitus wrote, "Ever-newer waters flow on those who step into the same rivers." You can't twice step in the river at the same place, as the river has moved on. The old adage says, "same-ol', same-ol' won't work." Churches need to constantly adapt their orthopraxy: Orthodoxy is *right doctrine* and orthopraxy is *right organization*. Staff support systems need to grow with the church.

5. Senior pastor transitions are challenging and need careful planning. Founding pastors can have a difficult time letting go of responsibilities and power. Read a case study on the transition from Gene Getz to Jeff Jones.[21] Read Jeff's lessons learned in his article, *Succession Thoughts*.[22] Hiring a senior leader from outside your church can bring new vision and direction. Hiring an insider can enhance your church's culture.

---

[20] Samuel R. Chand, *Culture Trumps Vision* (Dallas: Leadership Network, June 23, 2015) available from leadnet.org/culture-trumps-vision/, adapted from Chapter 1 of *Cracking Your Church's Culture Code* by Samuel R. Chand.

[21] David R. Fletcher, *Exit of a Founding Pastor* (Austin, Texas: XPastor) available from https://www.xpastor.org/strategy/10-year-planning/exit-of-a-founding-pastor-jeff-jones-slated-to-replace-gene-getz/.

[22] Jeff Jones, *Succession Thoughts* (Austin, Texas: XPastor) available from https://www.xpastor.org/strategy/10-year-planning/succession-thoughts/.

Steps

❑ Gather Insider History

Defining culture can be like nailing Jell-O® to the wall. Before you dig into compensation, thoroughly understand the culture of your church. An adage says, *past performance is an indicator of future outcomes.* If you know of past issues, you can put an action plan in place to chart a new history. Talk face-to-face with the insiders of your church. Have a meal together to understand not just the facts but the context and feelings behind those facts:

- When and why was the church begun?
- Who were and are the key leaders?
- What influences have shaped your church to be what it is today?

Knowing the insider history will help you avoid past pitfalls. When someone says, "We have tried that before," you can give a knowledgeable answer. A good response can then be, "That was then and the world is more complicated now ... let's examine new solutions to our problem."

❑ Evaluate Your Church

Once you have a firm grip on the history of your church, you can evaluate its current status. Do not focus on compensation issues here. Look at overall ministry. Examine your mission statement. Ask for stories of ministry from key leaders. Those stories should exemplify the implementation of the mission statement.

- What are your church's strengths in people, program and culture?
- What are current ministry limitations, concerns and issues? What ministry opportunities and challenges are on the horizon?
- Describe in detail how your mission statement is being fulfilled in existing and upcoming ministry.

Write down your findings. Give concrete examples in your notes with names, descriptions of ministry and results. When you get to the steps of analyzing role descriptions and compensation, this data will be invaluable.

❑ Form a Compensation Team

Bring together those who are wise in money management and are aligned with your church's mission. The Compensation Team may be a subset of the Finance Team or report directly to your governing board.

If you already have a Compensation Team ...

- If you are new to working with your Compensation Team, it is essential to gather the insider history. Learn of past issues, decisions and red-flagged items. Read all minutes and material from the Compensation and Finance Teams. Review the last seven years of minutes of the governing board.
- Review the team's charter. Ensure that the charter includes elements of what the team does and does not do. Be specific in the tasks. Include in the charter the ability to create or renovate the compensation guide, subject to the approval of your governing board.
- Include term limits and how new Compensation Team members are selected. The approval process may be a part of your constitution. If not, it must be in the church policy and the policy must be approved by your governing board.
- Good church governance dictates that your governing board formally appoint the Compensation Team. The governing board must also appoint your Finance Team.

The Compensation Team should ...

- Review your compensation guide and its alignment with staff salaries. Empower the team to fully examine and walk through your compensation system.
- Review staff leadership decisions about raises, bonuses and other salary changes.
- Recommend a raise pool amount or percentage to the Finance Team and/or governing board. Good governance recommends that adequate checks and balances be maintained on confidential salary changes.
- Make recommendations to the governing board about the salaries of senior leadership. This enables the church leadership to inform the congregation of sufficient process and decision-making in setting those salaries. Preempt the question, "Did you give yourself a raise?"

The Compensation Team can ...

- Participate in the setting of individual salaries. This is cumbersome as a church staff grows. Larger churches have the Compensation Team review salary changes before they are enacted.
- Review ministerial housing allowances and recommend them for approval to the governing board. This is often done in conjunction with, or solely by, the Finance Team. Choose a method for approval of the housing allowances and always follow that method.

Questions to Consider

One

In thirty years, Pastor Wilson led the church's growth from five families to 1,500 people. At the end of his tenure, what do you consider to be the strengths and limitations of WheatFields?

	Strengths	Limitations
1		
2		
3		
4		
5		
6		
7		

Two

Dan Black led the discussion with the Compensation Team. Was he well prepared for this meeting? Did he have a strategic agenda? With the perfect hindsight of 20/20 vision, how would you have advised to lead the meeting?

_____
_____
_____
_____
_____
_____
_____
_____
_____

Three

What are the major issues or red flags in the discussions with your Compensation Team? How can you better address the issues of the team members? What presentation methods would enhance your team meetings?

_____
_____
_____
_____
_____
_____
_____
_____

Tools

This section provides you with material that was introduced or finalized in this chapter. These items are also available at https://www.xpastor.org/smart. The password for this page is: smart money.

Sample—Compensation Team Charter

We value each person's service to the mission of our church. We want wages that allow staff to live a reasonable lifestyle in our community. Jesus tells us to be generous and the apostle Paul says that a worker is worthy of their wages. We desire to be fair and generous.

Compensation Team members are appointed by our elders. As our policy states, "The term is three years with a one-year rotation off the team."

Confidentiality is vital. All discussions are confidential. Members will only discuss compensation issues or salary data when in Compensation Team or Elder Board meetings.

The Team Shall ...

- Regularly review the *Big Burrito* Salary Spreadsheet and its alignment with the compensation guide. Senior staff will give reasonable explanations about salaries, especially those below Quad 1 and above Quad 4. Concerns should be reported to the Elder Board.
- Raises must align with our six values for merit increases:
    1. Experience—years in jobs that impact their current role.
    2. Education—formal education as seen in a bachelor's degree, master's degree or doctorate. Ongoing education that signifies the person as a life-long learner.
    3. Responsibility—the ability to carry out their work in a timely and effective manner. Key staff carry the weight of more ministry responsibility.
    4. Team spirit—contributes to the morale of the staff and is excited to be here.
    5. Missional alignment—implements the vision of the church in their area.
    6. Special considerations—published songs, books, national speaking engagements, teaching that enhances high performance of local ministry.

- Give counsel to senior staff about the scope of raises, bonuses or lack thereof.
- Every three years, review the compensation guide for comparable salaries and benefits. Senior staff present proposed changes to the guide and the team recommends revisions to the elders. We base our salary data on: other local churches; churches in national compensation surveys; local non-profits, police departments and public school teachers.
- Receive recommendations from senior staff about a pool of raises and/or bonuses. The team recommends to the elders the size of that pool.
- Recommend to the elders the salaries of the senior pastor and executive pastor.

- Review ministerial housing allowances and recommend them to the elders.
- Assist the elders and staff in severance issues.

The Team Shall Not ...

- Change its charter but may make recommendations to the elders.
- It shall not determine salaries for staff. Senior staff shall set all salaries other than their own.

- 3 -

WHO IS
A PASTOR?

Putting Staff in the Right Classifications

Dan Black drove to work on Monday morning and planned his first week of solving the compensation crisis. He thought, "Who is a pastor?" It seemed like a simple question but then he saw the aging sign of WheatFields Good News Church. "We've been around a long time and probably have lots of history on this issue. The straightforward answer is, people with the title of *pastor*, but are things ever that easy?" Dan questioned. "Except, we have staff with other designations who do ministry, such as ministry directors and weekday preschool leaders. I suppose that other churches have teachers, missionaries and others who could be included."

Some staff have a slice of their duties in hands-on ministry, such as a bookkeeper, accountant or business administrator. Can any of them be considered a pastor? If any or all of these people can be considered ministerial, there are legal, tax and financial implications. Dan stumbled into the broader issue of "What does it take to be ministerial and receive the ministerial exception?" Was it possible that WheatFields had erred in their prior answer to the question, "Who is a pastor?"

The long brewing compensation crisis at WheatFields had finally come to a boiling point. Four months into his new role as the executive pastor, Dan came face-to-face with his first crisis. Money was at the root of the problem. However, it was not a lack of money but a surplus that compounded the crisis. The church had bountiful resources for raises but did not have a cogent compensation system. For thirty years, the practice at WheatFields had been to give across-the-board raises. With 128 staff members, the Compensation Team's angst was palpable—they needed a rational methodology for compensation. The team wanted it posthaste! Dan had a skimpy three weeks to draft a not-so-skimpy compensation guide.

From Dan's initial research, he wondered if the employees were in the right job classifications. The HR files had scant documentation about the ministerial status of staff members. It was possible that the church was out of compliance about who should be licensed, commissioned or ordained.

Dan needed to discover the legal and ecclesiastical issues inherent in the question, "Who is a pastor?" This journey would lead him to understand the ministerial exception and his church's policy on ministry functions. To begin the journey, Dan formulated three pivotal questions:

- Who is currently licensed, commissioned or ordained?
- Who does ministerial work but lacks ministry credentials?
- Who is paid as a minister but shouldn't be?

The issue of "Who is a pastor?" was Dan's starting point for creating his compensation guide. He had little idea how complicated the issue was or how it might affect the staff at WheatFields.

Assembling Necessary Documentation
Review Board Minutes

Dan worked to answer his first question, "Who is licensed, commissioned or ordained?" The research would need to examine thirty years of Elder Board minutes and the church's HR files. WheatFields had an Elder Board but Dan knew the process would be the same if a church had a Board of Deacons, Trustees or other structure. The highest level of authority in a church needed to either credential or accept the credentials of ministerial staff.

Dan asked his Executive Assistant, Nancy Rearson, to work on the project:

Dan: "I'd like you to examine each and every page of board minutes for credentialing. While you're doing that, I'll review the HR files. And while you're at it, see if there's any mention of housing allowances or approvals in those elder minutes ... and see if you can get it done by lunch time ... that's a joke, of course."

Nancy: "I'm less than thrilled with this assignment. At eleven elder meetings per year for thirty years, that comes to 330 meetings. You really want me to read the minutes for each one?"

Dan: "That's right. I've been an elder here for twenty of those years, but don't remember much in the way of board motions to commission pastors."

Nancy: "But, but ... but that's ten binders of minutes! There must be over a thousand pages. That could take me weeks!"

Dan: "We don't have weeks, just days. The scope of your review should only be for motions concerning licensing, commissioning or ordaining staff—or approval of policy for the same. This will make your task easier. And while you're doing that, I'll do other research."

Nancy's only reply was a glare. Dan knew that the clock was ticking on his three-week timetable!

From his initial study on the topic of titles and credentialing, Dan knew that churches used different nomenclature concerning ministry staff. "Did I just use that word, *credentialing*? A week ago I didn't even know what it meant in the church world," Dan thought. He found many documents online that gave him plenty of food for thought. Two articles were particularly helpful, both from the Evangelical Council for Financial Accountability: *Pastoral Ordination, Licensure, or Commissioning Procedure*[23] and *Qualifications for Ministerial Tax Status*.[24]

There is a wide latitude of church policy and polity on titles and credentialing. The titles range from senior or lead pastor, executive or senior associate pastor, assistant pastor to youth pastor, worship minister to lay minister, missionary to counselor, evangelist to chaplain … the list goes on.

Denominational churches often have national guidelines that define titles and the formal recognition of ministry staff. They may have district or regional committees for ordination. These certify the integrity and worthiness of the individual for the ministry role. National guidelines can provide avenues of nurture, counsel and discipline for the recipient. Like many independent or unaffiliated congregations, WheatFields has their Elder Board set policy concerning ministry credentials for licensing, commissioning and ordaining.

Licensing

Ministry staff can be licensed as a ministry credential. Some churches and denominations license a new pastor during a watch-care period in the steps leading to ordination. Other churches license non-paid staff to empower them to perform weddings, lead funerals, deliver communion and other sacerdotal tasks. Still other churches use a license as the mechanism to denote all ministry staff. A ministry license can convey a title, such as pastor, community pastor, lay minister or ministry director.

A license may be time constrained to an ordination program and lapse if the candidate fails to complete the process. If not in an ordination program, a church may license an individual for a select period of time or be open-ended. A license may be revoked for cause in cases of moral turpitude when the individual trespasses the church's code. In its policy documents, WheatFields chose not to license their ministry staff.

---

[23] Evangelical Council for Financial Accountability, *Pastoral Ordination, Licensure, or Commissioning Procedure* (Winchester, Virginia: ECFA) available from www.ecfa.org/Content/Pastoral-Ordination-Licensure-or-Commissioning-Procedure.

[24] Dan Busby, *Qualifications for Ministerial Tax Status* (Winchester, Virginia: ECFA) available from www.ecfa.org/Content/Qualifications-for-Ministerial-Tax-Status, excerpted from *Zondervan Church & Nonprofit Tax & Financial Guide* and *Zondervan Minister's Tax & Financial Guide* by Dan Busby, Michael Martin and John Van Drunnen.

Commissioning

Commissioning is another vehicle for a church or denomination to credential ministry staff. Churches often commission missionaries, paid staff and non-paid ministry workers. The process is often more informal than ordination or licensure, but still requires proper documentation. While the hiring process may be the path for some churches to interview the candidate, the governing board is required to perform the commissioning. Commissioning can convey a title, such as pastor or ministry director.

A commission tends to be for the duration of work in a specific local church or ministry, such as a missionary on assignment to a specific field. Like licensing, a commission may be revoked for moral turpitude or other causes.

WheatFields chose to only use commissioning as their way to certify ministry workers. For a goodly number of years, as WheatFields commissioned ministry staff, men were pastors and women were ministry directors. Over time, these titles evolved and created tension in the staff, as Dan knew all too well.

Ordaining

As for ordination as a method to credential ministers, the term has wide differences of meaning. The usages range from "conferring holy orders on" to "publicly or privately denoting an individual as a pastor." Some churches have a multi-year ordination process that includes a watch-care licensing period. Many churches ordain a candidate after a council interviews the candidate for theological competency and personal holiness. Other churches invest the title without an ordination council.

There may be a public ordination ceremony, a private laying on of hands or simply an action by the governing board. Like a ministry license and commission, ordination may be revoked. Generally the title of pastor, minister or reverend is conveyed in ordination. Ordination generally is conferred to an individual for life, while less often it is for the duration of work at a specific church or ministry.

When WheatFields drafted its policy on ministry credentials, the ordination of women was highly controversial. Dan remembered the challenging discussions at the elder meetings on this topic. The controversy was compounded by the church being unsure about conveying to a woman the title of pastor. WheatFields chose to forgo ordination but decided to recognize ordination from other churches or denominations for incoming staff. Over its thirty-year history, WheatFields had a tinge of iconoclasm. While following established church culture on most issues, they could discard traditional ecclesiastical mores. This happened in the initial discussion on the policy on credentialing. The elders thought it unfair, and not biblically based, to have an ordination process that was exclusive to men. Though they were unwilling to call women *pastors* in the early years of the church, they decided to have men and women be commissioned for ministry in the same process. The church put into policy two titles for ministry staff—*pastor* and *ministry director*.

Initially, the title *pastor* was given to men who were in full-time, vocational ministry. This was fairly straightforward as the staff was comprised of two men, Pastor Wilson and Associate Pastor Burnham. According to the church's policy, the term *ministry director* was applied to women who had shepherding roles. With a graduate degree in theology, Sheila Compton was hired as the first ministry director for women. Later, Kelsey Eck, a 40-year-old mom, reentered the workforce as WheatFields' Ministry Director for Worship. Though Kelsey lacked seminary training, her life experience was rich in ministry activity.

Problems of Blurred Roles and Titles

As WheatFields hired more staff, the lines of demarcation blurred between pastor and ministry director. Informally at first, ministry directors began to include men who were exploring vocational church work. While a student at a local college, Ed Davis became a part-time ministry director for youth. Billy Kovakian was a thirty-year-old who sensed that God was leading him out of the business world. He was exploring a ministry role and became the ministry director for adults. Then, the term *ministry director* expanded further to include men who were recent seminary graduates but did not have significant ministry experience. The church's hiring team cited Emory Verde as "too raw" to be considered as a pastor, so he received the title, Ministry Director.

WheatFields had backed themselves into a dilemma of staff titles. Pastors had become the big men on campus. Ministry directors were women, people exploring ministry or others not experienced to be called a pastor. The ministry directors, especially the women, began to feel like second class staff. It took nearly a decade for WheatFields to realize the dilemma and another number of years to solve it.

When WheatFields realized the problem of titles for ministry staff, the elders entered into a long and closely-held discussion. Before coming to any conclusions, the elders expanded the dialogue to key staff and then to all staff. Then, the elders began conversations with the congregation. The elders reasoned that as women had shepherding gifts, they should be called pastors. Dan remembered that some of the congregation said, "But aren't pastors also elders? Our constitution calls for elders to be male." The leaders studied the Scriptures and found the church had made a false assumption about elders and pastors. The elders drafted a statement that said:

> Pastors often function as overseers (another word for elder) but only one of our pastors is in the office of elder. At this time, only Senior Pastor Wilson is on our Elder Board. While we affirm our constitution that men are called to be in the office of elder, we do not see that the

Bible says that only men can be pastors. Thus, we affirm that men and women can be called pastor. We will continue to use the term, *ministry director*, for men and women who are either new to ministry or who have little or no theological education.

Though the church members had that tinge of iconoclasm, this was a major shift. With the biblical reasoning about the shepherding gifts and abilities of women, the church members slowly accepted the change.

The term *pastor* was enshrined in the policy documents to be applied to any man or woman who, through ministry or life experience, demonstrated a pastoral calling and then had been commissioned by the elders. It was expected that all pastors be theologically competent. Generally this entailed some level of on-site or online seminary education. The term *ministry director* was applied to men and women who were exploring or just beginning a ministry career. *Ministry director* also applied to individuals who did some pastoral work in their church positions but lacked theological expertise. *Pastors* were to be the theological experts in the church and *ministry directors* needed to have some degree of biblical knowledge.

As WheatFields wrestled with titles over fifteen years, they crafted a clear and biblically-reasoned policy. This was a major asset to Dan in his research. He remembered the elder discussions that he had been a part of. His research reminded him that:

- The definitions of ministry roles were clear. They had a solid biblical base and were consistent with the theological views of the church.
- The titles aligned with IRS regulations that all ministry workers be licensed, commissioned or ordained.
- If ever called into court, Dan could defend the WheatFields' policy. The views were the deeply held religious convictions of his church.

While the policy was clear, Dan knew that the implementation was murky. "It all gets back to the family business model of Pastor Wilson," he thought. "I don't want to throw Pastor Wilson under the bus. He was God's man to build this fantastic church … but he left me with some huge issues!" Dan continued, "But I was on the Elder Board, I was in the room making decisions, so all of us elders share responsibility if our practices failed to live up to our policies."

Dan mused, "I have a bad feeling about where my research is heading. If I had to stand before a judge, I might not be able to declare that WheatFields was acting in accordance with the law or our policy."

Review Ministry Descriptions

While Nancy's review of the elder minutes was underway, Dan reviewed the staff role descriptions from the HR files. "This is dismal. Many staff members lack even a bare bones job description." He found no role descriptions for:

- Three pastors
- Four directors
- One coordinator
- Two administrative assistants
- Six facility workers
- Thirty preschool lead teachers, thirty teachers and thirty assistant teachers

For these staff without a job description, Dan asked for each person, or their supervisor, to send three to five bullet points listing their roles. He asked that each description include the scope of the role, its primary functions and if any ministry was performed.

The staff were quick in their responses. Many dug up an aged file that had little reflection of their current duties and others emailed bullet points. Dan reviewed the full and partial job descriptions. He summarized, "The staff responded well and now everyone has at least something in print about their roles." As Dan reviewed the ministry descriptions, he found:

- The eleven pastors easily had a ministry function—pastors of college/young adults, discipleship, executive, family, high school (two), junior high, mission, preschool, senior and worship.
- The ministry functions of the nine directors had wide latitude— accounting director, assistant directors (two) of preschool, creative director, database director, facility director, information technology director, media director and worship director.
- The role of the worship intern could have a ministry component.

It was clear that some staff had no direct ministry function in their roles, such as his executive assistant, as well as the administrative assistants, coordinators and facility workers. Dan made a note to do a comprehensive review of all role descriptions after the compensation guide was drafted.

He asked the worship pastor to come and talk about the role of the worship intern. "There is a valid ministry component in the role," Hank said, and continued, "But, as we rotate interns each year, I would recommend that we not commission the various interns." That was good input and Dan would make the final determination later.

For the nine directors, things would be harder. Dan began by talking to the finance director:

> Janet: "All nine directors are being paid as ministerially exempt. They have the title of *director*."

> Dan: "That's it? Because of the title?"

> Janet: "Pastor Wilson said that the policy commissioned all directors, so we paid them as such. No FICA was taken out and they all have self-determined housing allowances as a portion of their salary."

> Dan: "Well, the policy says that ministry directors *can* be commissioned as ministerial staff."

> Janet: "I'm not privy to the policy and was just doing what Pastor Wilson said."

In the next few days, Dan would need to meet with each of the nine directors. "Does that conversation center on the amount of ministry that each person does? I'm not ready for those conversations because I don't yet understand enough about pastoral roles. I don't get this thing with the IRS and who really is a minister." Dan realized that he had significant challenges ahead.

Review Housing Allowances

While still waiting for the results of the Elder Board minutes, Dan wondered more about housing allowances. He checked in with the Finance Office:

> Janet: "No, I've never seen elder minutes approving housing allowances."

> Dan: "No paperwork at all?"

> Janet: "We just got that information verbally from Pastor Wilson."

> Dan: "I've been on the Elder Board for twenty years and don't remember approving a motion for housing allowances. Do you think it possible that in our thirty-year history, that we never officially approved any housing allowances?"

> Janet: "That's above my pay grade. That's an elder deal."

Dan: "Pastor Wilson isn't just at fault in this. It looks like all of us elders failed our responsibility."

If the board of WheatFields had never approved housing allowances, the church had violated the law for its ministerial staff. Dan's learnings informed him that in order to legally receive a housing allowance, approvals must happen before the employee is paid.

Dan sorted the formal job descriptions and bullet point summaries into three categories— pastoral, non-pastoral and to be determined. He called a friend:

Attorney: "Essentially, you got it right! With a church staff, the ministerial and non-ministerial differentiation is key for financial, legal and tax code issues."

Dan: "I'm working on that right now. What about the Fair Labor Standards Act and ministry staff?"

Attorney: "Ministry workers are licensed, commissioned or ordained by your governing board. These are the only church staff who can receive a housing allowance free of federal income tax."

Dan: "I think I understand that part."

Attorney: "Pastors and other ministry staff are considered professional ministry personnel and so are exempt from wage and hour regulations. Do all the ministers have proper credentials on file?"

Dan: "No, that's the problem! In twenty years on the Elder Board, I don't recall commissioning anyone ... Where is this heading?"

Attorney: "You could have a problem, for sure."

Dan: "And what if the church has never approved housing allowances for our pastors or ministry directors?"

Attorney: "You and those staff would be in big trouble. For that, you need to consult with a CPA and then the church's attorney."

Dan: "What might be the tax implications if every pastor and director has been filing false income tax forms for their entire employment at WheatFields?"

Attorney: "The tax and legal issues will be enormous, could run into the hundreds of thousands of dollars, maybe a million. There will be fines, financial paperwork and lots of legal fees. Ethically the church should pay the employee's tax liability, as it was your fault."

Dan: "My compensation crisis may have discovered a disaster. But, you said 'my fault.' Am I really at fault?"

Attorney: "It's your problem to fix. You're sitting in the chair of responsibility. Get used to it."

Dan was stewing on the problem when Janet brought the worksheets that pastors and ministry directors had submitted for their housing allowances. Worksheet was an overstatement. "These are really just slips of paper with the requested portion of salary to be designated as housing allowances. I don't know much about this housing allowance thing, but if it's like the rest of the regulations on pastoral pay, I doubt that we're doing a good job of it," Dan thought. He made a note that sometime soon, perhaps this week, he needed to more clearly understand the type of expenses that qualify for a housing allowance.

"If any of the nine ministry directors have never, or no longer perform any ministry or shepherding, what do I do?" Dan thought. "Either I have to insert a ministry role into their job description or delist them as ministry directors. That's not going to be a fun discussion." He continued, "They will hate me for taking away their housing allowance, let alone the status that they feel as a ministry director." Dan's crisis now had the potential to upset the morale of nine ministry directors.

Opting Out of Social Security

From Janet in the Finance Office, Dan discovered that two pastors had opted out of Social Security. "I have never heard of this," he said aloud to an empty office. "I didn't know that anyone could opt out of Social Security. That sounds fantastic and makes great economic sense to me," Dan concluded. Digging online he realized, "I need to check out IRS *Form 4361*."[25] Unfortunately, in the scant personnel files, Dan found no paperwork from the two pastors regarding their decision to opt out of Social Security.

"I'm going to send an email to Dan Busby, President of the ECFA, and see if he will reply. Maybe he knows if we should have copies of this opting out stuff in our files." Dan received this reply from Dan Busby:

---

25 U.S. Department of Treasury, Internal Revenue Service, *Form 4361: Application for Exemption From Self-Employment Tax for Use by Ministers, Members of Religious Orders and Christian Science Practitioners*, revised January 2011," available from https://www.irs.gov/pub/irs-pdf/f4361.pdf.

Form 4361 should be in their personnel file. Of course, most ministers have lost their completed *Form 4361*. If so, that should be noted and perhaps they should be asked to obtain a copy from the IRS. If the form was filed eons ago, retrieving it from the IRS may be challenging.[26]

He made a note for HR to work on that documentation. Dan's future to-do list was growing.

Dan did a search on the web and found that only for religious earnings can ministers opt out of Social Security. IRS *Form 4361* must be completed within the second tax filing year of religious employment. The form has detailed stipulations:

> I certify that I am conscientiously opposed to, or because of my religious principles I am opposed to, the acceptance (for services I perform as a minister, member of a religious order not under a vow of poverty, or Christian Science practitioner) of any public insurance that makes payments in the event of death, disability, old age, or retirement; or that makes payments toward the cost of, or provides services for, medical care. (Public insurance includes insurance systems established by the Social Security Act.)[27]

Form 4361 continues:

> I certify that as a duly ordained, commissioned, or licensed minister of a church or a member of a religious order not under a vow of poverty, I have informed the ordaining, commissioning, or licensing body of my church or order that I am conscientiously opposed to, or because of religious principles I am opposed to, the acceptance (for services I perform as a minister or as a member of a religious order) of any public insurance that makes payments in the event of death, disability, old age, or retirement; or that makes payments toward the cost of, or provides services for, medical care, including the benefits of any insurance system established by the Social Security Act.[28]

Dan thought, "In a heartbeat, I would opt out of Social Security for financial reasons but I would have to lie to do it. I don't have a 'conscientious religious principle' to base my decision on. Bummer for me." As he had seen on *Form 4361*, a minister can opt out of government insurance only based on *conscientious religious principles*.

---

[26] Personal email from Dan Busby to the author, March 22, 2018.

[27] IRS *Form 4361*.

[28] IRS *Form 4361*.

In terms of finances, those who opt out do not receive Medicare based on their ministry earnings. Dan learned in his research about pastors who had opted out of Social Security in the 1960s and 1970s. In those decades, medical costs were manageable. With the current high cost of medical insurance, those retired pastors found the lack of Medicare to be a substantial loss. In retirement, those pastors pay thousands of dollars each year from their savings for medical insurance. "While I would like to opt out of Social Security," Dan reasoned, "I want to have Medicare available to me in retirement!"

Opting out of Social Security insurance is essentially an irrevocable election. Since opting out is based on deeply held religious views, and not financial considerations, the Social Security Agency rarely opens a window to reenter the system. One such window expired in 2002 and has not been opened since.

Who Pays FICA and SECA?

Dan researched to determine who needed to pay into the Federal Insurance Contributions Act (FICA) and who needed to pay into the Self-Employment Contributions Act (SECA). He found that non-pastors are statutory employees and ministers are common law employees. In the online article, *Church Employees or Independent Contractors,* the ECFA discusses church employees:

> There are basically two types of employees defined by the Tax Code: statutory employees and common law employees. Statutory employees have specifically defined jobs that on the surface might appear to be self-employed positions were it not for the statutes that define the work as that of an employee. The common law employee is the category which affects local churches most often.[29]

The ECFA article goes on to state:

> A common law employee is generally anyone who performs services that can be controlled by the employer. That is, the employer has the legal right to control (even if not enforced) the means, methods, and results of the services provided. If the employer/employee relationship is deemed to exist based on the facts in each case, it does not matter what it is called, nor how the payments are measured or paid, nor if the services are performed full time or part time. The employer must determine any taxable amounts paid, withhold appropriate taxes for lay employees, make appropriate tax payments, and report those taxes

---

[29] Pensions and Benefits USA, The Church of the Nazarene, *Church Employees as Independent Contractors,* posted with permission by the Evangelical Council for Financial Accountability, available from www.ecfa.org/Documents/ChurchEmployees_IndependentContractors.pdf.

to the IRS. Virtually all pastors, associate ministers, church custodians, church secretaries, paid choir directors, paid nursery workers, etc., are viewed by the IRS as common law employees. Their compensation is reported on Form W-2.[30]

"This is utterly confusing and seems to be legal mumbo-jumbo," Dan said aloud as his head swam in the unique classifications of church employees. "What have I gotten myself into?"

In the business world and for non-ministerial church employees, people pay into FICA. FICA is comprised of two equal parts. The employer and employee each pay 7.65% of wages. Each of the shares of 7.65% of gross wages is split into 6.2% for Social Security and 1.45% for Medicare. The total amount of FICA contributions is 15.3% of wages.

As many pastors stay in Social Security, they must pay into SECA. For the purposes of federal income tax and Social Security, pastors are technically classified as self-employed. The church cannot pay SECA. At least quarterly, ministers are responsible to pay their estimated taxes, which includes the full 15.3% of the government's insurance plans. For SECA, ministers pay both the 7.65% employee portion and the employer's portion of 7.65%. Further, the church cannot deduct SECA contributions from the pastor's pay. The pastor may ask the church to send federal and state estimated tax payments to the government. This is a convenience issue only and not a requirement on the church or pastor.

Dan ran some quick numbers on what those numbers might mean. He found:

Non-Pastors Earning $50,000
If a non-pastor earns $50,000 a year, the employer must contribute the FICA amount of 7.65% of gross wages, which is $3,825. This employer contribution is virtually unseen by the employee. Since FICA is a federal requirement, employees earning $50,000 rarely consider their compensation to be what the employer actually pays, $53,825. The employee must contribute their 7.65% share of FICA, which on a salary of $50,000 is another $3,825. These amounts must be deducted and remitted by the employer. The total contribution for a salary of $50,000 is 15.3%, which comes to $7,650. Not accounting for other benefits or costs, non-pastors with an annual salary of $50,000 will take home and have an income tax liability of $46,175.

Pastors Earning $50,000
For a pastor earning $50,000, their taxable wage is the full $50,000.

---

[30] Pensions and Benefits USA, *Church Employees as Independent Contractors*.

They must contribute 15.3% in SECA on those wages, which is $7,650. When filing federal income tax to the IRS, this amount may be partially or fully offset by savings though a ministerial housing allowance and any deductible part of self-employment tax on *Form 1040*, line 24. Not accounting for other church benefits or costs, after paying $7,650 in SECA, the pastor will have an annual take home pay of $42,350.

Pastors with a SECA Equivalency Bonus

Some churches compensate their pastors with extra salary to offset the 7.65% employer portion of what would have been contributed to FICA. This is essentially a bonus to their salary. For a pastor earning $50,000, a church can pay what would normally be the 7.65% employer's portion of FICA, which for a $50,000 salary is $3,825. This bonus is taxable income to the pastors. The pastor's taxable earnings rise to $53,825. They pay SECA $8,235 on those wages. Not accounting for other benefits or costs, the pastors earn $45,590.

"With all these pastoral taxation issues, my head is in a muddle. I wonder how the ministerial housing allowance changes the amount of tax due?" Dan thought. "Sorting through the employment and tax issues is a deep dive. I'm accustomed to dealing with business employees where the rules are fixed and seemingly consistent. This pastoral pay stuff is a real challenge." Dan had found that ministerial compensation is riddled with complexity.

The Fair Labor Standards Act

With his head buzzing, Dan researched further on pastoral compensation. "It doesn't make much sense to me," he mused. "But I'd better understand correctly who is a minister and who isn't. I may have some staff that don't really fall in the right classification. Isn't there a test of time that requires a minister to perform a certain amount of ministry? Are pastors really exempt from wage and hour laws?"

Continuing his search on the internet, Dan found more to consider about the ministerial exception and the Fair Labor Standards Act. Dan found an article, *Lesser Known Exemptions: The 'Ministerial' Exception to the FLSA* by Franczek Radelet, a nationally-noted labor law firm based in Chicago.[31] He also found *Questions and Answers from the General Information Overtime Webinars* from the U.S. Department of Labor.[32]

---

[31] Franczek Redelete Attorneys and Counselors, *Lesser Known Exemptions: The 'Ministerial' Exception to the FLSA* (Chicago: Wage Hour Insights, April 7, 2015) available from https://www.wagehourinsights.com/2015/04/lesser-known-exemptions-the-ministerial-exception-to-the-flsa/.

[32] U.S. Department of Labor, *Questions and Answers from the General Information Overtime Webinars*, revised January, 2018, available from https://www.dol.gov/whd/overtime/final2016/webinarfaq.htm.

Dan wondered why he had joined a church staff. "I have some employees who the Department of Labor says are not employees. Some employees have anti-discrimination coverage and others don't. Some get a housing allowance and some don't."

He discovered a Wikipedia article that noted Supreme Court Justice Clarence Thomas who "eschewed the use of any specific test for determining who qualifies as a minister, writing that he would like to defer to a religious organization's good-faith understanding of who qualifies as a minister."[33] Dan realized, "This stuff has even made it to the Supreme Court. I'd better walk carefully on this topic!"

He learned that the amount of time that a commissioned minister serves in ministry or shepherding is not a factor. The Supreme Court noted:

> It is not one that can be resolved by a stopwatch. The amount of time an employee spends on particular activities is relevant in assessing that employee's status, but that factor cannot be considered in isolation, without regard to the nature of the religious functions performed.[34]

"Now I have more insight on how to resolve issues at WheatFields," Dan thought. "Role descriptions need to describe the ministerial function of every pastor and ministry director. While the amount of time in ministry is not the sole issue, I need to determine if each person is actually doing ministry."

Findings from the File Cabinet

Nancy, Dan's assistant, finished the task of reviewing the elder minutes. "Hey, Dan, at fifty pages an hour, it took me 23 hours to review over 1,150 pages in ten binders. It's not that I'm bored or anything but that was three solid and dull work days," she quipped. The final list included the name of each person, the date of elder action and whether each person was licensed, commissioned or ordained.

Dan looked at the report and added his findings from the HR files. He found numerous issues:

- Two pastors had been ordained at another church. The ordination of one was noted in the minutes and the other was not. Neither had copies of their ordination certificates in their personnel files. He thought, "The first place that the IRS would look would be the personnel files."

[33] Wikipedia, *Hosanna Tabor Evangelical Lutheran Church & School vs. the Equal Opportunity Employment Commission* (San Francisco: Wikimedia Foundation, page last edited on April 13, 2018) available from https://en.wikipedia.org/wiki/Hosanna-Tabor_Evangelical_Lutheran_ Church_&_School_v._Equal_Employment_Opportunity_Commission.

[34] Wikipedia, *Hosanna Tabor*.

- When Pastor Wilson and Associate Pastor Burnham had retired, both were given the lifetime title of *Pastor Emeritus*. There was no record of this in the elder minutes or personnel files.
- Six pastors had been commissioned by the elders and were noted in the minutes. "I have no recollection of ever commissioning these folks," Dan thought. And none have any record of the commissioning in their personnel files." He made a note to add the information to the HR files.
- Five pastors had never been commissioned by the elders or, if they were, it wasn't recorded in the minutes. "That list includes me and Steve Borneo!" Dan mused, "I feel uncomfortable in getting commissioned, as I've never worked in a church before. Yet, now I'm called a pastor. Yes, I have twenty years of church board experience but I need some formal biblical and theological training to feel more qualified on theological issues." Such are the thoughts of many new executive pastors who come from the business community.
- Two of the five directors were commissioned by the elders.
- There was no record that the Elder Board had ever approved housing allowances for pastors or directors. If the elders had made those approvals, they had not been recorded in the minutes.

Dan was dismayed. "This challenge is so much bigger than I thought. The report on the Elder Board minutes has many troubling areas. And this doesn't include the problems with job descriptions and ministry functions. What are we going to do about the elders never approving housing allowances?"

Then it came to Dan, "A week into this project and I haven't even started to examine salaries! The days are just blurry images. The whole week passed like lightning. What will next week be like?"

Toolbox

Principles

1. The first element of *Smart Money for Church Salaries* is: **Invest** in staff salaries with skill, towards fulfillment of the church's vision statement, so that God will entrust spiritual riches. The second element is:

   Handle worldly wealth with excellence and trustworthiness, using money to serve God ... and not the other way around.

2. Handling money makes people nervous. Scripture says:

   For the love of money is the root of all evils. Some people in reaching for it have strayed from the faith and stabbed themselves with many pains. But you, as a person dedicated to God, keep away from all that. Instead pursue righteousness, godliness, faithfulness, love, endurance, and gentleness. 1 Timothy 6:10-11

3. Handling worldly wealth well requires a focus on righteousness and godliness. Money is simply a tool that must be used with skill. In itself, money is not evil but the love of it is a root of evils. We want to be excellent in studying the good use of finances and found trustworthy in that use.

Core Concepts

1. Ministry staff must pay 15.3% of their wages in SECA. They can ask the church to forward that money to the government. Churches can give a bonus to help cover the SECA differential. Ministry staff can opt out of Social Security on the grounds of deeply held religious beliefs. All non-ministry staff pay 7.65% FICA and the church must contribute 7.65% in employer-matching funds.

2. Role descriptions are essential for understanding the function of ministry staff. Without careful attention, staff roles and titles can blur over time. The Supreme Court determined that the amount of time in ministry is not the determinate factor for whether a person is considered ministry staff. A local church can license, commission or ordain ministry staff. Some denominations have procedures that must be observed for credentialing; some denominations handle the entire process of credentialing.

3. Ministerial housing allowances must be approved by the church before they can be applied to salary. Allowances cannot apply to prior earnings.

Church policy should be clear on the role of ministry staff. Consistent implementation is essential. If it cannot be implemented, then it should be changed.

Steps

❑ Ask Staff Role and Tax Questions

1. Examine the job descriptions for all staff. A one-page description with percentages of time is ideal. For staff that lack a job description, begin with three to six bullet points of their roles. For ministry staff, ensure that a valid ministry function is included.

2. Gather the ministry staff and teach on the difference between FICA and SECA. Instruct that ministers must make, at a minimum, quarterly tax payments on April 15, June 15, September 15 and January 15. They alone are responsible for remitting all their taxes. Ministry staff can ask the church to send money to the government from their wages, but the church is not required to do so.

3. Review your ministerial housing allowance form. Ensure that your form or worksheet lists all the options that can be included in a housing allowance. See the Tools section in Chapter 4 for examples.

4. Teach ministry staff to understand and fully utilize the benefits of the ministerial housing allowance. Many staff mistakenly omit items like furniture, computers and gardening equipment.

❑ Review Internal Controls

1. Scour your church policy and ensure that it answers the question, "Who is a pastor?" Ensure that job descriptions, titles and functions consistently implement your policy.

2. Read board minutes for the past approvals of ministerial housing allowances. Create a list of prior approvals.

3. Place all necessary records in each employee's HR file. This includes housing allowance forms; certificates of license, commission or ordination; forms for opting out of Social Security.

❑ Think Biblically on Tax Issues

Benjamin Franklin quoted Daniel Defoe, saying: "In this world nothing can be said to be certain, except death and taxes." While there are spiritual truths that can be added to the quote, taxes are ever present. Few enjoy paying taxes and many try to avoid them. Jesus taught on taxes:

> Show me the coin used for the tax." So they brought him a denarius. Jesus said to them, "Whose image is this, and whose inscription?" They replied, "Caesar's." He said to them, "Then give to Caesar the things that are Caesar's, and to God the things that are God's. Matthew 21:19-21

The apostle Paul wrote:

> For this reason you also pay taxes, for the authorities are God's servants devoted to governing. Pay everyone what is owed: taxes to whom taxes are due, revenue to whom revenue is due, respect to whom respect is due, honor to whom honor is due. Romans 13:6-7

While a Christian may not enjoy paying taxes, Scripture requires that we do so. Church staff must pay a variety of taxes, such as: FICA or SECA; federal, state and local income taxes, and taxes on unused ministerial housing allowances. Ministers can opt out of Social Security and Medicare for theological and deeply held beliefs—and never receive those benefits based on their church earnings.

As a church leader, you must instruct staff on what Scripture says about paying taxes. You must model honesty and uprightness in paying your own taxes. You must hold staff to high ethical standards if they are thinking about opting out of Social Security.

As Paul says:

> So the person who resists such authority resists the ordinance of God, and those who resist will incur judgment (for rulers cause no fear for good conduct but for bad). Do you desire not to fear authority? Do good and you will receive its commendation, for it is God's servant for your good. But if you do wrong, be in fear, for it does not bear the sword in vain. It is God's servant to administer retribution on the wrongdoer. Therefore it is necessary to be in subjection, not only because of the wrath of the authorities but also because of your conscience. Romans 13:2-5

Questions to Consider

One

Dan Black had spent a week sorting through, "Who is a pastor?" List the pertinent criteria and issues that Dan found:

	Criteria for "Who Is a Pastor?"	Unique Issues of Pastors
1		
2		
3		
4		
5		
6		
7		

Two

Dan learned the difference between FICA and SECA as well as ministers being able to opt out of Social Security. Dan needed to write a summary of his learnings to send to the pastors and directors. What should he say?

_____

_____

_____

_____

_____

_____

_____

_____

Three

The first week of Dan's three-week project had come to a close. With mind-numbing detail, he had learned who could be considered a pastor. The Finance Office provided a list of all salaries and Dan labeled that *original* as he knew he would be making changes to it—see the Tools at the end of this chapter. Now Dan needed to plan his strategy for the next week. What are the steps that Dan should take in the next five days?

Day 1 _____

Day 2 _____

Day 3 _____

Day 4 _____

Day 5 _____

Tools

This section provides you with material that was introduced or finalized in this chapter. These items are also available at https://www.xpastor.org/smart. The password for this page is: smart money.

Spreadsheets that Dan received in Week 1

WheatFields Good News Church
Overview—Original File

Area	Salary
Pastors & Directors	$1,220,392
Support Staff	$2,471,357
Benefits Budget	$721,572
Total	**$4,413,321**
4% Across the Board Raises	**$176,533**

Pastors and Directors—Original File

Title	Salary
Finance Director	$65,000
Assistant Director for Preschool	$42,000
Assistant Director for Preschool	$42,000
College & Young Adults Pastor	$55,000
Creative Director	$38,366
Database Director	$42,000
Discipleship Assistant Pastor	$53,000
Executive Pastor	$99,000
Facility Director	$62,000
Family Pastor	$93,000
High School Pastor	$62,000
High School Assistant Pastor	$43,000
IT Director	$75,238
Junior High Pastor	$40,000
Media Director	$48,744
Mission Pastor	$59,000
Preschool Pastor	$62,000
Senior Pastor	$115,000
Worship Pastor	$85,111
Worship Director	$38,933
20	**$1,220,392**

SMART MONEY FOR CHURCH SALARIES

Support Staff—Original File

Title	Salary
Administrative Assistant	$40,000
Administrative Assistant	$40,000
Coordinator	$37,000
Coordinator	$37,000
Executive Assistant	$40,000
Facility Overseer	$42,000
Facility Worker	$35,000
Facility Worker	$35,000
Facility Worker	$35,000
Facility Worker	$35,000
Facility Worker	$35,000
Receptionist	$22,800
Receptionist	$22,800
Secretary	$33,000
Secretary	$33,000
Stage Hand	$15,080
Worship Administrative Assistant	$34,522
Worship Intern	$24,815
30 Preschool—Lead Teacher	$737,100
30 Preschool—Teachers	$610,740
30 Preschool—Assistant Teachers	$526,500
108	**$2,471,357**

- 4 -

SALARIES
FOR PASTORS

Getting Staff Buy-In

The first week of Dan Black's compensation crisis had come to a close. Sunday was coming soon. The new senior pastor, coupled with a fantastic worship team, were creating a sensation in the region. Growth was climbing each week and donations were skyrocketing. This fueled the compensation crisis.

The week's research had been a deep dive for Dan and Nancy, his assistant. They looked into records, minutes, policy and legal issues. Dan was mentally worn out on Friday afternoon. On the drive home he surmised, "The ministerial compensation issue is far more complicated than I could ever have dreamed ... SECA, opting out of Social Security, IRS rules and regulations, ministerial housing allowances, this crazy non-employee yet employee status, taxes, who is a minister, and even the Supreme Court. Regular old business was so much easier!"

In beginning his pastoral life a few months ago, Steve had cautioned Dan to take off one day a week. "If it was good enough for God," Steve counseled, "then it's good enough for you. Sunday is not a day of rest for pastors, so take Friday to unplug and get away from it all. It's a new rhythm of Sunday being a full day of work." Dan had failed to heed Steve's advice. He had worked Sunday through Friday.

On Saturday, Dan shared with his wife, Doris, what his week had been like.

> Doris: "What did the staff say about compensation?"
>
> Dan: "All I did this week was research ... but I did talk to the worship pastor on one issue."
>
> Doris: "What? You haven't gotten input from *all* the pastors and directors?"
>
> Dan: "Give me a break. I was too busy to talk to much of anyone."
>
> Doris: "Don't get testy with *me* on this. They work there too! You need to involve them in the discussion ... don't you? Sooner or later they'll hear about this. It's better to get staff input before you make a decision."

SMART MONEY FOR CHURCH SALARIES

Dan: "I'm not ready to agree to this. It's a leadership decision and we leaders need to make it."

Doris: "Did you just mutter that to me or to yourself? In business, you moved at the speed of light and you needed to so as to stay competitive ... but, but ... don't looked irked that I'm giving *you* advice. I know that look ..."

Dan: "Humph."

Doris: "... perhaps you need to move a little slower, Mr. Greased Lightning."

Dan: "Humph."

Doris: "Now listen to me on this. You and Steve are the new guys in staff leadership. Make sure that you have people following you or you'll be leading no one."

Dan: "I'll think about it."

Doris: "While you're thinking, why don't you do some praying too? You haven't mentioned a word about asking what God thinks about all these changes."

Dan felt the sting of her words. She was right and that made the sting all the sharper. He hated it when she was right! Dan needed to gain staff perspective on matters that would affect each of them.

The next day in the sermon, Steve touched on the vision of WheatFields, *Family, Mission and Worship.* He was speaking on the words of Jesus from John 13:35, "Everyone will know by this that you are My disciples—if you have love for one another." In the skilled way of a great communicator, Steve applied the principle of love to each of the three words in the vision statement.

Dan reflected on what Doris and Jesus had said, "Hmmm ..." he thought, "I wonder how I can love the staff in this compensation crisis. Maybe I need to adjust my game this week and have some discussions with the staff."

Monday morning began with Dan and Steve's weekly meeting.

Dan: "I was talking with Doris and thinking about your message yesterday. I think I need to have some discussions with the pastors and directors about compensation."

Steve: "That's a great next step. Why don't you share your research with the core leaders at this morning's meeting? Then this afternoon, talk with all the pastors and directors. But your challenge will be to not trash the reputation of Pastor Wilson, while simultaneously sharing that we do have a problem."

Dan: "With that many people in the room, I just don't want to convey that they will be making the decision."

Steve: "Ask for their input. Let's lean into the wisdom of the team and see what they have to offer."

In business, Dan was accustomed to a small executive team. He knew how to work well with a few hand-picked leaders. Talking to twenty people about these issues would be a challenge for him.

Forthright Staff Discussions
Core Team Meeting

The Core Team of WheatFields consisted of the senior pastor, executive pastor and the pastors of family, mission and worship. At the Monday morning meeting, Dan summarized his findings. He was careful to say that the problems were the responsibility of the elders and not of any one person.

Dan presented nine key issues:

1. The challenge of a thirty-year history of across-the-board raises.
2. The review of board minutes—some pastors had not been commissioned and housing allowances had never been approved by the elders.
3. The need for an improved housing allowance form.
4. The need for better job descriptions for most staff.
5. Questions about the ministry functions of the nine directors.
6. Opting out of Social Security.
7. Differences in net earnings for a non-ministerial staff person earning $50,000 and taking home $46,175 and a pastor earning $50,000 and taking home $42,350. The impact of the ministerial housing allowance still needed to be factored.
8. The FLSA and how it does not apply to pastors but does apply to other staff.
9. Dan's confusion about the layout and organization of the salary spreadsheet.

The Core Team responded with a shocked silence. Mark Houdini, the Worship Pastor, broke the ice:

> Mark: "Is that all you did last week? Really though, that's good work but hard to hear about and harder to understand."

People joked about Mark's last name but he claimed to be related to the great magician. It was no joke that he was like magic on the worship stage.

Ed Baker, the Mission Pastor, added:

> Ed: "It's beyond me to solve it and I'm glad that you're doing it. We've been needing this for some time."

Dan sensed that there was something behind Ed's comments. Mark and Ed's comments opened the door for a healthy discussion of the major issues. The suggestions from the team were manifold. Family Pastor Liz Jackson shared a key take-away and three others followed:

> Liz: "You need to give at least cost of living increases to staff. All my family and preschool people can't be losing money due to inflation."

> Mark: "Gauge the speed of change based on the discussion today with the pastors and directors."

> Ed: "You may be surprised at what the directors have to say!"

> Steve: "Let's get out an email today to the elders to get *all* pastors commissioned and *all* housing allowances approved."

Dan and Steve got a few minutes together after the Core Team meeting.

> Steve: "Well, that went exceedingly well."

> Dan: "Yes, I was surprised how much they had sensed certain problems. They didn't know what the problems were, but they knew something wasn't right! I was totally amazed at how open they were to possible solutions."

> Steve: "They're good folks, and they've been living with tensions in the salary structure for some time, especially Ed Baker. I heard that we

hired him years ago at a pretty low salary. He took it because that's what he made on the mission field, where his money went a long way further."

Steve had given Dan some insight about Ed's comments.

Pastors and Directors Meeting

Just as he had done with the Core Team, Dan had a forthright discussion with the pastors and directors. This new step was a risk for Dan, but it seemed the right thing to do. Steve set the stage for the discussion with all the pastors and directors:

> Steve: "It's coming up on that time of year when we give raises. Every one of you is working so hard in this season of growth. There are wonderful challenges with all the newcomers and I want you to know how much I appreciate you."

Dan had a deep admiration for how Steve could encourage and bring people together with just a few words:

> Steve: "Dan and I met this morning. He and his team did crucial research last week and several issues emerged. Let me have him share those with you."

That was a terrific set-up for Dan. Steve's preface had gotten the group quiet and serious:

> Dan: "Steve and I had a good discussion with the Core Team over nine important issues. I hope that we can have a similar open and honest conversation. No one is taking verbatim minutes, so please speak your mind."

He paused and continued:

> "You are giving advice here and we want to hear from everyone. And if you think of something after the meeting, please stop by my office. Even though I may be immersed in something, please come in and talk. I want to hear from you."

All eyes were on Dan but he felt that his introduction was not as friendly as he wished. In business, Dan rarely managed by walking around. He was beginning to see the positive aspects of that process. He added:

Dan: "And I'll be coming around to your offices to talk. I really want to be with you in these vital issues."

After Steve's and Dan's introductory comments, you could have heard a pin drop on the carpet. The pastors and directors were apprehensive but there was a warmth to their presence. Dan felt like he was about to have a fireside chat with twenty family members.

Dan laid out all nine major issues. He gave just the facts and no personal opinions. Dan did not share the results from the Core Team discussion. He wanted the pastors and directors to give their own views, uncolored by the leadership team.

What ensued was a lively discussion—and that is a gross understatement. Perhaps at no other time in the church's history had there been such animated sharing. On the fly, Steve tossed out all other agenda items. Even with a one-agenda meeting, it lasted 45 minutes longer than usual. Nearly everyone had something to say, often with strong emotion. Dan made notes on the salient statements:

Emotional Responses
Commissioning
Julie Stairs, Preschool Pastor: "I'm *shocked* that Pastor Wilson and the elders never commissioned me. Does this mean that I'm really not a pastor here? What do I tell my husband? That I'm not really a pastor?"

Raises
Colton Manta, College Pastor: "I've always hated, hated, *hated* the across-the-board raises. There is no motivation for me in that. My team works hard, puts in extra hours for all sorts of evening events and we get the same raise as the janitor."

José Mendoza, Facility Director: "Don't be making fun of my staff like that! They work as hard as anyone."

Colton: "Oh, sorry, my bad. It was a junk analogy."

Job Descriptions
Charlie Ethelridge, Media Director: "Why don't I have a job description? I have been yelling for one for years. How am I supposed to know if I'm doing what my boss wants me to do?"

Ed: "We all know what we're supposed to do, so it doesn't bother me."

Charlie: "That's easy for you to say in missions, but my area is different. Media is everything and anything."

FLSA

Hank Fogarty, IT Director: "I thought that the FLSA didn't apply to anyone in a church. Several of my staff have been working overtime and we've never paid them for that. Have I been breaking the law? Could I go to jail or be fined? I can't afford a fine and penalty from the Feds. What gives here? I'm *mad* about this!"

Solid Input

Raises

John Stanley, Discipleship Pastor: "Inflation was 2% last year. If we don't get a raise, then my salary just went down 2%. I have kids who need clothes and summer camp. It's financially tight as it is."

Will Martinez, High School Pastor: "I hear that some of you don't like across-the-board raises. I like them because they treat everyone the same and fairly. But, I would add, I've never had to assign raises before and my opinion might change if I did. My wife makes great money as a doctor, so I may be seeing through rose-colored glasses."

Irene Steele, Worship Director: "My husband's a doctor. I can tell you that raises at the hospital are not across-the-board. It's pay for play— the top players get the best merit increases."

Opting Out of Social Security

Irene: "I wish that I was told I could have opted out of Social Security. It won't be around when I retire. My husband has a nice retirement plan."

Liz Jackson, Family Pastor: "I researched this for Pastor Wilson. You can't opt out for economic reasons, only theological ones."

Irene: "I would have wanted to make the decision for myself."

Housing Allowances

Tamika White, Assistant Director for Preschool: "If my housing allowance wasn't approved, do I have to refile my taxes for the last nine years of my employment? Ugh. I'll have to pay a big fine and back taxes. Will the church cover that?"

Julie: "And can we get a better housing allowance form? How am I supposed to know what I can include? I'm not a tax expert and my CPA says this stuff is bizarre."

Director Issues

Todd Petrey, Database Director: "Needing to do ministry stuff in my role is interesting, at best. I've never been settled about my ministry role as a director."

José: "In my role as facility director, I don't think that I have a ministry function. I've never really been happy being in the pastor category for my taxes. I've always felt it odd at best, wrong at worst."

Derek Mays, Creative Director: "If I had a better job description, I might feel better about paying my own SECA. It really seems like I should be a non-ministerial employee. I'd like to not be a ministry director and for the church to pay my FICA."

Grace Peterson, Assistant Director for Preschool: "Every time that I submit a ministry housing allowance form, I feel like a cheater. My role as an assistant director really doesn't fit that mold."

No Comments

Dan: "I didn't hear any comments on two topics. No one talked about the differences in net earnings for a non-pastor and pastor. That's a difficult and numbers-filled issue. And no one said anything about the organization of the salary spreadsheet. Well, only Steve and I see the spreadsheet, so that makes sense."

Though some staff comments were heated, the mood was good in the room. The venting allowed people to express long-suppressed thoughts. No one crossed the line into inappropriate comments. As the meeting closed, there were a few final thoughts.

Final Comments to be Savored

Irene: "I'm so glad that we're finally working on these issues. Dan, go full steam ahead."

Ed: "Dan, you need to be fair in your decisions, but don't take too long. Thanks for letting us give input. I've always wanted to have this kind of discussion. I've had concerns about our salary rates for a long time. From your days as an elder, you've always had my trust … now you have it all the more."

Will: "Dan, these issues are way beyond my comfort level. I don't think well in these areas. I'm a shepherd and do best in counseling, not finances. But you've been an elder for twenty years ... when I was just a kid, I grew up respecting you. You led the team that brought Steve here four years ago and now you're the executive pastor. We trust you and thank you for trusting us to have this conversation. That took leadership courage! We're thankful for leaders like you and Steve. Go for it!"

Steve prayed and adjourned the meeting. There were plenty of hugs and handshakes as the staff left. Several of the staff were teary-eyed.

After the meeting, Steve and Dan reconnoitered:

Steve: "That was lively ... and you did a fantastic job letting people share. Good job on not prefacing the conversation with the input from the Core Team."

Dan's head was throbbing from the discussion:

Dan: "Yes, we elders got a bit of a well-deserved drubbing. We let Pastor Wilson do some things that were not right and now we need to make amends. It's our fault as elders. We are the fiduciary leaders of this church."

Steve: "And you didn't throw Pastor Wilson under the bus. Good job on that too. You held your tongue!"

Dan: "What surprised me was that so many of the directors saw that they were not really in ministerial roles. And did I just use that word, 'ministerial?' A week ago I never would have used that word."

Steve: "You're in a new land. Get used to it. Welcome to a new world!"

True to his word, Dan wandered the halls for the rest of the afternoon. He stopped into as many offices as possible. The discussions were fruitful but didn't raise any new thoughts. Dan's meandering gave a warmth to his leadership style and he made a mental note to do it more often. "Hey," he thought, "a crisis can teach me some new things."

At home that night, Dan expressed thanks to Doris for recommending that he talk with the staff.

Doris: "See, I knew that your team would have some great ideas. They don't want to make those decisions but do want to give input. And ... I've been telling you for years to manage by walking around."

Dan: "And the amazing thing is that we never talked about anyone's salary numbers ... all we talked about were the core ideas of compensation and who is a minister."

Dan thought to himself, "Last week was research, today was all talk, and I still haven't addressed the salaries. I thought this was going to be all about money. Amazing!"

Monday of the second week had come to a close.

Improving the Salary Spreadsheet

Tuesday morning came early and Dan was working well before sunrise. "Finally I get to be on home turf and deal with salaries! This is something I am an expert on. Let's look at the salary spreadsheet that the Finance Office provided." Dan brought up the page on his computer and saw the summary:

Overview of Salary & Benefits

Area	Salary
Pastors & Directors	$1,220,392
Support Staff	$2,471,357
Benefits Budget	$721,572
Total	**$4,413,321**

"Well, that's pretty basic and needs more detail. Today, my goal," he reasoned, "is to sort through all the salaries of the pastors and directors."

Dan looked further at the spreadsheet. It was the first time that he had examined it:

Pastors and Directors

Title	Salary
Finance Director	$65,000
Assistant Director for Preschool	$42,000
Assistant Director for Preschool	$42,000
College & Young Adults Pastor	$55,000
Creative Director	$38,366
Database Director	$42,000
Discipleship Assistant Pastor	$53,000
Executive Pastor	$99,000

Facility Director	$62,000
Family Pastor	$93,000
High School Pastor	$62,000
High School Assistant Pastor	$43,000
IT Director	$75,238
Junior High Pastor	$40,000
Media Director	$48,744
Mission Pastor	$59,000
Preschool Pastor	$62,000
Senior Pastor	$115,000
Worship Pastor	$85,111
Worship Director	$38,933
20 Staff	**$1,220,392**

"This just won't do. Maybe I need to start with just the pastors. There are lots of problems here," Dan said out loud and woke his wife. Doris mumbled something indiscernible and rolled over. Dan returned to the list and began to make adjustments.

First, he sorted the pastors from the directors. "I know that all the pastors are ministerial, so let's start with them. They're a separate class of employee and easy to define." Dan added a column for the FLSA status, which he named *Type*:

Pastors

Title	Type	Salary
College & Young Adults Pastor	Ministerial	$55,000
Discipleship Assistant Pastor	Ministerial	$53,000
Executive Pastor	Ministerial	$99,000
Family Pastor	Ministerial	$93,000
High School Pastor	Ministerial	$62,000
High School Assistant Pastor	Ministerial	$43,000
Junior High Pastor	Ministerial	$40,000
Mission Pastor	Ministerial	$59,000
Preschool Pastor	Ministerial	$62,000
Senior Pastor	Ministerial	$115,000
Worship Pastor	Ministerial	$85,111
	Total	**$766,111**

"This doesn't have any organizational sense to it. It's just an alphabetical list. I want to have employees listed by their departments. I want to see all the employees for each department with the total departmental cost."

Dan made notes on how the Finance Office needed to change the spreadsheet:

1. Sort employees by department. Add the following:
    *   The name of every department and its accounting number.
    *   Each employee's title and full name.
    *   The FLSA status: ministerial, exempt or non-exempt.
    *   Full-time or part-time status.
    *   Salaried staff should have their salaries listed.
    *   Hourly staff should have their hourly rates, budgeted weekly hours and annualized wages totaled.
    *   Core Team members need to be listed in bold.

2. Include every church-provided benefit:
    *   FICA amounts for all non-ministerial staff.
    *   The participation level by percentage in the church's 403B retirement program and the cost to the church for each person.
    *   List staff that participate in the church's medical insurance program. Employees contribute 21% of their premium. Have columns for the employee contribution and the total premium cost to the church.
    *   The costs for each employee in Dental, Vision and Life Insurance programs.
    *   Include a column for taxable auto allowances.
    *   Include a column for tax-free cell phone allowances.[35]
    *   Add columns for any other church-provided benefit, taxable or not.

3. Summarize the total cost to the church for each staff member.

Dan sent off the list to Janet Williams, the Finance Director, with a terse, "Update this asap." He wondered how she would react to the level of detail that he wanted. He instantly regretted asking for the changes by email. "There is going to be an interesting conversation with Janet when I get in. I may need to apologize for being terse. It may take her team a while to gather all the data from their various files and accounts."

Sorting Ministerial Salaries by Categories

Dan thought through the categories of staff. He needed a definition for classes of staff. These classes would be used for issues with payroll, HR, medical insurance, retirement account and other benefits.

---

[35] U.S. Department of Treasury, Internal Revenue Service, *IRS Issues Guidance on Tax Treatment of Cell Phones; Provides Small Business Recordkeeping Relief,* September 14, 2011, available from https://www.irs.gov/newsroom/irs-issues-guidance-on-tax-treatment-of-cell-phones-provides-small-business-recordkeeping-relief.

The role of senior leadership came from the church's constitution. The definitions for Core Team, pastor and ministry director were defined in church policies. There was nothing in print to define the titles of assistant pastor or assistant ministry director, so Dan created temporary definitions for these roles.

"No wonder there's a confusion of titles. The assistant roles have never had a formal definition for HR and the Finance Office to follow. The website even removes the word *assistant*, so all the ministerial staff are listed as either pastors or directors," Dan thought. He brought all the ministerial titles and definitions together in one document:

Senior Leadership
The church constitution defines this team as the senior pastor and executive pastor. Senior leaders have an umbrella responsibility for the entire church. Nothing is outside of their purview or ultimate responsibility.

Core Team
Church policy says, "Approved by the Elder Board, the Core Team takes the three elements of vision—*Family, Mission and Worship*—and implements them into strategic initiatives. The Core Team speaks into church-wide issues and looks beyond the needs of their own departments."

Pastors
People who have at least five years of church, business or life experience that pertain to their ministry area. These people demonstrate wisdom in action and experience in ministry. The spiritual qualifications of an elder must be met. The pastors carry the weight of theological and ministry expertise at WheatFields.

Assistant Pastors
Those with less experience in ministry. High potential must be demonstrated but not extensive experience. The spiritual qualifications of a deacon must be met. Dan added: *Definition pending approval.*

Ministry Directors
Some may not meet the church's policy guidelines for being a pastor or assistant pastor. Their role description must have some ministry aspect but might not have a main focus on pastoral work. Others may be students, recent college or seminary graduates. Some ministry directors may not desire to pursue the biblical education required by

WheatFields to be a pastor. This category allows the church to signify their work as being at the ministry level. The spiritual qualifications of a deacon must be met.

Assistant Ministry Directors

Like assistant pastors, this level is for those just starting out in church ministry. The spiritual qualifications of a deacon must be met. Dan added: *Definition pending approval.*

Dan hoped that his working definitions were good starting places and he was willing to negotiate those definitions with the staff.

Having working definitions for each role, Dan began to sort the salaries of the pastors and directors. He added columns for the department name and account number.

Then he sorted the pastors and departments by the vision of WheatFields—*Family, Mission and Worship.* "I'm going to put the preschool in a separate category. As a huge and income-producing entity, I want to separately see all the preschool salaries."

Pastors—Core Team in Bold

Department	D#	Title	Type	Salary
Family	**37**	**Family Pastor**	**Ministerial**	**$93,000**
Family	37	High School Pastor	Ministerial	$62,000
Family	37	College & Young Adults Pastor	Ministerial	$55,000
Family	37	High School Assistant Pastor	Ministerial	$43,000
Family	37	Discipleship Assistant Pastor	Ministerial	$53,000
Family	37	Junior High Pastor	Ministerial	$40,000
Mission	**47**	**Mission Pastor**	**Ministerial**	**$59,000**
Worship	**27**	**Worship Pastor**	**Ministerial**	**$85,111**
Leadership	**17**	**Senior Pastor**	**Ministerial**	**$115,000**
Leadership	**17**	**Executive Pastor**	**Ministerial**	**$99,000**
Preschool	67	Preschool Pastor	Ministerial	$62,000

While the initial sorting of the pastors was easy, Dan needed a tighter focus. "There are some interesting disparities of wage and titles. I need to look at just the Core Team salaries," Dan thought.

Core Team Salaries

Department	D#	Title	Type	Salary
Family	37	Family Pastor	Ministerial	$93,000
Mission	47	Mission Pastor	Ministerial	$59,000
Worship	27	Worship Pastor	Ministerial	$85,111
Leadership	17	Senior Pastor	Ministerial	$115,000
Leadership	17	Executive Pastor	Ministerial	$99,000

"Essentially, our Core Team salaries demonstrate the priority of our ministry vision of *Family, Mission and Worship*. Our highest salaries should go to those who implement the vision of the church through strategic initiatives."

Dan further reflected on each pastor on the Core Team:

"Liz, as Family Pastor, oversees so many people and departments: nursery, weekday preschool and Sunday preschool, elementary, junior high and high school. Reporting to Liz is Julie Stairs, Preschool Pastor. Julie has responsibility for 600 children in our weekday school. Also, Liz was the righthand leader for Pastor Wilson and her book on *Family Ministry* is a bestseller. Her salary makes sense."

"Mark in Worship excels in his ministry. Everyone knows that worship at WheatFields is exceptional—he *is* a Houdini! He has a large team with plenty of people and events to manage. We can't have Mark get stolen away by some other church who offers a better salary. He might need to be paid the same as Liz in Family. If we did that, Mark would get a raise of $7,889."

Worship Pastor Salary Issue

Department	D#	Title	Type	Salary
Family	37	Family Pastor	Ministerial	$93,000
Worship	27	Worship Pastor	Ministerial	$85,111
			Delta	$7,889

"Ed's salary in Missions is the strange one. He makes $34,000 less than Liz. Missions is about 23% of our $5 million ministry budget. What's going on here? He has lots of responsibility and is doing a fantastic job. Ed is in high demand as a speaker around the country and earns a little from that. Maybe Pastor Wilson thought of a speaking gigs as Ed's way of making up for his low salary. Ed is a national figure in missional thinking. He brings the best thinking and excellent plans and execution

SMART MONEY FOR CHURCH SALARIES

to our church. He looks woefully underpaid. I bet that's why he made some interesting comments yesterday, first in the Core Team and then in the pastors and directors meetings."

Mission Pastor Salary Problem

Department	D#	Title	Type	Salary
Family	37	Family Pastor	Ministerial	$93,000
Mission	47	Mission Pastor	Ministerial	$59,000
			Delta	$34,000

Dan thought about the three pastors on the Core Team with himself and Steve. "Perhaps those three pastors should be paid the same amount. They carry equal weight of responsibility. They make significant decisions and plenty of people report to each one. That's something I need to talk to Steve and the Compensation Team about."

Dan turned his attention to the other six pastors on staff:

Pastoral Salaries

Department	D#	Title	Type	Salary
Family	37	High School Pastor	Ministerial	$62,000
Family	37	College & Young Adults Pastor	Ministerial	$55,000
Family	37	High School Assistant Pastor	Ministerial	$43,000
Family	37	Discipleship Assistant Pastor	Ministerial	$53,000
Family	37	Junior High Pastor	Ministerial	$40,000
Preschool	67	Preschool Pastor	Ministerial	$62,000

Dan saw two issues.

"David Yang, Junior High Pastor, earns $3,000 less than JB Jones, High School Assistant Pastor. I shouldn't have an assistant pastor earning more than a pastor. That isn't right. Either David in junior high is underpaid as a pastor or he should be classified as an assistant pastor. He's only been in ministry for a year and is relatively inexperienced. Should I change David's title from *pastor* to *assistant pastor*? That would feel like a demotion. I need advice from the Core Team about that. We could leave the title as is and let David grow into the full pastor role—not an ideal solution but politically achievable."

"John Stanley, Discipleship Assistant Pastor, has ten years' experience and is paid similarly with three people who have the title *pastor*. That looks like an easy fix to change his title to *pastor*. But I'd better talk to the Core Team about that as well."

Dan compiled his list of issues:

1. The Finance Office had a huge to-do list for a revised spreadsheet.
2. The worship pastor may need a merit increase of $7,889.
3. The mission pastor is underpaid and needs a merit increase of $34,000.
4. The junior high pastor should have been hired as an assistant pastor.
5. The assistant discipleship pastor should have the title of *pastor*.

"I haven't yet looked at raises but now I know the status of our pastoral salaries. It should be easy to fix the titles. Those merit increases should happen this year. Janet in Finance won't be happy with me when I get to the office ... and Ed's salary is gnawing at me."

Dan made notes about other items for the future—a few needed work as early as next week:

1. A list needs to be made of severance agreements in place, if there are any.
2. Any intellectual property agreements need to be listed.
3. The ministerial housing form needs drastic improvement.
4. An 8-year salary history should be compiled.
5. The HR files need to include commissioning dates and certificates (or the certificate from another church and the acceptance date by our elders), job descriptions and annual reviews.

"Now I'm ready to get to the office," Dan thought. "Last night I was supposed to email the elders about commissioning five of the pastors and approving all the housing allowances, but didn't. Got to get to that asap."

Before he got to the door of the church office, Dan met Janet from Finance.

> Janet: "That ain't going to happen for a month. Collecting all that info will take days of work. It just can't happen quickly."

> Dan: "Look ... well, I mean, well ... I apologize that I sent that email. I should have talked to you in person. I'll do that in the future. Can you accept my apology?"

> Janet: "Okay, I'm cooling down some. But that spreadsheet that you want is a ton of work."

> Dan: "Nancy finished the research on the elder minutes last week. What if she helps your staff compile all the numbers?"

Janet: "Deal. With her help, we can probably get it to you by next Monday."

Dan: "Just so I don't mess up again, let me make sure that Nancy has the bandwidth to help."

Janet: "Yeah, don't send her one of those emails like I got."

Dan: "I deserved that! Again, sorry for that email. Are we okay?

Janet: "Yeah, we're good. Thanks for letting me vent."

Dan spent the rest of Tuesday in meetings and other church work. He didn't get to the salaries of the directors. He did make individual appointments with each director for the next day. Before he knew it, the afternoon had come and gone. The work of Tuesday was done.

Toolbox

Principles

1. Let's review the first two elements of *Smart Money for Church Salaries*:

   > 1—**Invest** in staff salaries with skill, towards fulfillment of the church's vision statement, so that God will entrust spiritual riches.
   > 2—**Handle** worldly wealth with excellence and trustworthiness, using money to serve God ... and not the other way around.

   The third element of *Smart Money for Church Salaries* is:

   > **Implement** a fair and generous compensation guide that neither underpays nor overpays.

2. One role of church leaders is to create, gain approval and implement a compensation guide. Jesus presents a challenging parable about fair and generous wages. While it speaks to God's Kingdom plan, it can apply to *Smart Money for Church Salaries*:

   > For the kingdom of heaven is like a landowner who went out early in the morning to hire workers for his vineyard. And after agreeing with the workers for the standard wage, he sent them into his vineyard ... When he went out again about noon and three o'clock that afternoon, he did the same thing ... each received a full day's pay. And when those hired first came, they thought they would receive more. But each one also received the standard wage. When they received it, they began to complain against the landowner, saying, 'These last fellows worked one hour, and you have made them equal to us who bore the hardship and burning heat of the day.' And the landowner replied to one of them, 'Friend, I am not treating you unfairly. Didn't you agree with me to work for the standard wage? ... Or are you envious because I am generous?'
   > Matthew 20:1-15

3. The goal in church compensation is to be fair to all workers, and still be generous with others. The parable shows the hurt that can arise. The landowner can be generous to the point of overpaying those who only worked an hour. Church leaders are stewards of funds and cannot overpay staff. A compensation guide gives a sane and rational way to pay church staff.

Core Concepts

1. Listen to the advice of your spouse. Pilate should have listened to his wife: "As he was sitting on the judgment seat, his wife sent a message to him: 'Have nothing to do with that innocent man; I have suffered greatly as a result of a dream about him today.'" Matthew 27:19

2. Engage in *four-wall discussions*. The name comes from the fact that what is said stays in the four walls of the room.[36] These are safe places for people to vent, share insecurities and pain. Staff can talk without being right on every issue. If you can't have *four-wall discussions* with a trusted team, who can you talk with?

3. Church policy must adequately describe each category of staff. Seek input from leaders. Include in the discussion those who will be affected by the decision.

4. Imbalanced compensation never remains a secret for long. Whether through inadvertent asides or outright sharing of salary information, people soon get an idea of the salaries of others.

---

[36] David R. Fletcher, *Four-Wall Discussions* (Austin, Texas: XPastor) available from https://www.xpastor.org/hey-fletch/four-wall-discussions/.

Steps

❏ Have Forthright Discussions

1. Listen to advice from your spouse. It is not necessary to share confidential salary information with your spouse. Share concepts and be attentive to the person who knows you best. They know the limitations in your communication style and can remind you how to defray those limitations.
2. Engage senior leaders in your church. Manage your information both upwards and with parallel leaders. Don't surprise other leaders with major decisions.
3. Seek input from a trusted leader from outside your church.
4. Conduct *four-wall discussions*.[37] Listen to staff, both key leaders and the rank-and-file. Compensation affects everyone's paycheck. Possible changes in compensation and benefits can scare staff and their families. Expect a wide variety of responses. Don't answer questions so much as listen for input.

❏ Analyze Ministry Staff Salaries

1. Discover existing categories from church policy and practice. Ensure that the use of titles and terms matches your constitution and policy. If they do not match, or there are new categories to add, then draft needed wording. Common categories include:

   - Senior pastor: also commonly called pastor, lead pastor, teaching pastor or preaching pastor.
   - Executive pastor: also commonly called senior associate pastor or associate pastor.
   - Core Team: also commonly called Leadership Team, Strategic Team or Management Team. Some churches do not have an explicit Core Team but have one by common practice. These are insiders that the senior pastor or executive pastor goes to for input.
   - Pastor: also commonly called minister.
   - Assistant pastor: also commonly called associate pastor, assistant or associate minister.
   - Ministry director: also commonly called ministry associate or descriptive titles by area.
   - Assistant ministry director: also commonly called assistant ministry associate or descriptive titles by area.

2. Sort the salaries into your church's ministry staff categories.
3. Analyze the salaries of pastors and ministry directors. Discover and note salary discrepancies, those that stand out as possibly being too low or too high.

---

[37] David R. Fletcher, *Four-Wall Discussions*.

4. Search for problems of titles and compensation—for example, where an assistant pastor is being paid for the work of a pastor.

5. Keep notes of related items as they arise. This could include work needed on intellectual property; ministerial housing allowance forms; creation of a five or eight-year salary history file; list of dates and certificates of license, commission or ordination; job description review; and annual reviews.

❏ Create the *Big Burrito* Salary Spreadsheet

1. List items to include in your full salary spreadsheet. Include all pertinent data—every employee, every cost, every benefit and the total cost per employee. See the Tools section for recommended items to include. In a separate area from staff, list any cost centers, such as a preschool, bookstore or café.

2. Give accounting leaders sufficient time and manpower to assemble the data for the *Big Burrito*. Negotiate with staff on the due date and give assistance when you make a sizable request like this.

3. Review the spreadsheet. Check that medical insurance contributions are accurate for each employee, as are the percentage of retirement contributions by the church. Compare the salary numbers to data provided by your payroll firm or Finance Office. Leave nothing to chance and double check all data. Expect errors and omissions.

Questions to Consider

One

Dan Black made a list of items that he wanted added to the salary spreadsheet. For your church, what would you add or subtract from his list? See the Tools section for his version.

	Data to Include on a Salary Spreadsheet
1	
2	
3	
4	
5	
6	
7	

Two

Dan needs to address issues on the titles of the junior high pastor and the discipleship assistant pastor. What would you advise him to do?

_____

_____

_____

_____

_____

_____

_____

_____

Three

Mission Pastor Ed Baker is paid $34,000 less than Family Pastor Liz Jackson. Should the three pastors on the Core Team be paid the same? For Ed, should Dan consider back pay or a bonus to cover prior years, a raise all at once, or raises over the next two years to bring him to the right salary level?

_____

_____

_____

_____

_____

_____

_____

SMART MONEY FOR CHURCH SALARIES

Tools

This section provides you with material that was introduced or finalized in this chapter. These items are also available at https://www.xpastor.org/smart. The password for this page is: smart money.

Your Church *Big Burrito* Salary Spreadsheet

Employees
- **Department**—list and sort by the department name and accounting number.
- **Employee**—title and full name. Show Core Team or key staff in bold.
- **FLSA Status**—ministerial, exempt or non-exempt.
- **Full-Time or Part-Time Status**—show salaries as applicable; hourly rates as applicable with budgeted weekly hours and annualized wages.

Benefits
- **FICA**—amounts for all non-ministerial staff.
- **Retirement**—the participation level by percentage in the church's retirement program and the cost to the church for each person.
- **Medical**—staff that participate in the church's medical insurance program. Have columns for the employee contribution dollar amount, if any, and the total premium cost to the church.
- **Other Benefits**—cost for each employee in the Dental, Vision, Life Insurance and other benefit programs.
- **Allowances**—taxable auto allowances and tax-free cell phone allowances.

Summary
- **Total Cost**—the complete cost to the church for each staff member.

- 100 -

Dan's *Big Burrito* Salary Spreadsheet Template

This and other items can be downloaded at https://www.xpastor.org/smart. The password for this page is: smart money.

Department	D#	Title	FLSA Status	Last	First	Hours	Hourly	Salary	FICA

In Dan's spreadsheet, the table below came after the "FICA" column

403B %	403B $	Medical Insurance	CoPay 21%	Dental	Vision	Life	Auto	Cell	Total Cost

2017—WheatFields' Ministerial Housing Allowance Form

Liz Jackson 2017 Housing Allowance

Liz Jackson	
Rent	$0
Mortgage	$10,300
Taxes	$6,262
Repairs	$3,900
Utilities	$1,800
Total	**$22,262**

Liz Jackson 2017 Taxable Income

Federal Taxable Income	
Church Salary	$93,000
Housing Allowance	$22,262
Taxable	**$70,738**

SMART MONEY FOR CHURCH SALARIES

2018 WheatFields' Ministerial Housing Allowance Form

Liz Jackson's 2018 Housing Allowance

Name: Liz Jackson	Title: Family Pastor
Date allowance should begin:	June 1, 2018
Date licensed, commissioned or ordained:	February 21, 2005

Kinds of Expenses	Annual Estimates
Rent	$0
Down payment for a house	$0
Loan principal & interest	$10,300
Real estate commissions & fees	$0
Property taxes	$6,262
Property taxes on contents	$0
Liability insurance	$450
Repair, maintenance & improvements	$3,900
Landscaping & pest control	$1,200
Furnishings—purchase & repairs	$2,000
Decoration & Renovation	$2,000
Utilities—gas, electric, water, telephone, trash, internet	$3,200
Homeowner's dues or fees	$500
Other—such as gardening equipment, computers	$0
Other—	$0
Unanticipated items	$6,000
Total	**$35,812**
Fair Rental Value of Home Plus Furnishings and Utilities	**$36,000**

Exclude income for federal income tax: The lower of your actual expenses or the fair rental value of your home (plus furnishings and utilities), up to your approved housing allowance. Pay 15.3% SECA on your total compensation. This form must be approved in advance of applicable compensation. This housing allowance applies until a new allowance is approved. Report unused housing allowances on your tax form.	
Date: May 1, 2018 Signature: *Elizabeth L. Jackson*	
Finance Team Approval: May 9, 2018	

Liz Jackson's 2018 Taxable Income

Federal Taxable Income	
Church Salary	$93,000
Housing Allowance	$35,812
Taxable	**$57,188**

- 5 -

SALARIES
FOR DIRECTORS

Defining the Director Role

On Wednesday's calendar, Dan had meetings scheduled with each of the nine directors. The topics would be their job descriptions, possible ministerial exemption and payroll issues if they were not exempt.

Dan looked at his schedule and shuddered. "Those may be some dicey conversations. Well, at least on Monday we got the ball rolling in the pastors and directors meeting. They've had two nights to sleep on it."

The file in front of Dan showed five relatively complete director job descriptions. A week ago, four other directors had no role descriptions. Now those four at least had a bullet point summary with, as his email asked for, "the scope of your role, your primary functions and any direct ministry you do." In reading all the job descriptions, Dan thought, "I'll just call these temporary until I meet with each one. I'd like to hear every director describe their role to me. Perhaps together we can come to a decision about their ministerial status. That would be better than me making a top-down decision and upsetting folks."

Director Issues

The file also contained the report from his executive assistant on the research from the elder minutes. Only two of the nine directors had been commissioned by the elders. "So, we did commission some of them. I have no recollection of doing that. It's tough to remember everything that the elders vote on."

Dan's salary spreadsheet showed the nine directors:

Directors

Title	Salary
Finance Director	$65,000
Assistant Director for Preschool	$42,000
Assistant Director for Preschool	$42,000
Creative Director	$38,366
Database Director	$42,000
Facility Director	$62,000
IT Director	$75,238
Media Director	$48,744
Worship Director	$38,933

"Bummer, no organization to the directors' information, just a list. I need that revised salary spreadsheet from the Finance Office. But this is what I have to work with today, so it will have to do."

Dan began to think about the upcoming meetings. "If some of these staff are not ministerially exempt, they may be professionally exempt from the Fair Labor Standards Act." He created a template to record his findings about each director:

Qualifications for FLSA Exemption

Title	Ministry Function?	Managerial Qualification?	Salary Qualification?	Exempt Determination
Finance Director				
Assistant Director for Preschool				
Assistant Director for Preschool				
Creative Director				
Database Director				
Facility Director				
IT Director				
Media Director				
Worship Director				

"I need a bullet point list of rules for FLSA managerial exemptions. This FLSA stuff for churches is murky to me. It seems that there are honest differences in interpretation of the federal guidelines." Dan did more research on the FLSA exemptions but was interrupted before he could finish.

It was time for his first interview with a director.

Interviews with Exempt Directors

Dan reminded himself that the first series of director meetings were with staff members that earned $38,366, $42,000 and $48,744. "If those folks are ministerially exempt, then salary is not a factor for exemption. If they are not ministerially exempt, then salary will be a major factor for possible managerial exemption. California has a unique salary level for managerial exemption, but that needs more study."

Irene Steele came promptly for her 9:00 am appointment. She came into the office and looked at Dan, waiting for the executive pastor to start the conversation:

Dan: "Welcome, great to ..."

Irene: "So, let me start with a little background info. I work twenty hours a week as worship director. The church has many times offered me a full-time role. Each time I declined. My husband loves working three twelve-hour days as an Emergency Room doc at WheatFields Memorial. He takes the Wednesday night shift, when I have rehearsal. He also works weekends, which makes him popular with the other docs. That's my take-it-or-leave-it negotiating position."

Dan: "Well, um, we take it."

Irene: "Let's get to it. You did a great job on Monday prepping everyone about the possible changes for directors. There wasn't any blood!"

Dan: "Thanks, I hoped that ..."

Irene: "That was the first time in a long time—if ever—that all the pastors and directors had a real discussion. I like that. People should have good two-way discussions. That's how my husband and I roll. You can't operate until you prep the patient."

Dan: "So, let's talk about ..."

Irene: "Yep, let's talk about the ministerial director thing. I have scrubbed our church policy on the subject, as I'm sure that you have."

Dan: "Yes, it's clear ..."

Irene: "My job description contains ministerial work—no cancer here. I made sure of that. Some staff have been howling for better job descriptions for years. I didn't have much of one for two weeks when I started. But for some reason they listened to me and we got one written."

Dan: "You have one of the most complete job descriptions ..."

Irene: "And you also saw that I was commissioned by the Elder Board on Tuesday, March 18, 2008?"

Dan: "That jogs my memory a bit about ..."

Irene: "Yep, I asked for my husband to be there, too. The elders prayed and placed hands on me for that commissioning. I asked for a certificate for my records. Just like in the hospital, you've got to have a good record retention plan. Here's a copy for your files. HR probably lost the one that I gave them in 2008."

Dan: "So, we have all the elements ..."

Irene: "Yep, I know the law too. You have the job description, date of commissioning, certificate of commissioning, ministerial work being done in accordance with the job description. I think that we're done here. Let's sew up this patient and I'm outta here."

Before Dan knew it, Irene had risen, shaken his hand and left his office. "Well," Dan thought, "I could do without the hospital imagery ... and I wouldn't have minded finishing my sentences either. Was I the doctor or the patient here? But we got it done, or should I say, *she* got it done." It was 9:03.

Between the appointments for Irene and the next director, Dan did more research on FLSA standards for exemption. At 9:30, Tamika White, Assistant Director for Preschool, came for her appointment.

Dan: "Hi, Tamika, have a seat."

Dan paused, bracing for a similar take-over as Irene had done. Tamika waited:

Dan: "So, let's talk about the ministerial role that you have as a director."

Tamika: "You're not going to demote me, are you? My husband was pretty upset that we might lose the housing allowance. And I may be underpaid as well."

Dan: "No, we're not going to demote you. But let's make sure that everything in your role fits and complies with the law."

Tamika: "I brought my job description that talks about my ministry to families. I regularly meet with the moms and dads. I assess the spiritual needs of the family. I share the gospel and pray with them. I write and send out a weekly devotional guide to all the parents. I lead the daily chapel. Each day I have a different age group attend."

Dan: "I do have your job description and there is plenty of ministry in it. Also, we searched the elder minutes and found that you were commissioned on Tuesday, June 12, 2001."

Tamika: "Oh, I didn't know that I had been commissioned by the elders."

Dan: "So really, there is no change in your status. Everything looks fine."

To be polite to Tamika, Dan asked her about her work and family. He didn't want to end the meeting after two minutes. They chatted on until 9:45 then Dan hastily filled in his summary sheet for the first two meetings:

Directors—Ministerially Exempt

Title	Ministry Function?	Managerial Qualification?	Salary Qualification?	Exempt Determination
Assistant Director for Preschool	Yes & Board Commissioned	—	—	Ministerial
Worship Director	Yes & Board Commissioned	—	—	Ministerial

"The morning is flying by," Dan realized.

Interviews with Non-Exempt Directors

Dan's next appointment arrived at 10:00. Dan was expecting Creative Director Derek Mays. However, Derek's supervisor, Media Director Charlie Ethelridge, also entered:

Dan: "Are you guys coming together to double team me?"

Derek: "I really wanted my boss to be with me. I don't understand this stuff."

Charlie: "Is that okay? If not, I can leave."

Dan: "No problem with me. You know, your titles don't make it easy to know who reports to whom."

Charlie: "That's a long story for another day."

Dan: "Okay, let's get to it. Perhaps we can work on the issues for both of you. What were your thoughts from Monday's discussion with all the pastors and directors?"

Charlie: "I'm supposed to be leading Derek, but neither of us have job descriptions. We sent in bullet point summaries to you ... at least that's a start."

Derek: "Charlie's a great boss, and we get along great and do really good work, but a real job description would be nice."

Dan: "On behalf of the church, I apologize that we haven't provided you with job descriptions. We didn't do what we should have been doing. We blew it. I'm sorry and want to move forward on a good footing. You are two of four directors who don't have adequate job descriptions. How do you see the ministry aspect of your jobs?"

Derek: "Charlie and I talked about that. I work for Charlie and do lots of work with videos, slide decks, worship service stuff ..."

Charlie: "And in the creative area, I oversee the design of all of our ministry material. But really, Derek and I don't see that we do much of any hands-on ministry. We're not part of the *On Call* list for people who come or phone in with issues. We don't do funerals or weddings—and wouldn't have a clue how to do them. We really don't do or want to do that kind of pastoral stuff."

Derek: "We're concerned, though, about the financial effects of losing the ministerial housing allowance."

Dan drew a deep breath. This was the challenging moment. He had to address salary implications for directors who would lose their ministerial housing allowances.

Dan: "Right now, you're paying the 15.3% of SECA."

Charlie: "What do those initials stand for?"

Dan: "That's the Self Employment Contributions Act ..."

Derek: "But I thought that we were church employees, not self-employed."

Dan: "The rules are hard to understand. For tax purposes, ministry staff are considered self-employed, but not self-employed for HR or other policies."

Charlie: "Clear as mud to me. We're creative types and don't get this CPA stuff."

Dan: "I had to take a deep dive into this last week. It was hard to get a handle on, so don't fret that you don't get it. If you're not ministry directors, then the church would pay your FICA—the Federal Insurance Contributions Act. Just like employees when I was running a for-profit business, the employer pays 7.65% of the salary and the employee pays 7.65%."

Charlie: "So that would make up the difference if we lose the housing allowance, right?"

Dan: "It would be pretty close for most folks."

Charlie: "Both Derek and I are younger and our salaries are on the low side. Would you also consider an increase to help us feed our families?"

While Charlie called himself a creative type, he was also a shrewd negotiator. The conversation continued for thirty minutes. Dan promised to review their salaries. Both Derek and Charlie agreed that if the compensation was fair, they would move to non-ministerial status.

"Four conversations down, and I'm not bruised or beaten up," thought Dan. "I hope the talks with the other directors go as well."

Todd Petrey, the Database Director, arrived late for his 11:00 am meeting. "Sorry about being late but we had an emergency bug that needed fixing. If I didn't get to it right away, our system might have crashed," he explained. The conversation with Todd was a repeat of that with Charlie and Derek. They were done in five minutes and Todd returned to further fix the latest software bug.

Grace Peterson, Assistant Director for Preschool, arrived at 11:30:

Grace: "I'm confused, wondering why I'm considered ministerial staff. I answer phones as the preschool receptionist."

Dan: "That's what we need to work out."

Grace: "I'm really an assistant *to* the director, not an assistant director."

Dan: "That's a good distinction!"

Grace: "And right now with young children, I can't handle more responsibility. I need to leave each day at 5:00 pm sharp to get home to my babies. Maybe I can do more when my children are grown."

Dan: "Well, we don't need to change that."

Grace: "And my husband hates this ministerial housing thing. I ain't a minister but will I lose money in this new deal? We can't afford to be losing any salary. We're a two income family as it is. We need every dollar that I earn."

Dan had learned what he needed. The rest of the conversation helped ease Grace's concerns. They continued on and talked for some time about Grace's children.

Dan updated his chart. He paused to consider the issues. "All four directors meet the federal salary minimum but three of them are not managerial. Charlie in media is managerial but may not meet the California salary standards. I need to better define those California salary issues. I'll mark him non-exempt for now."

Non-Exempt Directors

Title	Ministry Function?	Managerial Qualification?	Salary Qualification?	Exempt Determination
Assistant Director for Preschool	No	Yes	No	Non-Exempt
Creative Director	No	No	No	Non-Exempt
Database Director	No	No	No	Non-Exempt
Media Director	No	No	Yes	Non-Exempt

"That table looks pretty good for starters. Four non-exempt directors completed so far. The next three director meetings will be different. Whatever the California minimum salary is for being managerially exempt, their compensation will exceed it."

Eating lunch at his desk, Dan began to review federal and state regulations, especially as they applied to the salaries of being managerially exempt. As Dan thought, he asked Nancy to schedule a combined meeting for the accounting, information technology and facility directors. "Tell them that we won't be discussing individual salaries, but only issues of management exemption" he added.

FLSA Exemption Standards

"I hate getting back into this FLSA stuff," Dan fumed. "But, I'd better be ready for the meetings with the next three directors. They're sharp people."

Dan found the Department of Labor's 2004 regulations where a minimum weekly salary of $455 was set for employees to be exempt from the FLSA.[38] Plus, employees have to qualify by their job description.

Federal FLSA Standards

	Weekly	Annualized
FLSA Minimum Salary	$455	$23,660

In 2015, the Department of Labor published a Notice of Proposed Rulemaking in the Federal Register. They proposed that a new guideline would take effect on December 1, 2016. That proposal set the new salary minimum to $47,476 which was just over double the existing amount. The proposed 2016 changes were tabled and the 2004 salary level was left in place. However, these issues are still being debated. The DOL noted in January 2018:

> The Department of Labor is undertaking rulemaking to revise the regulations located at 29 C.F.R. part 541, which govern the exemption of executive, administrative, and professional employees from the Fair Labor Standards Act's minimum wage and overtime pay requirements. Until the Department issues its final rule, it will enforce the part 541 regulations in effect on November 30, 2016, including the $455 per week standard salary level.[39]

"Whoa, they may try again to increase the minimum. If they do, that would be a whopping change."

Dan also found an updated page from January 2018 from the U.S. Department of Labor, Wage and Hour Division's, *Fact Sheet #17A: Exemption for Executive, Administrative, Professional, Computer & Outside Sales Employees Under the Fair Labor Standards Act (FLSA).*[40]

"Okay," Dan thought. "I know about the federal salary standards. Now onto the issues of who are executive, administrative, and professional employees." Dan consulted the

---

[38] U.S. Department of Labor, Wage and Hour Division, *Defining and Delimiting the Exemptions for Executive, Administrative, Professional, Outside Sales and Computer Employees; Final Rule*, April 23, 2004, available from https://www.dol.gov/whd/overtime/regulations.pdf.

[39] U.S. Department of Labor, *Overtime*, revised January, 2018, available from https://www.dol.gov/whd/overtime/final2016/.

[40] U.S. Department of Labor, *Fact Sheet #17A: Exemption for Executive, Administrative, Professional, Computer & Outside Sales Employees Under the Fair Labor Standards Act (FLSA)*, revised July 2008, available from https://www.dol.gov/whd/overtime/fs17a_overview.pdf.

Federal Register for the Department of Labor, Regulations on *Defining and Delimiting the Exemptions for Executive, Administrative, Professional, Outside Sales and Computer Employees; Final Rule.*[41]

Dan was reminded that job titles are insufficient "to establish the exempt status of an employee." He summarized his learnings from the regulations about the nature of the roles:

Executive Qualifications
- Primary duty is management.
- Regularly directs the work of two or more other employees.
- Authority to hire or fire employees or whose suggestions and recommendations as to the hiring, firing, advancement, promotion or any other change of status of other employees are given particular weight.

Management Qualifications
Includes activities such as interviewing, selecting, and training; setting rates of pay and hours of work; directing the work of others; maintaining records for use in supervision or control; appraising productivity and efficiency for the purpose of recommending promotions or other changes in status; handling employee complaints and grievances; disciplining; planning work; determining techniques to be used; apportioning work; planning and controlling the budget; monitoring or implementing legal compliance measures.

Administrative Qualifications
- Primary duty is the performance of office or non-manual work directly related to management.
- Primary duty includes the exercise of discretion and independent judgment with respect to matters of significance.
- An executive assistant or administrative assistant to a senior executive generally meets the duties requirements for the administrative exemption if such employee, without specific instructions or prescribed procedures, has been delegated authority regarding matters of significance.

Dan thought about his executive assistant. "Though she meets the requirement of the duties in the administrative qualifications and her salary meets federal guidelines, yet she may not meet the California salary minimum. I'll leave her as a non-exempt employee for now."

---

[41] U.S. Department of Labor, *Defining and Delimiting the Exemptions*.

California Exemption Standards

"Hey, wait a minute," Dan thought. "The State of California has some special requirements added to the federal ones, but I don't know those amounts" Dan realized. States can add to the FLSA requirements but not subtract from them.

Dan found a summary article from the Society for Human Resource Management. He learned of an important addition by the State of California.[42] The wage level for professional exemption was double the state's minimum wage. "Oh great, just when I thought that things were getting easier, I need to consider new variables ... double minimum wage for exemption."

Going to the State of California, Department of Industrial Relations website, Dan found the Labor Commissioner's Office scale of minimum wage.[43] He knew that the state legislature had set a yearly increase and wanted that information straight from the source. "My info has to be accurate." Dan found the scale for minimum wage and added to it the annualized figure for double minimum wage:

California Minimum Wage

Date Beginning	Hourly Rate	Annualized Full-Time	Double Annualized
January 1, 2018	$11.00	$22,880	$45,760
January 1, 2019	$12.00	$24,960	$49,920
January 1, 2020	$13.00	$27,040	$54,080
January 1, 2021	$14.00	$29,120	$58,240
January 1, 2022	$15.00	$31,200	$62,400

"Whew, that is a huge increase for minimum wage. When I get to the support staff salaries, I'm going to need that info. I wonder how we'll afford it for those who earn minimum wage? I'll ask Janet to see if we have anyone who doesn't earn the current minimum wage."

"But for now, I need to remember that California doubles the minimum wage amount for someone to qualify for FLSA exemption. What a maze of facts and numbers!"

[42] Society for Human Resource Management, *What Is the Difference Between California Overtime Exemption Requirements and Federal Overtime Exemption Requirements?* (Alexandria, Virginia: SHRM, December 26, 2017) available from https://www.shrm.org/resourcesandtools/tools-and-samples/hr-qa/pages/californiaexemptionrequirements.aspx.

[43] State of California, Department of Industrial Relations, Labor Commissioner's Office, *Minimum Wage*, December 2016, available from https://www.dir.ca.gov/dlse/faq_minimumwage.htm.

He continued to think about those who may be managerially exempt and ran some numbers for future implications:

California 5-Year Increases

Date Beginning	Management Salaries	Increase	Percent
January 1, 2018	$45,760		
January 1, 2022	$62,400	$16,640	36.4%

"If someone is managerially exempt in our church, I have to ensure that their future salary will qualify. In seven years, that annual salary is going way up. They may earn $45,760 this year but in 2022 they're required to earn $62,400 to maintain their exempt status. I wonder what other states do? Well, that's not my problem. I just have to worry about the rules in California."

Interviews with Exempt Directors

At 2:30 pm, three directors came into Dan's office: Director of Finance Janet Williams, Director of Information Technology Hank Fogarty and Facility Director José Mendoza. Dan began with some ground rules for the discussion:

> Dan: "Each of you makes well above the current minimum for federal and state exemption from FLSA. The federal level is $23,660 and the state level is $45,760."

> Janet: "Well, yeah, we oversee huge areas."

> Dan: "The state level is going to rise to $62,400 on January 1, 2022."

> José: "All three of us are probably already near that level."

> Dan: "In this discussion, let's assume that. Also, let's not talk specific salaries here. Our church likes to keep individual salaries private as much as possible."

> Janet: "Well, my staff and I know all the salaries and we're as quiet as church mice."

> Dan: "Before we get caught up in the salary discussion, give me your thoughts about Monday's round table with the pastors and directors."

There ensued a frank and sometimes emotional discussion about the question, *Who is a pastor?* In varying degrees, from lukewarm to hot, all three were opposed to being considered ministers.

> Dan: "We're all agreed that according to your job descriptions and desires, none of you want to continue to be ministerially exempt."

> José: "Amen to that. As facility director, it has never seemed right to me."

> Dan: "Since each of you qualify for state and federal FLSA exemption based on your current salaries, let's talk about the management qualifications."

> José: "I'm often at the church at 6:00 am and leave sometimes at 6:00 pm. The church couldn't afford overtime for me ... and I wouldn't want it."

> Dan: "That's right, so let's see if you fit the qualifications to be exempt."

So that everyone could see the qualifications, he connected his computer to the video screen in his office:

Management Qualifications

Includes activities such as interviewing, selecting, and training; setting rates of pay and hours of work; directing the work of others; maintaining records for use in supervision or control; appraising productivity and efficiency for the purpose of recommending promotions or other changes in status; handling employee complaints and grievances; disciplining; planning work; determining techniques to be used; apportioning work; planning and controlling the budget; monitoring or implementing legal compliance measures.

Everyone looked at the qualifications for a minute.

> Dan: "Why don't each of you tell me how you fit within these qualifications."

> Janet: "It seems to me that my work in 'planning and controlling the budget' fits clearly."

José: "You have given me a loud voice on hiring, disciplining and terminating the facility staff."

Hank: "As information technology director, I don't see that I qualify."

Janet: "What do you mean? You have a staff that you oversee. You plan work and 'determine techniques to be used.' If you did any more legal compliance on communications issues, like how we used to have recorded music on our website, then you'd be an attorney. You are *there*, buddy."

The conversation then turned to how to make the change from ministerial to non-ministerial. Just as Charlie, Derek and Grace raised questions about the effects of losing their ministerial housing allowances, so did Hank, Janet and José.

Changes for Directors

Dan now had two hours of think time. He needed to process all of the gleanings from the day. He had learned in business not to over-schedule his day with meetings. Dan tried to leave significant margin at the end of the day to reflect and work through issues.

Dan finalized the chart of directors:

Determination of FLSA Status

Title	Ministry Function?	Managerial Qualification?	Salary Qualification?	Exempt Determination
Finance Director	No	Yes	Yes	Exempt
Assistant Director for Preschool	Yes & Board Commissioned	—	—	Ministerial
Assistant Director for Preschool	No	Yes	No	Non-Exempt
Creative Director	No	No	No	Non-Exempt
Database Director	No	No	No	Non-Exempt
Facility Director	No	Yes	Yes	Exempt
IT Director	No	Yes	Yes	Exempt
Media Director	No	No	Yes	Non-Exempt
Worship Director	Yes & Board Commissioned	—	—	Ministerial

Looking at his notes in chronological order, Dan made a list of action items:

Change Titles to Include Ministry
- Irene Steele: Change title to Worship Ministry Director.
- Tamika White: Change title to Assistant Ministry Director of Preschool.
- Inform staff that we will be using approved titles from our policy documents. Clear up confusion between the roles of directors and ministry directors.

Change of Title to Exclude Ministry
- Grace Peterson: She should have been hired as an administrative assistant or coordinator. Her tasks aren't really those of an assistant director. Should I change her title? It would seem like a demotion ... but she may have given the answer when she said her role was being an assistant *to* the preschool director. That's the title change we need.

Change of Status from Ministerial to Non-Exempt
- Change to non-exempt: Derek Mays (Creative Director), Todd Petrey (Database Director) and Grace Peterson (Assistant to the Preschool Director).
- Examine whether Charlie Ethelridge (Media Director) should be managerially exempt. Initial recommendation is no.
- Educate each on FLSA non-exempt status.
- Educate all non-ministerial staff on FLSA requirements. Include information about overtime, breaks, not working in the evenings without recording hours, cell phone and email after hours, etc.

Change of Status from Ministerial to Managerially Exempt
- Janet Williams (Accounting Director), Hank Fogarty (Information Technology Director) and José Mendoza (Facility Director).
- Educate each on FLSA exempt status.

Back Pay for Minimum Wage Issues
- Receptionists Carolyn Morrison and Janet Smithey were earning $10.96. They needed back pay to January 1, by 4 cents an hour. Stage Hand Jeanie Wilson needed back pay of 50 cents an hour.

Compensation Work
- Examine salary implications of non-ministerial directors losing their housing allowances. Consider a merit increase, if needed.
- Add FICA to the salary spreadsheet for the non-ministerial directors. Examine the cost to the church.
- Consider the raise requests from Derek Mays (at $38,366) and Charlie Ethelridge

(at $48,744). Todd Petrey (at $42,000) and Tamika White (at $42,000) may be underpaid. Salary comparisons are needed to validate this.

- Irene Steele, Worship Ministry Director, is part-time. $38,933 is great money for twenty hours a week. Does Irene receive any benefits?

Dan reflected, "For years we considered the directors as ministerially exempt from the Fair Labor Standards Act. They didn't turn in a time card, take rest breaks nor meal breaks as required for non-exempt workers. They often worked more than forty hours a week and were not paid overtime. Now, four of them will be non-exempt and need to do those things. That will be a culture shift."

With a little time left in the work day, Dan turned his attention to the salaries of the directors who were not ministers. Like he had done with the spreadsheet for pastors, Dan added columns for the department name and accounting code. He then sorted the employees by department. Finally, he added a column for the new FICA contribution that the church would have to make.

New FICA Contribution for Directors

Department	D#	Title	FLSA	Salary	FICA
Worship	27	IT Director	Exempt	$75,238	$5,756
Worship	27	Creative Director	Non-Exempt	$38,366	$2,935
Worship	27	Media Director	Non-Exempt	$48,744	$3,729
Operations	57	Finance Director	Exempt	$65,000	$4,973
Operations	57	Database Director	Non-Exempt	$42,000	$3,213
Operations	57	Facility Director	Exempt	$62,000	$4,743
Preschool	67	Assistant Director for Preschool	Non-Exempt	$42,000	$3,213
			Total		$28,561

"So, by doing the right thing and changing the classifications of seven staff to non-ministerial, we will now have to pay $28,561 in FICA. I hate to do that but it's the right thing to do. Well, at least we can easily afford it with our current donation surplus."

"I still need names added to this spreadsheet. I don't do well with just titles. Without names, sooner or later I'm going to make a mistake. I've known these people for years, but need to see all the data in one place."

Dan created a spreadsheet to consider the ramifications of seven staff losing their housing allowances. He began by doing some estimates on the current taxes that they were paying. "I'll just assume a 15% federal tax rate for all of them, to make things easy."

Dan created this file to estimate the federal income tax and SECA:

Directors—With a Housing Allowance

Title	Salary	15.3% SECA	Housing Allowance	Federal Tax Basis	Federal Tax Estimate	Federal Tax & SECA
IT Director	$75,238	$11,511	$35,000	$40,238	$6,036	$17,547
Creative Director	$38,366	$5,870	$22,000	$16,366	$2,455	$8,325
Media Director	$48,744	$7,458	$24,000	$24,744	$3,712	$11,169
Finance Director	$65,000	$9,945	$30,000	$35,000	$5,250	$15,195
Database Director	$42,000	$6,426	$25,000	$17,000	$2,550	$8,976
Facility Director	$62,000	$9,486	$32,000	$30,000	$4,500	$13,986
Assist. Dir. for Preschool	$42,000	$6,426	$28,000	$14,000	$2,100	$8,526

He knew that the tax numbers were rough. "Form 1040, line 27 has a deduction for the 'deductible part of self-employment tax,' but I'm not going to get to that level of detail. Form 1040, Line 7, people must include 'excess housing allowance,' but to get that exact I would need to see everyone's taxes ... fat chance on that ... not that I want to wade through all their stuff. This is a good start."

Next, Dan created a spreadsheet of what would happen to those directors when they lose their ministerial housing allowances:

Directors—Impact of Losing Housing Allowances

Department	D#	Title	Salary	Federal Tax Estimate	7.65% FICA by Employee	Federal Tax & FICA	Potential Gain or Loss
Worship	27	IT Director	$75,238	$11,286	$5,756	$17,041	$506
Worship	27	Creative Director	$38,366	$5,755	$2,935	$8,690	-$365
Worship	27	Media Director	$48,744	$7,312	$3,729	$11,041	$129
Operations	57	Finance Director	$65,000	$9,750	$4,973	$14,723	$473
Operations	57	Database Director	$42,000	$6,300	$3,213	$9,513	-$537
Operations	57	Facility Director	$62,000	$9,300	$4,743	$14,043	-$57
Preschool	67	Assistant Dir. for Preschool	$42,000	$6,300	$3,213	$9,513	-$987

"It looks like a slight gain for three employees and a loss for the creative director and database director. Grace in the preschool will lose the most at $987—that hurts," Dan reflected.

Dan was done for Wednesday. "That was a full day of work. Sorting through the federal and state issues took most of the day. The salary piece was not too hard once all the people were in the right classifications."

On the drive home he called Pastor Wilson:

> Dan: "Pastor Wilson, I'm calling to bring you up to date on some issues regarding some of the directors."
>
> Wilson: "That's nice of you to call. Remember, though, I'm not going to give any input. I'm enjoying just being a member of our church. I'm not in leadership any longer. I'm retired."
>
> Dan: "I know. This is a courtesy call so you can say you were informed and support what we're doing ..." and Dan shared his thoughts.
>
> Wilson: "Those all sound like good next steps for the church."
>
> Dan: "Wow! Since you're not 'head of the family' any longer, you're so relaxed!"
>
> Wilson: "That's right. I get to focus on pure ministry now. No leadership responsibilities ... and I love it. I'm about done with my next book, too. Keep up with the good work!"

Dan ended the call and continued his drive home. "Thursday will be a focus on support staff issues. That should be as easy as pie," he hoped.

The next day would show whether Dan's thought was fact or fiction.

Toolbox

Principles

1. In preceding chapters we have seen the first three elements of *Smart Money for Church Salaries*:

   1—**Invest** in staff salaries with skill, towards fulfillment of the church's vision statement, so that God will entrust spiritual riches.
   2—**Handle** worldly wealth with excellence and trustworthiness, using money to serve God ... and not the other way around.
   3—**Implement** a fair and generous compensation guide that neither underpays nor overpays.

   The fourth element of *Smart Money for Church Salaries* is:

   Follow federal or state regulations with integrity.

2. Webster's *Dictionary* begins the definition of *integrity* with, "Firm adherence to a code of especially moral or artistic values: Incorruptibility."[44] That is a good place to start. Church leaders must adhere to local, state and federal rules.

   A second definition from Webster of integrity is: "An unimpaired condition: Soundness."[45] A church antonym of integrity could be: "Impairing the moral and legal status of your church."

3. Consider what the Bible says about integrity:

   The one who conducts himself in integrity will live securely,
   but the one who behaves perversely will be found out. Proverbs 10:9

   The integrity of the upright guides them,
   but the crookedness of the unfaithful destroys them. Proverbs 11:3

   The Lord abhors a person who lies,
   but those who deal truthfully are his delight. Proverbs 12:22

4. When we follow rules and regulations with integrity, we don't have to fear standing

[44] Merriam-Webster, *Integrity* (Springfield, Massachusetts: Merriam-Webster, updated on April 17, 2018) available from https://www.merriam-webster.com/dictionary/integrity.
[45] Merriam-Webster, *Integrity*.

before a court of law. We have done the best to uphold civil law. In Mark Twain's notebook from 1894, he wrote: "If you tell the truth you don't have to remember anything." The problem with dis-integrity is that we have to remember the small deceits, the outright lies, the prevarications.

5. You don't want a local reporter asking the question, "Is it true that your church evaded the law on fair hiring, on equitable pay, on overtime wages?"

Steps

❏ Explore the Roles of Directors

1. You may have exempt and non-exempt directors. Examine each person's role description to establish any ministry function.

2. If you desire to make a change to a director's status, conduct a face-to-face discussion. Have them describe their role in their own words. Ask if they see their role as ministerial in nature. If someone is a ministry director, see the preceding chapter as the directors in this chapter do not have a ministry function.

3. You may need to change the status of a director from ministerial to exempt or non-exempt. Calculate any potential loss from losing the ministerial housing allowance. Consider an increase in salary to cover this loss. Add to your budget the FICA amount that the church will need to contribute.

❏ Analyze the Salaries of Directors

1. Sort the salaries of your church's directors into staff categories.

2. Analyze the salaries of your directors. Discover and note salary discrepancies, those that stand out as possibly being too low or high.

3. Create a chart of the qualifications for FLSA exemption. Learn the FLSA qualifications for exempt managers and administrators. To be exempt, the employee's work must meet the standard for their FLSA category.

4. Create a chart of your state's salary qualifications for exemption. The federal salary minimum for exemption is $23,660. Your state may impose a higher standard, which may increase over time. California's salary qualification is double the minimum wage and rising annually.

5. Compile a list of changes as you work through issues. Don't wait until the end of your analysis.

❏ Create *Think Time*

Ministry schedules crowd out time to think and reflect. Major issues and strategic alignment require sufficient time for thorough analysis. Put at least an hour a day in your calendar as *think time*. This allows you the opportunity to move your event horizon from today's urgent needs to the important issues facing your church in the next six to twelve months.

Dwight Eisenhower said: "I have two kinds of problems, the urgent and the important. The urgent are not important, and the important are never urgent." Follow the thinking of a president of the United States. Give yourself sufficient space to focus on important issues.

Questions to Consider

One

With the proposed changes at WheatFields, seven staff would lose their status as ministerially exempt. The church would begin to pay $28,561 in FICA on those wages. The employees would lose their housing allowances but would stop paying SECA. Each would pay federal income tax on their full salary, instead of their salary less the housing allowance.

What is your recommendation on how to settle any pay differences for each affected employee on this issue?

Change of Compensation for Losing Housing Allowance

Department	D#	Title	Potential Gain or Loss	Change Compensation? How much?
Worship	27	IT Director	$506	
Worship	27	Creative Director	-$365	
Worship	27	Media Director	$129	
Operations	57	Finance Director	$473	
Operations	57	Database Director	-$537	
Operations	57	Facility Director	-$57	
Preschool	67	Assistant Dir. for Pre-school	-$987	

Two

Dan had a dilemma with Charlie Ethelridge, Media Director. His salary of $48,744 was eligible for a federal salary FLSA exemption. Was his role managerial? If they made him managerial, then when California minimum wages increased in coming years, he would require significant raises. What would you advise Dan?

_____

_____

_____

_____

_____

_____

_____

Three

If you had been Dan during these Tuesday meetings, what would you have done differently? Are there mistakes that Dan made? How would your gifts and abilities have changed the meetings?

_____

_____

_____

_____

_____

_____

_____

SMART MONEY FOR CHURCH SALARIES

Tools

This section provides you with material that was introduced or finalized in this chapter. These items are also available at https://www.xpastor.org/smart. The password for this page is: smart money.

Federal FLSA Exemption

Be aware of the federal salary minimums for exemption:

FLSA Salary Minimum

	Weekly	Annualized
FLSA Minimum Salary	$455	$23,660

Executive Exemption Qualifications
- Primary duty is management.
- Regularly directs the work of two or more other employees.
- Authority to hire or fire employees or whose suggestions and recommendations as to the hiring, firing, advancement, promotion or any other change of status of other employees are given particular weight.

Management Exemption Qualifications
- Includes activities such as interviewing, selecting, and training; setting rates of pay and hours of work; directing the work of others; maintaining records for use in supervision or control; appraising productivity and efficiency for the purpose of recommending promotions or other changes in status; handling employee complaints and grievances; disciplining; planning work; determining techniques to be used; apportioning work; planning and controlling the budget; monitoring or implementing legal compliance measures.

Administrative Exemption Qualifications
- Primary duty is the performance of office or non-manual work directly related to management.
- Primary duty includes the exercise of discretion and independent judgment with respect to matters of significance.
- An executive assistant or administrative assistant to a senior executive generally meets the duties requirements for the administrative exemption if such employee, without specific instructions or prescribed procedures, has been delegated authority regarding matters of significance.

For full definitions, see the Federal Register, Department of Labor, Regulations on *Defining and Delimiting the Exemptions for Executive, Administrative, Professional,*

Outside Sales and Computer Employees; Final Rule.[46]

State Issues

California's Qualifications for FLSA Exemption

Date Beginning	Hourly Rate	Annualized Full-Time	Double Annualized
January 1, 2018	$11.00	$22,880	$45,760
January 1, 2019	$12.00	$24,960	$49,920
January 1, 2020	$13.00	$27,040	$54,080
January 1, 2021	$14.00	$29,120	$58,240
January 1, 2022	$15.00	$31,200	$62,400

Your State Exemption Salaries

Date Beginning	Hourly Rate	Annualized Full-Time	Computed Annualized
January 1, 2018			
January 1, 2019			
January 1, 2020			
January 1, 2021			
January 1, 2022			

States with Higher Exemption Salary Levels[47]

	2017	2018	2019
Alaska—two times the state minimum wage	$40,768	$40,934	
Arizona—at least state minimum wage	$20,800	$21,840	$22,880
California—two times the state minimum wage			
California—26 or more employees	$43,680	$45,760	$49,920
California—25 or fewer employees	$41,600	$43,680	$45,760
Colorado—executive or supervisor must earn in excess of the equivalent of the state minimum wage. The administrative and professional exemptions only require that an employee be salaried.	$19,344	$21,216	$23,088
Connecticut	$24,700	$24,700	

---

[46] U.S. Department of Labor, *Defining and Delimiting the Exemptions.*

[47] Daniel L. Thieme and Sebastian Chilco. *Exempt Employee Pay Minimums Will Increase in 2018 in Various States,* (San Francisco: Littler Mendelson, December 11, 2017) with 2018 author's additions from various state labor departments, available from https://www.littler.com/publication-press/publication/exempt-employee-pay-minimums-will-increase-2018-various-states.

Iowa	$26,000	$26,000	
Maine—annual rate must exceed 3,000 times the state minimum wage or the FLSA rate, whichever is higher.	$27,000	$30,000	$33,000
Oregon—salary is no less than the state minimum wage multiplied by 2,080			
Oregon—general	$21,320	$22,360	
Oregon—urban	$23,400	$24,960	
Oregon—non-urban	$20,800	$21,840	
New Jersey—at least state minimum wage	$17,555	$17,888	
New York—executive or administrative must be paid a salary. The professional exemption does not include a salary requirement. Note: takes effect December 31.			
New York—New York City, 11 or more employees	$50,700	$58,500	
New York—New York City, 10 or fewer employees	$46,800	$52,650	
New York—Nassau, Suffolk & Westchester Counties	$42,900	$46,800	
New York—remainder of state	$40,560	$43,264	
Rhode Island—at least state minimum wage	$19,968	$21,008	$21,840
South Dakota—at least state minimum wage	$17,992	$18,408	

Chart of Directors

FLSA Status at WheatFields

Title	Ministry Function?	Managerial Qualification?	Salary Qualification?	Exempt Determination
Finance Director	No	Yes	Yes	Exempt
Assistant Director for Preschool	Yes & Board Commissioned	—	—	Ministerial
Assistant Director for Preschool	No	Yes	No	Non-Exempt
Creative Director	No	No	No	Non-Exempt
Database Director	No	No	No	Non-Exempt
Facility Director	No	Yes	Yes	Exempt
IT Director	No	Yes	Yes	Exempt
Media Director	No	No	Yes	Non-Exempt
Worship Director	Yes & Board Commissioned	—	—	Ministerial

Your Church FLSA Exempt Staff

Director Level Staff	Ministry Function?	Managerial Qualification?	Salary Qualification?	Exempt Determination

Your titles may be different than director. List people who are managers, program leaders, lead coordinators, team leaders, etc. Consider those on your staff who are not pastors but may have ministerial functions. List all who have a possible managerial qualification to be exempt from the Fair Labor Standards Act.

- 6 -

STAFF SALARIES
AND STAFF ISSUES

Support Staff Salaries

"Today," Dan asserted on Thursday morning, "I'm going to jump into the support staff salaries. Maybe I can skip looking at FLSA and other regulatory issues. Haven't I seen everything already?" He was hopeful in his thinking but realistic that the day could include more compliance issues.

To date, Dan had not closely looked at the support staff salaries. When he finally did, he thought "I can't make heads or tails of this! It's just a bunch of titles and numbers—I need names." Taking the full list (see the Tools at the end of this chapter), Dan summarized the positions and wages:

Support Staff Salaries

	Support Staff	Annual	Total
2	Administrative Assistant	$40,000	$80,000
2	Coordinator	$37,000	$74,000
1	Executive Assistant	$40,000	$40,000
1	Facility Overseer	$42,000	$42,000
5	Facility Worker	$35,000	$175,000
2	Receptionist	$22,800	$45,600
2	Secretary	$33,000	$66,000
1	Stage Hand	$15,080	$15,080
1	Worship Admin. Assistant	$34,522	$34,522
1	Worship Intern	$24,815	$24,815
30	Preschool Lead Teacher	$36,400	$1,092,000
30	Preschool Teacher	$30,160	$904,800
30	Preschool Assistant Teacher	$26,000	$780,000
108			**$3,373,817**

"So, none of these folks are ministerially exempt. Many make more than the $23,660 federal minimum for possible managerial or administrative FLSA exemption, but none meet California's 2018 exemption level of double minimum wage, $45,760. All of our support staff are non-exempt and must comply with the FLSA rules and regulations," Dan summarized.

"Creating the compensation guide, I have the categories pretty much laid out. But, I can't believe that raises were given by category. I guess that's what happens when you do across-the-board raises and generally make annual wages come out to even dollars."

"Perhaps I'm done here. That was so easy." Dan thought.

Support Staff and the FLSA

Dan asked Janet to come and give an update on the revised salary spreadsheet.

> Dan: "Hey Janet, how do you do it? There are no names for these positions?"
>
> Janet: "I've been running payroll for so long with raises by category of worker, that I'm used to it. And I don't really use the salary spreadsheet that much. That's mostly for the Compensation Team."
>
> Dan: "I just learned of a church near us where FICA was deducted for the lead pastor. His return got flagged by the IRS at tax season and he had to pay a year's worth of SECA! We need to double check who is exempt and non-exempt, asap!"
>
> Janet: "And that's a lot of initials! I'll have my team double check the exemption status of each employee."
>
> Dan: "How is the spreadsheet revision going?"
>
> Janet: "We're about done and might have it to you by EOD. I've been thinking about our conversation yesterday ..."
>
> Dan: "Is this good news or bad news?"
>
> Janet: "Two things. First, did you know that a church can opt out of paying FICA if they file *Form 8274*?"[48]
>
> Dan: "Believe it or not, I found that in my research. There's an IRS page, called *Elective FICA Exemption for Churches*,[49] or something like that. But, it means that every employee would have to pay 15.3% SECA. Even

---

[48] U.S. Department of the Treasury, Internal Revenue Service, *Form 8274: Certification by Churches and Qualified Church-Controlled Organizations Electing Exemption From Employer Social Security and Medicare Taxes*, revised August 2014, available from https://www.irs.gov/pub/irs-pdf/f8274.pdf.

[49] U.S. Department of the Treasury, Internal Revenue Service, *Elective FICA Exemption for Churches*, last reviewed or updated, August 4, 2017, available from https://www.irs.gov/charities-non-profits/churches-religious-organizations/elective-fica-exemption-churches-and-church-controlled-organizations.

having the weekday preschool still allows us to qualify. But I don't want all of our people to have to pay SECA."

Janet: "Okay, you got me there. But did you know that a church is automatically exempt from the Fair Labor Standards Act?"

Dan: "Yep, I did more research than I wanted to last week. Let me put up on the screen what it says."

Department of Labor, Wage and Hour Division Opinion Letter

Enterprise coverage does not apply to a private, non-profit enterprise where the eleemosynary, religious or educational activities of the non-profit enterprise are not in substantial competition with other businesses, unless it is operated in conjunction with a hospital, a residential care facility, a school or a commercial enterprise operated for a business purpose.[50]

Dan: "Many churches can opt out. We, however, run a school and that puts us under what is called Enterprise Coverage. Some churches are unable to opt out because they have more than $500,000 of business income."

Janet: "Are donations considered business income?"

Dan: "No, business income would be from a café, bookstore, internet sales, rental of office or parking spaces. Plus, they may have to pay UBIT on that profit. But, the preschool automatically qualifies our church in the enterprise category of the FLSA."

Janet: "So before we had the preschool, we were following the law with regard to our staff being exempt from the FLSA?"

Dan: "Yes and no. Some employees may have been exempt before we had the school, some not."

Janet: "That's confusing!"

---

[50] U.S. Department of Labor, Wage and Hour Division, *Opinion Letter FLSA2005-12NA*, September 23, 2005, available from https://www.dol.gov/whd/opinion/FLSANA/2005/2005_09_23_12NA_FLSA.htm.

Dan: "Welcome to my world. Though a church may not have enterprise coverage, individuals may be covered if they participate in interstate commerce."

Janet: "But we don't sell anything to another state."

Dan: "If your email goes to another state, if you buy something online, if we ship some of Pastor Wilson's books to Arizona ... do I need to go on?"

Janet: "Sounds rather complicated, again."

Dan: "For a church that qualifies and chooses to be exempt from the FLSA, they may have a cook or janitor who doesn't buy anything from out of state. That person would not be individually included."

Janet: "Okay, the cook or janitor are not under FLSA."

Dan: "But what about an administrative assistant? For the first year, just doing office work, they work overtime and it's okay. But in the second year, they start making travel arrangements to New Mexico for a youth or mission trip, suddenly they're covered under the individual provisions of the FLSA. And I haven't seen if California added anything to these federal rules. States can't subtract from FLSA but they can add to it."

Janet: "Got it. So because of that interstate thing, its easiest and best if all non-exempt staff are under FLSA."

Janet left and Dan returned to his analysis.

Dan compiled a list of issues that HR would have to monitor for all non-exempt staff. "This is going to take some explaining and perhaps a change in culture."

FLSA Compliance Issues

Non-exempt staff can't volunteer in their own department. For example, the worship administrative assistant can't volunteer to be the choir secretary on Wednesday evening.

Non-exempt staff can volunteer in another department. The worship assistant can go on youth trips and not be paid.

Non-exempt staff can do after-hours email and take phone calls. They must document their time and be paid for it. The facility overseer often gets cell phone calls in the evenings and on weekends. That may need to be paid at overtime rates.

Interns are non-exempt at WheatFields. If one goes on a retreat, they can only work eight hours a day, otherwise overtime must be paid. As a California employee, if the trip is longer than six days they must receive a day off, otherwise overtime must be paid.

Dan hoped that there were no other issues that touched on compensation and HR for support staff.

Overtime for Non-Exempt Staff

Dan needed to tackle how overtime was paid at the church. In researching hourly wages, Dan learned about the computation of hours from the Department of Labor's FLSA rules:[51]

The definitions included:
- The workweek is a fixed and regularly recurring period of 168 hours—seven consecutive 24-hour periods.
- It need not coincide with the calendar week. It may begin on any day and at any hour of the day.
- Different workweeks may be established for different employees or groups of employees.
- Averaging of hours over two or more weeks is not permitted. Normally, overtime pay earned in a particular workweek must be paid on the regular pay day for the pay period in which the wages were earned.

Federal FLSA rules:
- Unless exempt, employees covered by the Act must receive overtime pay for hours worked over forty in a workweek at a rate not less than time and one-half their regular rate of pay.
- There is no limit in the Act on the number of hours employees aged sixteen and older may work in any workweek.
- The Act does not require overtime pay for work on Saturdays, Sundays, holidays, or regular days of rest, unless overtime is worked on such days.

"So," Dan thought, "I bet that we've been allowing workers to time-shift overtime to the next work week. That has to stop!"

---

[51] U.S. Department of Labor, Wage and Hour Division, *Overtime Pay*, available from https://www.dol.gov/whd/overtime_pay.htm.

Dan found that California law adds to the federal standard for non-exempt employees:

- Time and a half pay when an employee works over forty hours a week.
- Time and a half pay when an employee works over eight hours a day.
- Double time pay when an employee works over twelve hours a day.
- When an employee works seven days in a row, time and a half pay for the first eight hours of work and double time thereafter.

California also has rules for meal breaks for employees:[52]
- For a work period of more than five hours per day, a meal period of not less than thirty minutes, except that if the total work period per day of the employee is no more than six hours.
- A second meal period of not less than thirty minutes, if an employee works more than ten hours per day, except that if the total hours worked is no more than twelve hours.
- Unless the employee is relieved of all duty during his or her thirty minute meal period, the meal period shall be considered an "on duty" meal period that is counted as hours worked which must be compensated at the employee's regular rate of pay.
- If the employer requires the employee to remain at the work site or facility during the meal period, the meal period must be paid.
- If an employer fails to provide an employee a meal period, the employer must pay one additional hour of pay at the employee's regular rate of pay for each workday that the meal period is not provided. This additional hour is not counted as hours worked for purposes of overtime calculations.

"I don't really want to know, but need to know our compliance on meals and overtime issues in the past," Dan realized. "But I'll draft a note to HR and the Finance Office to look into it."

Medical Insurance for All Staff

WheatFields has ninety teachers in the weekday preschool that runs from 7:00 am-5:00 pm. Before the Affordable Care Act, it may have been permissible to not offer them medical insurance. "I'm not sure about that now." Dan called their representative, Wade Wilkerson, at GuideStone:[53]

---

[52] State of California, Department of Industrial Relations, *Meal Periods*, revised July 11, 2012, available from https://www.dir.ca.gov/dlse/faq_mealperiods.htm.

[53] Based on email dialogues between the author and Wade Wilkerson, Regional Manager, Insurance Plans, GuideStone Financial Resources in March and April, 2018.

Dan: "We're using GuideStone for our health insurance for our church staff. Do we need to offer insurance for our weekday preschool staff?"

Wade: "How many hours do they work each week? Are they seasonal employees?"

Dan: "They work forty hours a week, 52 weeks a year. I don't think they work overtime but I'm not sure. So, they are regular, full-time employees."

Wade: "Under the Affordable Care Act, and probably before, you need to offer them health insurance. You're going to have to pay a fine of $188.33 per month for 2017."

Dan: "Well, we'd better get on this asap."

Wade: "GuideStone offers non-ERISA plans, so you can create categories of employees. You have to offer minimum essential coverage to all staff."

Dan: I haven't heard of categories of employees. What is that?"

Wade: "You're required to offer basic medical insurance to all employees that work over thirty hours a week. In a non-ERISA plan, you can have different plans for pastors, support staff, facility workers and preschool teachers. No employee can contribute more than 9.56% of their pay to the health insurance plan. For California, with your minimum wage at $11.00 or $22,880 a year, that means a worker cannot contribute more than $2,187 of their wages for medical insurance."

Dan: "Let's go with two plans, one for church staff and another for preschool teachers."

Wade: "You have a Platinum plan for your staff. That's top notch. You can offer a Gold or Silver plan to your preschool teachers. And you're only required to offer the employee coverage. Their spouse or dependents can enroll and pay the full premium amount."

Dan and Wade finished their conversation. Dan opted for the Gold coverage and would receive the paperwork in a few days from Wade.

A Smattering of Issues
HR Issues

Dan noted a few other items that HR would need to look into:

- Workers' Compensation compliance.
- HR files—making sure to separate medical insurance from performance files.
- Vacation time payout upon an employee exiting employment.
- Final check to a departing employee on their last day.

The Worship Department had five members of the band who were paid as contract workers. "This is a tricky area and churches take lots of positions on this," Dan thought. "I bet that they need to be considered employees." He sent an email to the worship pastor asking him for more information about his musicians.

Dan knew that Pastor Wilson had a severance agreement and that one was being drafted for Steve. Dan made a note to ensure that a copy of Steve's would be placed in his personnel file. "We have some elders who insist on a severance agreement. They say, 'sooner or later you're going to leave, retire or die ... so let's get you taken care of.'"

Pastor Wilson had written a trilogy of books on *Family, Mission and Worship.* Dan had never seen an Intellectual Property Agreement about who owns the books or royalties. He sent Pastor Wilson an email. Ever prompt, Pastor Wilson replied:

> "We didn't worry about Intellectual Property as we never expected my books to sell very well. When they did fly off the shelf like hotcakes, I just gave the profits back to the church. My family and I did get a nice trip to Hawaii out of it! Come to think of it, Mark in Worship made some money with his songs. And Liz Jackson's book on *Family Ministry* was popular. I guess that we had more IP issues than I thought. Thanks for handling it now."

The IP for writing songs would need to be considered. From his business experience, Dan knew that without an IP agreement in place, all work by the employees done on church time or church equipment was "work for hire." The books and songs needed an IP agreement in order for some or all of the profits to go to the individuals. "The problem for the worship pastor is that we tested his new songs here, refined them in our band practice, and recorded them in our studio." Dan made another note to get an attorney to draft IP agreements for each person producing such work.

Cost Centers

Dan knew from his research that churches often have cost centers. A cost center essentially is a business unit in a church. The IRS notes that if the business income is "substantially related to the charitable, educational, or other purpose that is the basis of the organization's exemption," then it is free of federal income tax.[54] They add, "An exempt organization that has $1,000 or more of gross income from an unrelated business must file Form 990-T." This is called Unrelated Business Income Tax (UBIT).

It is vital to know the net operating income or loss from a cost center. You can charge the cost center for rent, utilities, insurance, maintenance and other fair expenses. You may decide that an annual monetary loss from a cost center is worthwhile as it fulfills the mission of your church. For example, few church cafés that are open during the week break even when all costs are assigned. The goal is to know exactly how much your church is investing in the café. Is it worth a loss of $5,000 or $55,000?

Typical categories of cost center salaries include:

- Assistance shop of clothing and furniture for the needy—manager and operator
- Bookstore—manager and operator
- Café—manager and barista
- Daycare center—manager and care-giver
- Elementary-high school—principal, divisional coordinator, lead teacher, teacher and assistant teacher
- Preschool—coordinator, lead teacher, teacher and assistant teacher
- Sports clinic—director, coach and helper
- Summer camp—director, leader, cook, counselor and helper

Before today, Dan had not thought much about cost centers in churches. "As a cost center, we need to determine the total income or loss of the preschool. My friend's church runs an assistance shop to provide clothing and furniture at a bargain price for the needy. He says that it aligns perfectly with their vision statement and he sent over their profit and loss summary." Dan looked over the summary:

Assistance Shop Cost Center

Area	Amount
Income	
Sales	$74,000
Restricted Donations	$225,000
Total Income	$299,000

---

[54] IRS *Unrelated Business Income Tax.*

Expenses	
Manager	$45,000
Operators	$148,000
Clothing & Furniture Sorters	$54,000
Fair Value Rent	$24,000
Utilities	$13,000
Umbrella Insurance	$10,000
Maintenance	$10,000
Accounting	$18,000
Total Expense	**$322,000**
Net Cost to Church	**$23,000**

"So, their net cost is $23,000 to run the shop. They've done a good job of summarizing the total cost. Of course, this is for internal use only. As it fits within the religious purpose of their church, a profit would be tax-free, no UBIT. I wonder what the actual profit is of our preschool?" Typical to Dan's style, he wanted to create a table but would have to wait on the *Big Burrito* spreadsheet from Janet.

Instead of eight hours working on support staff issues, it was turning into Dan's catch-all day.

Federal Laws and Size of Organization

Dan knew from his business experience that there are a growing number of regulations to follow as an organization gains more employees. "We'd better make sure that HR is following those that apply to us."

He found an article by Zenefits[55] which he summarized, "most of these apply to a church." Dan made a long list:

One and More Employees
- Consumer Credit Protection Act—wage garnishing issues.
- Employee Polygraph Protection Act—no lie detector tests.
- Employment Retirement Income Security Act (ERISA)—private pension and health plans issues, COBRA included. *Churches are exempt.*
- Equal Pay Act (EPA)—equal pay for equal work. *Ministerial exception here!*
- Fair and Accurate Credit Transactions Act—detailing how credit information is handled.

---

[55] Zenefits, *Compliance Checklist: Federal Employment Laws You Need to Know at Every Stage of Your Company's Growth* (San Francisco: YourPeople, June 12, 2017) available from https://www.zenefits.com/blog/compliance-checklist-each-company-size-threshold/.

- Fair Labor Standards Act (FLSA)—minimum wage, rest breaks, overtime and child labor. *A church may be exempt but individual employees might not be.*
- Federal Insurance Contribution Act (FICA)—to fund Social Security and Medicare. *Ministers are exempt and must pay SECA.*
- Federal Income Tax Withholding—*ministers are exempt and must pay their own estimated taxes at least quarterly by April 15, June 15, September 15 and January 15.*
- Health Insurance Portability and Accountability Act (HIPAA)—protection of employee health information. *A best practice is to have separate locations for health insurance and personnel files.*
- Immigration Reform and Control Act—required employee I-9 forms.
- National Labor Relations Act (NLRA)—unions can be formed. *Most churches are exempt.*
- Occupational Safety and Health Act (OSHA)—standards for work conditions.
- Sarbanes-Oxley Act—corporate responsibility, combat fraud and provide financial disclosures. *Churches are exempt.*
- Uniform Guidelines for Employment Selection Procedures—no discrimination on the basis of race, color, religion, sex, or national origin. *There are some first amendment considerations and overrides.*
- Uniformed Services Employment and Reemployment Rights Act—military duty with reemployment rights.

Eleven and More Employees

- The Occupational Safety and Health Act (OSHA)—records maintenance.

Fifteen and More Employees

- Americans with Disabilities Act (ADA)—no discrimination for disabilities in employment and public accommodation. *Churches are exempt.*
- Genetic Information Nondiscrimination Act (GINA)—no discrimination based on genetic information.
- Title VII, Civil Rights Act of 1964—prohibits sexual harassment and sex discrimination. Includes the Lilly Ledbetter Fair Pay Act and the Civil Rights Act of 1991. *There are some church overrides with the ministerial exception.*

Dan paused on the Title VII information. He did further research on that topic, wanting wording straight from the Equal Employment Opportunity Commission. Dan found, *Questions and Answers: Religious Discrimination in the Workplace,* which said:

Religious Organization Exception

Under Title VII, religious organizations are permitted to give employment preference to members of their own religion.

Ministerial Exception

Clergy members generally cannot bring claims under the federal employment discrimination laws, including Title VII, the Age Discrimination in Employment Act, the Equal Pay Act, and the Americans with Disabilities Act. Some courts have made an exception for harassment claims where they concluded that analysis of the case would not implicate these constitutional constraints.[56]

"So, we can ensure that new and existing employees are followers of Christ. There is no rule that forces us to hire someone outside of our faith tradition," Dan thought. "That's an important one for us to remember and to cite the EEOC page on it."

Dan continued his summary of the Zenefits article:[57]

Twenty and More Employees

- Age Discrimination in Employment Act (ADEA)—no discrimination in hiring workers age 40+. *There is a ministerial exception here!*
- Consolidated Omnibus Budget Reconciliation Act (COBRA)—must offer to continue health insurance for 18-36 months after employment. *Churches can be exempt.*

Fifty and More Employees

- Affirmative Action Program (AAP)—recruit and train minorities, women, disabled persons and veterans, with record keeping. *Churches can be exempt.*
- Affordable Care Act (ACA)—must offer health insurance with strict record keeping stipulations. 50+ full-time equivalent workers.
- Family and Medical Leave Act (FMLA)—up to twelve weeks of unpaid leave following the birth, adoption, or foster placement; or serious family illness.

One Hundred and More Employees

- EEO-1 Survey Filing (Title VII, Civil Rights Act of 1964)—diversity records for workplaces and individual employees.
- Worker Adjustment Retraining Notification Act (WARN)—notify employees at least sixty days in advance of workplace closings and mass layoffs.

"I never knew all of this. Perhaps when I was in business my HR department did ... but I didn't. Now I'm responsible to ensure that it's implemented at WheatFields."

---

[56] U.S. Equal Employment Opportunity Commission, *Questions and Answers: Religious Discrimination in the Workplace"* revised January 31, 2011, available from https://www.eeoc.gov/policy/docs/qanda_religion.html.

[57] Zenefits, *Compliance Checklist.*

"It's closing time on Thursday and I'm going home. What a week at the office."

Conclusion

Dan finished the office work for the second week of his compensation crisis. As he drove home he thought, "I'm glad that I shared with Janet that story about the local church that mis-categorized their lead pastor's salary. The church put him as non-exempt and took out FICA. At tax time, he had to pay 7.65% in SECA all at once. On $100,000 he would have to pay $7,650. Plus, he probably had to pay a late penalty and a fine. Maybe from that story Janet will get how rabid I can be about accurate salary information. I need to make a note to see the report from our payroll firm on who they have recorded as ministerially exempt from WheatFields."

Dan hoped to get some rest on Friday and Saturday. The heavy workload was wearing him out.

Toolbox

Principles

1. We have seen the first four elements of *Smart Money for Church Salaries*:

    1—**Invest** in staff salaries with skill, towards fulfillment of the church's vision statement, so that God will entrust spiritual riches.
    2—**Handle** worldly wealth with excellence and trustworthiness, using money to serve God ... and not the other way around.
    3—**Implement** a fair and generous compensation guide that neither underpays nor overpays.
    4—**Follow** federal or state regulations with integrity.

    The fifth element of *Smart Money for Church Salaries* is:

    Learn from information channels of those with deep knowledge of church finances, avoiding the "stupid tax."

2. Who likes the word *stupid*? Some parents don't allow their children to use the word. Good inflow of information can help you avoid the *stupid tax*. From books, online sources and conferences, find the right channels of information.

3. Find a coach or mentor who has worked through church issues. Learn vital lessons before you make dumb mistakes. Two or four hours a month with a coach can mean the difference between success and failure. It may be your first-time rodeo, but you can ride the bronco of church issues as a seasoned rider.

Steps

❑ Analyze Salaries of Support Staff

Analyze the salaries of your support staff. Discover and note salary discrepancies, those that stand out as possibly being too low or high. Use your chart of FLSA exemption qualifications to determine if any are exempt as managers or administrators. Remember federal and state salary minimums for exemption.

Search for problems of titles and compensation. For example, discover if an administrative assistant is doing the work of an executive assistant. As issues arise in your study, create a to-do list.

1. Sort the Salaries of Support Staff

Sort the salaries of your church's support staff into categories. You may need to define or refine your categories along the way.

Typical categories include:
- Administrative assistant—The title, *secretary,* is fading from use. The exempt status of administrative assistants can be challenging to determine:

  Routinely ordering supplies (and even selecting which vendor to buy supplies from) is not likely to be considered high-enough to qualify the employee for administratively exempt status. There is no 'bright line.' Some secretaries may indeed be high-level, administratively exempt employees (for example, the secretary to the CEO who really does 'run his life'), while some employees with fancy titles (e.g., 'administrative assistant') may really be performing nonexempt clerical duties.[58]

- Department coordinator—Depending on job function and salary, coordinators may be FLSA exempt.
- Executive assistant—The role of an EA is to "manage the life" of the senior leadership and give significant input into staff issues. These qualifications can make them administratively exempt from the FLSA.[59] For many EAs, the issue of qualification depends on their salary and state minimums.
- Facility maintenance and custodial
- Nursery supervisor and care-giver

---

[58] Chamberlain, Kaufman and Jones, Attorneys at Law (Albany: FLSA Home Page), *Coverage under the FLSA*, available at https://www.flsa.com/coverage.html.

[59] U.S. Department of Labor, Employment Standards Administration, Wage and Hour Division, *Opinion Letter FLSA2006-23NA,* October 26, 2006, available from https://www.dol.gov/whd/opinion/FLSANA/2006/2006_10_26_23NA_FLSA.pdf.

- Musician—Take special care if your church hires musicians for worship, special events, weddings or funerals. There are some musicians who perform in the church that genuinely qualify as independent contractors. These are instrumentalists and soloists that make special appearances, such as an occasional time in the worship service or a wedding. These independent contractors can be paid an honorarium and may need a *1099MISC* if they earn more than $600 each year. Musicians who sing or play on a regular basis, who must attend scheduled rehearsals and are assigned specific functions, these should be classified as employees. You will need to consider whether these employed musicians meet minimum wage standards for your state.
- Host for weddings, special receptions and funerals. These and other hosts are often not church employees. The same considerations given to musicians apply to hosts.
- Special events caterer
- Receptionist
- Worship leader, worship service producer, worship and a/v technician.

Your church will most likely have other categories of support staff. For creating a salary guide, attempt to keep the categories concise. Too many categories create an unwieldy guide; too few lacks the depth to adequately analyze salaries.

2. Sort the Salaries of Cost Centers
A cost center essentially is a business unit in your church. The goal is to know exactly how much your church is investing in the center. Is it worth a loss of $5,000 or $55,000?

Typical categories of cost center salaries include:
- Assistance shop of clothing and furniture for the needy—manager and operator
- Bookstore—manager and operator
- Café—manager and barista
- Daycare center—manager and care-giver
- Elementary-high school—principal, divisional coordinator, lead teacher, teacher and assistant teacher
- Preschool—coordinator, lead teacher, teacher and assistant teacher
- Sports clinic—director, coach and helper
- Summer camp—director, leader, cook, counselor and helper

3. Check and Re-Check
It is all too easy for some salaries not to appear on your salary spreadsheet. Part-time nursery workers are often overlooked. You may have someone paid by your mission fund or care fund. Technically they are an employee but many people see them as "doing some work in that area." Double and triple check that every staff member is accounted for on your spreadsheet. All staff means each and every one.

4. Educate Staff on FLSA Requirements

Your church may be FLSA exempt. Remember that if exempt, individuals who do interstate commerce are non-exempt. If your church has more than $500,000 in business income, or runs a school, then your church is considered an enterprise. An enterprise is non-exempt from FLSA regulations.

Ensure that your overtime policy is accurately conveyed to all staff. This includes phone calls made to or from non-exempt staff. For example, if a pastor calls their assistant at 7:00 pm for an update on a ministry event, then that must be counted as billable time to the church by the assistant. There are no exceptions for this with non-exempt staff.

Federal and state rules also have meal and rest break periods for non-exempt staff. If the receptionist is in the lunch room and gets called back to the phone for a few minutes, then this is billable time to the church. This is not counted toward overtime pay.

❑ "See the Doctor" on Medical Insurance

1. Most insurance carriers work through agents. Your insurance agency should have a wealth of resources for you about medical insurance issues. As the agency is paid 4-7% of your medical premium, they have motivated self-interest to serve you well. Get to know your agent and ask for help.
2. The Affordable Care Act dramatically changed the landscape of medical insurance. More changes may come in future years. Regularly have a detailed discussion with your insurance agent about current issues and proposed changes to the ACA.
3. Do a medical insurance check-up on your staff. Inform them of the available medical benefits. Generally this is done during an annual staff presentation by your agent. Each covered employee should receive a 5-20 page paper copy of their coverage.
4. Implement a health improvement program. Run a contest to encourage people to exercise. Give tax-free awards to those who complete a segment or the entire program. This could include money for a gym membership, a *fitbit* or an *Apple Watch*. Make it worth their time to earn the prize. A healthier staff will gradually lower your medical insurance premiums, yielding huge savings to your church.

❑ List the Smattering of Issues

As you work through your compensation study, other issues will surface. Keep a list as you find them. Examples include:

1. Intellectual Property Agreements are needed for sermons, songs and books. Without an IP agreement, any work done on church time or with church equipment belongs to the church.
2. Review the federal laws that pertain to the size of organizations. Ensure that you are fulfilling those requirements.

3. Consider the implications of the mis-categorization of staff and SECA contributions. Get a printed report from your Finance Office and payroll service. Double check that all staff are properly categorized in the payroll system.

4. Ask your Finance Office to prepare a document on the compensation reporting to the government. List the schedule of due dates and type of report. Review the amounts remitted and their timeliness.

5. You may find other pertinent items for your church. Write down those items as you discover them.

Questions to Consider

One

WheatFields could continue to not offer health insurance to the preschool teachers. They would pay a fine of $188.33 per month. Should WheatFields comply with the Affordable Care Act and offer insurance to the teachers or pay the fine?

_____
_____
_____
_____
_____
_____
_____

Two

At first blush, the Compensation Team thought they were requesting salary information only. Dan's evaluation uncovered many messy areas of WheatFields. What are the top three areas that you need to evaluate for your church?

1. _____
_____
_____

2. _____
_____
_____

3. _____
_____
_____

Three

Unless an Intellectual Property Agreement is in place, the creation of songs, sermons and books most likely belongs to your church. Is this an issue at your church? What steps can you take to clarify the issue?

_____
_____
_____
_____
_____
_____
_____

Tools

This section provides you with material that was introduced or finalized in this chapter. These items are also available at https://www.xpastor.org/smart. The password for this page is: smart money.

Original Support Staff List
that Needed Dan's Attention

Administrative Assistant	$40,000
Administrative Assistant	$40,000
Coordinator	$37,000
Coordinator	$37,000
Executive Assistant	$40,000
Facility Overseer	$42,000
Facility Worker	$35,000
Facility Worker	$35,000
Facility Worker	$35,000
Facility Worker	$35,000
Facility Worker	$35,000
Receptionist	$22,800
Receptionist	$22,800
Secretary	$33,000
Secretary	$33,000
Stage Hand	$15,080
Worship Administrative Assistant	$34,522
Worship Intern	$24,815
30 Preschool—Lead Teachers	$737,100
30 Preschool—Teachers	$610,740
30 Preschool—Assistant Teachers	$526,500
108	**$2,471,357**

- 7 -

FINDING COMPENSATION DATA

Researching Salaries for Comparison

It was Friday and Doris was at work. Though Dan wanted to take the day off, having worked Sunday through Thursday, he said, "I'll make an exception this week. I'll just do some internet research on compensation data. What else would I do with my day? I'm not accustomed to working on Sundays *and* having Fridays off."

Dan made a list of places he could find salary data:

- National church compensation databases—Christianity Today,[60] Leadership Network,[61] MinistryPay[62] and XPastor[63]
- Local churches
- Local nonprofit organizations
- Local school districts
- Local police departments

Dan considered firefighters, but reasoned that police departments had more employees and salary levels. "I don't have a network in place to talk with local churches or nonprofits. Perhaps I can do that next year."

School District Salaries

A number of miles away from WheatFields is Newport Beach. "Let's see what the Newport-Mesa Unified School District salaries are. We're not quite as well-heeled as that town, but close." The information was online, as it is for most public school districts. Dan found 28 salary levels for teachers.[64] He simplified it into a chart:

---

[60] Christianity Today, Church Law & Tax Report, *Church Salary* (Carol Stream: Christianity Today) available from ChurchSalary.com.

[61] Warren Bird, *Leadership Network Large Church Salary, Staffing, and Benefits Survey* (Dallas: Leadership Network, 2018) available from http://leadnet.org/salary/.

[62] The Church Network, *The Church Salary Survey of The Church Network* (Richardson, Texas: The Church Network and the National Association of Church Business Administration) available from https://www.ministrypay.com.

[63] XPastor, *Compensation Survey* (Austin, Texas: XPastor) available from https://www.xpastor.org/courses/church-compensation/.

[64] School Loop, *2016-2017 Teacher Salary Schedule 188 days, Newport-Mesa Unified School District, Salary Schedule #44*, approved January 31, 2017 (San Francisco: School Loop) available from nmusd-ca.schoolloop.com/file/1281197594254/1246559508790/561603266115719012.pdf.

2017 Teachers, Newport-Mesa Unified School District

Years	BA +30 or Credential	BA +60 or Master's	BA +75 MA or PhD	BA +75 with Certification
1	$54,043	$60,420	$65,350	$66,608
5	$58,538	$70,683	$76,451	$77,921
10	$58,539	$85,996	$93,014	$94,802
15	$58,539	$93,014	$100,604	$102,538
20	$58,539	$100,604	$100,604	$102,538
28	$58,539	$104,628	$117,692	$119,955

"That's some pretty good data but the starting salaries are high! Most of our church support staff have bachelor's degrees, but I can't pay them that much. All of our pastors have a master's, so that data may be helpful for them."

Dan then saw what a school leader makes:[65]

2017 School Administrators, Newport-Mesa

Title	Step 1	Step 3	Step 6
Coordinator III	$97,402	$105,349	$118,503
Coordinator II	$101,338	$109,608	$123,294
Coordinator I	$109,691	$118,642	$133,455
Asst. Principal Elementary	$101,856	$110,167	$123,922
Principal Elementary	$114,704	$124,064	$139,556
Asst. Principal High School	$115,551	$124,979	$140,584
Principal High School	$133,708	$144,619	$162,676

Dan also found that selected school administrators receive a $2,000-$4,500 automobile allowance.[66] "Wow, that's some pretty good money to run a school. I wonder how much the district leaders earn?"[67]

---

[65] School Loop, *Management Salary Schedule 2016-2017, Newport-Mesa Unified School District*, approved January 31, 2017 (San Francisco: School Loop) available from nmusd-ca.school-loop.com/file/1281197594254/1246559508790/8305085910870398259.pdf.

[66] School Loop, *Management Transportation Allowance, Newport-Mesa Unified School District*, (San Francisco: School Loop) available from nmusd-ca.schoolloop.com/file/128119759425 4/1246559508790/8156724607258361966.pdf.

[67] Transparent California, *2013-2016 Salaries for Newport-Mesa Unified* (Las Vegas: Nevada Policy Research Institute) available from https://transparentcalifornia.com/salaries/school-districts/orange/newport-mesa-unified/.

2017 District Administrators, Newport-Mesa

Title	Regular Pay	Other Pay	Total Pay	Benefits	Total
Director Elementary Education	$207,945	$9,000	$216,945	$68,127	$285,072
Director Secondary Education	$207,945	$9,000	$216,945	$68,550	$285,495
Assistant Superintendent	$215,372	$9,000	$224,372	$50,839	$275,211
Associate Superintendent	$225,000	$9,000	$234,000	$59,385	$293,385
Superintendent	$275,945	$10,200	$286,145	$79,906	$366,051

The Los Angeles Times reported in 2017 about Superintendent Fred Navarro:

> Newport-Mesa Unified School District Superintendent Fred Navarro will receive a bonus of $34,450 for his performance in the 2016-17 school year, for which he was rated "exceptional" by the Board of Trustees.
>
> Navarro's salary will rise 2.5% to $282,844 for the 2017-18 school year and to $289,915 in 2018-19, according to the district.
>
> The merit pay is in addition to salary increases the board approved last month for top district administrators, including the superintendent.[68]

"That's a lot of money. I doubt that we'll be paying Steve at the level of a district administrator. If our staff see these salaries, they may jump ship and go work for the school system." While looking up data for Orange County, California, Dan found files about Orange County, Florida. He found the wages for teachers[69] and administrators[70] in the Orlando area:

---

[68] Priscella Vega, *Newport-Mesa Schools Superintendent Gets $34,450 Bonus for 'Exceptional' Performance* (The Los Angeles Times, December 13, 2017) available from www.latimes.com/socal/daily-pilot/news/tn-dpt-me-nmusd-supt-20171213-story.html.

[69] Orange County [Florida] Public School System. *Orange County Public Schools 2016-2017 Instructional Grandfathered/Performance Salary Schedule*, board approved June, 14, 2016, available from https://www.ocps.net/UserFiles/Servers/Server_54619/File/Departments/Human%20Resources/Compensation/Salary%20Schedules/Salary%20Schedule%20docs%20WP/Open%20Range%20Schedule%202016-17.pdf.

[70] Orange County [Florida] Public School System, *Orange County Public Schools 2017-18 School Based Administrator Performance Salary Schedule*, board approved July 25, 2017, available from https://www.ocps.net/UserFiles/Servers/Server_54619/File/Departments/Human%20Resources/Compensation/Admin-School%20Based%202017-18%20Salary%20Schedule%20FINAL.pdf.

2018 School Salaries, Orange County, Florida

Title	Minimum	Maximum
Teacher Tier 1	$39,500	$43,175
Teacher Tier 2	$41,080	$49,035
Teacher Tier 3	$43,370	$56,428
Teacher Tier 4	$54,735	$72,600
Principal, Elementary School	$80,197	$117,295
Principal, Middle School	$82,384	$120,496
Principal, Senior High School	$92,347	$135,431

"Those numbers look pretty close to our current salaries. Orlando also includes supplements for advanced degrees."[71]

Orlando Teacher Supplements

Master's	$2,780
Specialist	$4,263
Doctorate	$5,622

Dan found that seven states don't have personal income tax: Alaska, Florida, Nevada, South Dakota, Texas, Washington and Wyoming. "So, the Florida employees are not paying our 10% California income tax. If we're paying similar salaries as Florida, then we may be underpaying our employees."

Dan also found a study conducted for the Hawaii Department of Education to examine Hawaii's teacher compensation:

> The scope of work called for a full investigation of the state's compensation system, including an examination of the structure of the state's salary schedule, a comparison of salary levels to those of comparison districts, a comparable wage study, and a set of recommendations for possible changes to the state's teacher compensation system.[72]

Dan liked what he saw. "This is great material. I get to see the inner workings of a national compensation study." Since the report was from 2014, Dan indexed the salaries for inflation to 2018. From the Hawaii study, he created a chart of many school districts:

---

[71] Orange County [Florida] Public School System, *Orange County Public Schools 2016-2017 Instructional Grandfathered/Performance Salary Schedule.*

[72] Augenblick, Palaich and Associates with Chris Stoddard, *Study of Hawaii's Compensation System* (Honolulu: Hawaii State Teacher's Association, November, 2014) available from www.hsta.org/images/uploads/Comprehensive_Salary_Study_Hawaii_1.27.15_Web.pdf.

2018 Indexed Teacher Salaries

Location	Minimum	Maximum
Wake County, North Carolina	$38,313	$74,000
Clark County, Nevada	$37,763	$78,857
Virginia Beach, Virginia	$44,230	$80,499
Houston, Texas	$50,960	$82,601
Miami-Dade County, Florida	$44,095	$84,407
Hawaii	$48,492	$88,956
San Diego, California	$45,957	$94,916
Fairfax County, Virginia	$50,907	$109,855
Montgomery County, Maryland	$50,530	$112,540

Dan noted the challenge of comparing total salaries, as the benefits piece was often difficult to ascertain. The report said:

> Direct comparisons are avoided here for two main reasons: First, the amount of data APA was able to collect from each district varied. Some districts have robust information posted online regarding benefits, stipends, and retirement. Other districts have limited data, were unable or unwilling to provide full details, even when contacted via phone. Second, the manner in which districts implement or provide benefits, stipends, and retirement varies widely, making direct comparisons difficult in some cases.

Dan thought, "I would wager that this will be true for churches also. I can compare base salaries, but the benefits piece is probably going to be hard to compare."

He remembered what he had read in the 2016 Washington Post article concerning the benefits of Dr. Karen Garza, the new Superintendent of the Fairfax County School District:

> Her new contract starts with a $300,000 base salary—a 7 percent increase from her current pay of $280,099—and runs through June 30, 2020. The contract also includes $25,000 in annual retirement savings, a monthly $2,000 housing allowance, and the use of a vehicle, laptop and cellphone for professional and personal purposes.[73]

---

[73] T. Rees Shapiro, *Garza Receives Four-Year Contract Extension as Fairfax Schools Superintendent* (The Washington Post, July 1, 2016) available from https://www.washingtonpost.com/local/education/garza-receives-four-year-contract-extension-as-fairfax-schools-superintendent/2016/07/01/fc7f1c18-3fb9-11e6-80bc-d06711fd2125_story.html.

"When I include insurance, I bet that her benefits come to almost $100,000 a year. I need to see what the ratio of WheatFields' salaries to benefits is."

Police Department Salaries

Dan searched on the internet and found the salaries of police departments. As Dan had data regarding the teacher's salaries in Newport Beach, he tried to find Newport's police salaries. The data on the internet was tedious to attempt to compile. He gave up.

Intrigued at Orange County, Florida, Dan found information on the Orlando Police:[74]

Orlando Police

	1st year	11th year
Officers	$48,276	$75,420

"There isn't much data online for Orlando, but what is there does fit many of our pastors. From year one to eleven, it's a nice salary spread. I wish I could see the quads for the entire department." Dan also found retirement guidelines for the Orlando Police Department.[75]

Continuing his search, Dan found a trove of readable data about the Seattle Police Department:[76]

2017 Seattle Police

	Start	6 Months	18 months	Max
Officer	$69,240	$74,244	$77,628	$90,672
Sergeant	$93,324	$97,344	—	$104,304
Lieutenant	$117,270	$122,034	$127,067	$132,142
Captain	$139,464	$145,080	$151,091	$157,144
Chief	$166,650	—	—	$266,614

"According to this data, we barely pay our Core Team what a sergeant makes. Steve isn't even in the starting grid for a lieutenant."

---

[74] City of Orlando, *Compensation*, available from www.cityoforlando.net/police/recruiting/compensation/.

[75] City of Orlando, *Police Pension Fund Participants' Retirement Options*, available from http://www.cityoforlando.net/pension/police-pension-fund-participants-retirement-options/.

[76] City of Seattle, *Salary and Benefits*, available from https://www.seattle.gov/police/police-jobs/salary-and-benefits.

Continuing to research, Dan found more data. "Now this is superlative info from the Chicago Police Department," he thought:[77]

2017 Chicago Police

	Start	Step 4	Step 8	Max
Officer	$48,078	$76,266	$90,024	$99,414
Detective	$70,980	$82,614	$97,440	$107,550
Sergeant	$76,932	$89,171	$101,422	$114,828
Lieutenant	$87,402	$100,668	$117,894	$128,346
Captain	$95,844	$111,018	$129,282	$138,138
Commander	—	—	—	$162,684
Deputy Chief	—	—	—	$170,112
Chief	—	—	—	$185,364
First Deputy	—	—	—	$197,724
Superintendent	—	—	—	$260,004

"The rates for officers, detectives and sergeants have a good range. I could almost just go with that for our pastors and Core Team salary range."

Dan found a listing of benefits for new recruits to the Hawaii police force.[78] "Benefit information is hard to come by, so I'll note these items," Dan thought.

Benefits for Hawaii Police
Overtime
Night differential pay and time-and-a-half for holiday work and overtime.

Time off
Holidays—thirteen paid days a year.
Vacation—21 working days a year. Accrued up to ninety days.
Sick leave—21 working days a year. Unused accrued toward retirement.
Military leave—fifteen days a year for active duty or annual training.
Funeral leave—three days for death of family member.
Accidental injury leave—up to 120 days for each work-related injury.

[77] Chicago Police Department, *2017 Position & Salary Schedule, Chicago Police Department, Sworn & Civilian Personnel*, revised July 14, 2017, available from directives.chicagopolice.org/forms/CPD-61.400.pdf.

[78] Hawai'i Police Department, *Police Officers, County of Hawai'i Jobs*, available from www.hawaiipolice.com/recruitment/police-officers.

Benefits

Health insurance—self or family medical, drug, vision and adult dental insurance partly subsidized.

Life insurance—fully subsidized group life insurance for $26,000.

Uniforms and equipment—furnished.

Automobile subsidy—monthly allowance for private automobiles in police use, plus fuel and oil and tax-exempt motor vehicle registration.

Retirement

Eligible with 25 years of police service.

"That's good food for thought for WheatFields' benefits," Dan summarized.

Church Salary Comparisons by Position

"I need to get a handle on what other churches pay their staff," Dan thought. "I wonder how our youth pastors compare to others. Outside of Liz, the head of the department, I'm going to focus on the pastors in our Family Department."

Dan created a chart of the salaries at WheatFields:

Family Pastor Salaries

Title	Last	First	Salary
High School Pastor	Martinez	Will	$62,000
College & Young Adults Pastor	Manta	Colton	$55,000
High School Assistant Pastor	Jones	JB	$43,000
Discipleship Assistant Pastor	Stanley	John	$53,000
Junior High Pastor	Yang	David	$40,000
		Average	$50,600

He found ChurchSalary.com from Christianity Today and did some research.[79] Dan found:

ChurchSalary.com Data—Youth Pastor Salaries
$37,176 is the national median salary. This is just salary, no benefits.

$53,000 is the national median compensation. This is base salary and a housing allowance (or parsonage value). No other benefits are included.

"I see that this CT data is from churches with more than 1,000 in weekly attendance. Our salaries run from $40,000 to $62,000 and our average for the five positions is $50,600.

---

[79] Christianity Today, *Church Salary.*

We are $2,400 below the national median. We do have a high cost of living in California and also a 10% state income tax. Our salaries seem to be a bit low."

"The Christianity Today site also lists benefits.[80] That's hard to come by."

Data—Youth Pastor Benefits

All Youth Pastor Respondents Reporting	Percent
Paid Vacation	98%
Health Insurance	66%
Housing Allowance	62%
Retirement	53%
Auto Reimbursement/Allowance	38%
Continuing Education	31%
Life & Disability Insurance	29%
Parsonage	6%

"There are churches with parsonages? I didn't know those still existed. I've never seen one in SoCal! I don't get why only 62% of youth pastors receive a housing allowance. That doesn't cost the church any money. Pastors create their own housing allowance number and then ask their board to approve the amount. I wonder if that is an error by the respondents."

To get more data points, Dan checked out the XPastor salary information for youth pastors.[81] "I'm going to condense that info into nine lines," Dan thought.

XPastor Data—Youth Pastor Salary

Area	Size	Role	Average $53,087
Northeast	1,400	Student Ministries Pastor	$40,926
Midwest	1,400	Youth Pastor	$47,763
West	1,700	High School Pastor	$54,093
South	1,700	Youth Pastor	$55,319
Midwest	1,800	Youth Pastor	$53,000
Midwest	1,900	Youth Pastor	$60,289
West	1,950	Pastor of Junior High	$44,381
West	1,950	Pastor of Student Ministries	$58,189
South	2,000	Youth Pastor	$63,825

---

[80] Christianity Today, *Church Salary*.

[81] XPastor, *Compensation* Survey.

"Our youth pastor salaries, those for assistant pastors, are probably a touch low. I'm going to need to consider whether we should give them raises."

Church Salary Comparisons In Toto

Dan had selectively copied data out of the XPastor Compensation Survey. While Dan was looking at the XPastor files, he considered what he wanted to see—all a church's major positions in the same table. He also liked knowing when the data was submitted and indexed for inflation. Dan was cautious of data that had hidden inflation indexes. "I read that the inflation index of the XPastor data is often accurate to within 1% of current salaries. I like that. I'm a 'give me all the information' kind of guy."

"Let's find a church in the West. Since XPastor uses U.S. government census data regions, let's find a church the size of WheatFields while Pastor Wilson was still pastor. Here's one with 1,400 in worship."[82]

1,400 in Worship

	2014 Data	2018 Data
Annual Budget	$3,300,000	$3,584,856
Payroll Budget	$1,380,000	$1,499,122
Benefits Budget	$220,000	$238,990
Total Employees—32		
Senior Pastor	$136,500	$148,283
Executive Pastor	$104,000	$112,977
Outreach Pastor	$80,000	$86,906
Small Groups Pastor	$68,000	$73,870
Worship Pastor	$55,000	$59,748
Children's Pastor	$50,000	$54,316
Business Administrator	$50,000	$54,316
Administrative Assistant	$45,000	$48,884
High School Pastor	$45,000	$48,884
Junior High Pastor	$42,000	$45,625
Facility Director	$35,000	$38,021

"Wow, those salaries are really close to ours. Pastor Wilson was making $140,000 when he retired a few months ago."

"The salaries for the SP and XP are higher than ours, but there could be some longevity issues to account for that. We have 35 church staff and they have 32. Our salary budget is $1.6 million and theirs is almost $1.5 million. For other staff, we tend to pay a bit more than this church of 1,400 in worship."

---

[82] XPastor, *Compensation Survey.*

"Let me see what XPastor has for a church in the West that is close to our current size:"[83]

2,100 in Worship

	2009 Data	2018 Data
Annual Budget	$3,000,000	$3,582,240
Payroll Budget	$1,121,641	$1,339,329
Benefits Budget	$198,111	$236,560
Total Employees—25		
Senior Pastor	$106,203	$126,815
Executive Pastor	$70,306	$83,951
Children & Youth Pastor	$67,590	$80,708
Education Pastor	$64,948	$77,553
Business Administrator	$62,447	$74,567
Outreach Pastor	$59,614	$71,184
Worship Pastor	$53,416	$63,783
Facility Director	$41,557	$49,622
Director of Media	$41,200	$49,196
Youth Staff	$40,000	$47,763
Administrative Assistant	$30,027	$35,855

"They have about the same number of people in worship as we currently do. Yet their annual budget is $3.5 million and ours is $5 million. Well, our community is affluent … so it makes sense that we have more staff."

"Let me do one more search, this time for a larger church than ours. Perhaps it can give me an idea of where our salary budget might go in the future."[84]

---

[83] XPastor, *Compensation Survey.*

[84] XPastor, *Compensation Survey.*

3,100 in Worship

	2013 Data	2018 Data
Annual Budget	$5,000,000	$5,519,650
Payroll Budget	$3,100,000	$3,422,183
Benefits Budget	$354,000	$390,791
Total Employees—65		
Senior Pastor	$221,000	$243,969
Executive Pastor	$95,000	$104,873
CFO	$92,300	$101,893
Worship Pastor	$74,000	$81,691
HR Director	$73,000	$80,587
Technical Director	$68,000	$75,067
Care Pastor	$68,000	$75,067
Student Pastor	$57,400	$63,366
Facility Director	$55,000	$60,716
Senior High Pastor	$48,000	$52,989
Worship Director	$40,000	$44,157
Executive Assistant	$36,000	$39,741
Outreach Director	$36,000	$39,741
Office Manager	$30,000	$33,118
Administrative Assistant	$24,000	$26,494

"Wow, I don't know what to make of this budget. They bring in the same amount of donations for the church as we do, $5 million. Yet, their SP earns more than double what Steve does. They have an XP, CFO and HR director on staff, all with good salaries. The other key staff are paid similarly to ours and they have double the number of church staff that we do."

The salary comparisons gave Dan plenty to consider. "I have enough solid data here to create a compensation grid for WheatFields. And the data provides enough variance that I can justify a range of potential salaries."

Local Cost of Living

"All those comparisons are great, a rich trove of data. But, I also need to consider what the cost of living is for our area compared to other areas. I could do a zip code analysis." Dan looked online and found something less granular than zip code data. "Here's some info on Orange County, California and Orange County, Florida. That should be interesting and both are close to Disney theme parks!" Dan made some notes:

Orange County, California

PayScale reported that the "cost of living in Orange County, California is 52% higher than the national average."[85]

The Living Wage Calculator from the Massachusetts Institute of Technology wrote that a family with two adults, one working, with two children needs $31.41 per hour in SoCal.[86]

"That's $65,332 annually to live in SoCal," Dan thought.

Orange County, Florida

PayScale reported that the "cost of living in Orange County, Florida is 5% lower than the national average.[87]

The Living Wage Calculator from the Massachusetts Institute of Technology wrote that a family with two adults, one working, with two children needs $25.21 per hour.[88]

"That's $52,665 annually to live in Florida. So, by MIT's figures the cost of living is 24% higher in SoCal than Orlando."

"I see the annual figures and percentages don't match, but they give me a range," Dan thought.

Dan tried to sort out the data from the PayScale page.[89] "Let me compare the cost of living from Orlando to here. The PayScale page says that if we hired a pastor from Orlando who earned $50,000 that their overall expenses would be 59% higher in SoCal. Groceries are 10% higher, housing is off the charts at 189% higher, utilities are lower by 6%, transportation is 45% higher and health care is 20% higher. The PayScale page says that an equivalent SoCal salary would be $79,500. There is no way that we can pay that kind of wage for an assistant pastor!"

[85] PayScale, *Cost of Living Calculator - Orange County, California* (Seattle: PayScale, 2018) available from https://www.payscale.com/cost-of-living-calculator/California-Orange-County.

[86] Amy K. Glasmeier, *The MIT Living Wage Calculation for Orange County, California* (Boston: Massachusetts Institute of Technology, 2018) available from livingwage.mit.edu/counties/06059.

[87] PayScale, *Cost of Living Calculator - Orlando, Florida* (Seattle: PayScale, 2018) available from https://www.payscale.com/cost-of-living-calculator/Florida-Orlando.

[88] Amy K. Glasmeier, *The MIT Living Wage Calculation for Orlando-Kissimmee-Sanford, Florida*, (Boston: Massachusetts Institute of Technology, 2018) available from livingwage.mit.edu/metros/36740.

[89] PayScale, *Cost of Living Calculator - Orange County, California*.

Dan compared the two numbers. "MIT says we are 21% higher and PayScale says 59%. I see that MIT does take into account our state income taxes.[90] So ... the experts have different numbers ... great! Well, either way, it's no wonder that we have so many dual income families here. We need two wage earners just to afford the housing."

WheatFields' Compensation Grid

"All those comparisons are helpful," Dan reasoned. "There is so much data that it's almost overwhelming. But I need to make some decisions, take a stand and get to our salaries. This is where I thought I would be starting!" Dan sighed.

"It's finally time for me to create a template for our compensation," Dan thought. He laid out the necessary elements:

Salary Comparisons
- Local public school teachers
- Local police
- Regional church salaries
- Church salary comparisons by position
- Church salary comparisons *in toto*
- National church salaries
- Local cost of living

Benefit Comparisons
- These are challenging to compile

Categories of Employees
- Ministerially exempt—pastors and ministry directors, ones paying SECA.
- Managerially exempt—directors meeting the FLSA criteria of work and salary.
- Administratively exempt—executive assistants meeting the FLSA criteria of work and salary (California's salary minimum is too high for employees at WheatFields to qualify as exempt).
- Non-exempt staff—directors, assistants (with varied titles), receptionists, stage hands, interns, facility workers, preschool teachers.

Salary Quad Grid
- Minimum pay
- Low to medium pay

---

[90] Carey Anne Nadeau, *Living Wage Calculator, User's Guide, Technical Notes for Amy K. Glasmeier, Department of Urban Studies and Planning, Massachusetts Institute of Technology* (Boston: Massachusetts Institute of Technology, 2017 Update) available from livingwage.mit.edu/resources/Living-Wage-User-Guide-and-Technical-Notes-2017.pdf.

- Medium to high pay
- Maximum pay

Grid numbers show ranges, not exact salaries. If anyone is below the minimum or above the maximum, list them in the final document with an explanation.

Criteria for Merit Increases

- Experience—years in jobs that impact their current role.
- Education—formal education as seen in a bachelor's degree, master's degree or doctorate. Ongoing education that signifies the person as a life-long learner.
- Responsibility—the ability to carry out their work in a timely and effective manner. Key staff carry the weight of more ministry responsibility.
- Team spirit—contributes to the morale of the staff and is excited to be here.
- Missional alignment—implements the vision of the church in their area.
- Special considerations—published songs, books, national speaking engagements, teaching that enhances high performance of local ministry.

Detail of Benefits

- Workers' Compensation.
- FICA for non-ministerial staff.
- Health insurance—generally for employees 30+ hours.
- COBRA—optional for churches.
- Retirement plan—generally for employees 30+ hours.
- Life insurance—$50,000 of coverage is tax-free, above that the individual pays tax on the premium, which is often $100-$200 in taxable income. The death benefit goes to the beneficiary free of income tax.
- Other insurance: dental, vision, accidental death and dismemberment and long-term disability.
- Automobile allowances—taxable. A mileage plan is not taxable but every trip must be recorded with the date, purpose and mileage.
- Cell phone allowances—non-taxable.

Define FICA and SECA

- Create text for the Compensation Team to understand the implications of SECA and the ministerial housing allowance.
- Define which employees must contribute to FICA and who cannot.

"Okay, I have my template. Now I need to sort our employees and create reasonable salary numbers for each level."

Filling in the Numbers

Dan had a challenge. "Without any annual reviews, I don't have much paperwork to use to base merit increases on." He sent an email to all supervisors to create summary sheets on their employees. "I'll follow up on that with some face-to-face discussions. Next year, we will do reviews in January and work on raises in February or March."

Senior Leadership

Dan began by examining the Core Team of WheatFields. "Since Steve and I have just begun here, I will put our salaries in Quad 1. Steve needs more money than I do, as I am set for life from my business career … but still, I need to receive fair compensation. Based on the salary comparisons, it seems equitable to have a $10,000 jump between the quads."

"That also moves the senior pastor salary closer to the Leadership Network[91] data from their chart. We are still a little below the national norms but can get there soon."

Leadership Network's *Large Church Salary Survey*

91 Warren Bird, *12 Salary Trends Every Church Leader Should Know: 2016 Large Church Salary Study, Complete Report,* chart *Senior/Lead Pastor Salary* used by permission, available from http://leadnet.org/salary/.

"The note with the chart from Warren Bird says that the box 'represents salary ranges from the 75th to 25th percentiles. 75th percentile means 25% made more and 75% made less. 25th percentile means 75% made more and 25% made less.' The dots are the 50th percentile of salary, the median."

Dan next looked at Leadership Network's data on executive pastors.[92] "My salary as executive pastor is pretty close to the norms. If anything, I'm at the high end."

Leadership Network's *Large Church Salary Survey*

"The other pastors on the Core Team have been here for some time, so their salaries will go into Quads 2 and 3. I want to leave some flexibility for raises for them, so I'll have Quad 4 be above their current salaries."

Dan concluded his review of the Leadership Network data.[93] "Looking at the LN data, our Core Team is like the position of senior associate pastor. Liz was certainly in that role with Pastor Wilson. I'd like to have the Core Team salaries fit with national norms. It looks like we are there."

---

[92] Warren Bird, *12 Salary Trends Every Church Leader Should Know*," chart used by permission: *Executive Pastor Salary*.

[93] Warren Bird, *12 Salary Trends Every Church Leader Should Know*, chart used by permission: *Senior Associate Salary*.

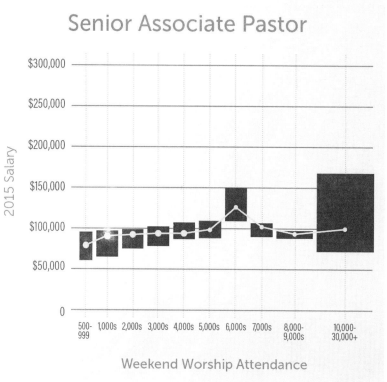

"The note said that high salary of the box was the 75% percentile. So, our Core Team is somewhere between 75% and 100% percentile. With our high cost of living and state income tax, it makes sense that we pay more than other churches."

"Our missions guy is woefully underpaid at $59,000. I'll mark him as an outlier to Quad 1. I think that I want his salary to match Liz Jackson's. We need to make up for the sins of prior years ... and do it now."

The first draft of Dan's compensation grid began to take shape:

Draft—WheatFields' Core Team

Ministerially Exempt	Quad 1	Quad 2	Quad 3	Quad 4	SECA
Senior Pastor	$115,000	$125,000	$135,000	$145,000	15.3%
Executive Pastor	$100,000	$110,000	$120,000	$130,000	15.3%
Core Team	$75,000	$85,000	$95,000	$105,000	15.3%

"Well, I finally got something accomplished on the compensation grid!"

Pastors and Ministry Directors

Dan moved on to the pastors, assistant pastors and ministry directors. "I'll start with the pastors. I'll put the highest pastor's salary, that of Will Martinez in high school, in Quad 3. Then, the other pastors will fit in well if I put them in Quads 1 and 2. For the pastor salaries, it seems good to have steps of $6,000 between the quads."

"If I do the same with the assistant pastors, I can have steps of $4,000 between quads. As for ministry directors, there is a broad range of salaries, so I will need steps of $5,000 between quads. The grid almost builds itself!"

Draft—Pastors and Ministry Directors at WheatFields

Ministerially Exempt	Quad 1	Quad 2	Quad 3	Quad 4	SECA
Pastor	$54,000	$60,000	$66,000	$72,000	15.3%
Assistant Pastor	$40,000	$44,000	$48,000	$52,000	15.3%
Ministry Director	$42,000	$47,000	$52,000	$57,000	15.3%

"I still have two salaries that are out of alignment. Junior High Pastor David Yang makes $40,000 and High School Assistant Pastor JB Jones makes $43,000. I'm going to mark both of these as outliers for now. They don't fit in well but I'll work on that later."

"Then there's Irene Steele, Worship Ministry Director. She makes $38,933 and works twenty hours a week. That's an equivalent of a full-time salary of $77,866. We don't pay any benefits to her but that's still an extremely strong salary. But she is utterly fantastic in leading worship. I need to mark her as an outlier too."

Directors and Staff

The exempt workers were easy to sort through. "The existing salaries fall into Quads 1 through 3. We have plenty of room for future raises in Quad 4."

Draft—Exempt Directors at WheatFields

Managerially Exempt	Quad 1	Quad 2	Quad 3	Quad 4	SECA
Director	$60,000	$67,500	$75,000	$82,500	—

Dan sorted through the non-exempt staff and created a grid for them:

Draft—Non-Exempt Staff at WheatFields

Non-Exempt	Quad 1	Quad 2	Quad 3	Quad 4	SECA
Director	$35,000	$40,000	$45,000	$50,000	—
Assistant, Secretary, Coordinator	$32,000	$35,000	$38,000	$41,000	—
Receptionist, Stage Hand, Intern (begins at minimum wage)	$21,632	$23,000	$25,000	$27,000	—
Facility Worker	$21,632	$26,000	$32,000	$36,000	—

"These were all straightforward and easy. Jeanie Wilson is at minimum wage and has always turned down raises. She works for the health insurance benefit. Someday I need to come up with a better title than *Stage Hand* for her. The facility workers all make $35,000. That's hard to believe. I wonder why we don't have some entry level facility workers at minimum wage?"

All that Dan had remaining were the ninety preschool teachers. "Right now, all the lead teachers make $17.50 an hour, the teachers make $14.50 and the assistant teachers make $12.50. Over time, I'd like to introduce some flexibility in those wages. Something doesn't feel right about the way that they add up. I'll have to wait for the full spreadsheet from Janet to get a better handle on these salaries."

Dan created a grid for the preschool teachers:

Draft—Preschool Teachers at WheatFields

Non-Exempt	Quad 1	Quad 2	Quad 3	Quad 4	SECA
Lead Teacher	$16.00	$17.00	$17.50	$18.50	—
Teacher	$13.50	$14.00	$14.50	$15.50	—
Assistant Teacher	$10.50	$11.50	$12.50	$13.25	—

Dan compiled his various tables into a master sheet:

Draft—The Compensation Grid of WheatFields

	Quad 1	Quad 2	Quad 3	Quad 4	SECA
Ministerially Exempt					
Senior Pastor	$115,000	$125,000	$135,000	$145,000	15.3%
Executive Pastor	$100,000	$110,000	$120,000	$130,000	15.3%
Core Team	$75,000	$85,000	$95,000	$105,000	15.3%
Pastor	$54,000	$60,000	$66,000	$72,000	15.3%
Assistant Pastor	$40,000	$44,000	$48,000	$52,000	15.3%
Ministry Director	$42,000	$47,000	$52,000	$57,000	15.3%
Managerially Exempt					
Director	$60,000	$67,500	$75,000	$82,500	—
Non-Exempt					
Director	$35,000	$40,000	$45,000	$50,000	—
Assistant, Coordinator	$32,000	$35,000	$38,000	$41,000	—
Receptionist, Stage Hand, Intern (begins at minimum wage)	$22,880	$24,500	$25,500	$27,000	—
Facility Worker	$22,880	$26,000	$32,000	$36,000	—
Preschool Teachers					
Lead Teacher	$16.00	$17.00	$17.50	$18.50	—
Teacher	$13.50	$14.00	$14.50	$15.50	—
Assistant Teacher	$11.00	$11.50	$12.50	$13.25	—

"We're in line with other churches from our region and around the country. This fits with the norms for school teachers and police. This is looking rather good."

"Let me see how the quads increase by percentages."

Increases by Quad at WheatFields

	Quad 1	Quad 2	Quad 3	Quad 4
Senior Pastor	Base	8.7%	8.0%	7.4%
Executive Pastor	Base	10.0%	9.1%	8.3%
Core Team	Base	13.3%	11.8%	10.5%
Pastor	Base	11.1%	10.0%	9.1%
Assistant Pastor	Base	10.0%	9.1%	8.3%
Ministry Director	Base	11.9%	10.6%	9.6%
Director—exempt	Base	12.5%	11.1%	10.0%
Director—non-exempt	Base	14.3%	12.5%	11.1%
Assistant, Coordinator	Base	9.4%	8.6%	7.9%
Receptionist, Stage Hand, Intern (begins at minimum wage)	Base	7.1%	4.1%	5.9%
Facility Worker	Base	13.6%	23.1%	12.5%
Lead Teacher	Base	6.3%	2.9%	5.7%
Teacher	Base	3.7%	3.6%	6.9%
Assistant Teacher	Base	6.3%	2.9%	5.7%

"Some of those increases, like the facility workers, are a little high. I'll need a couple of years to smooth those out. Some teacher increases are low, but that's what the job market is paying."

"Next week I'll look at individual salary increases and the outliers. Plus, I should have the full salary spreadsheet. Janet thought she would get it to me by last night, but it still hasn't arrived. If I receive it soon, I'll make next Wednesday night's deadline for the Compensation Team." Dan was hopeful at best, fearful at worst.

Dan compiled the data into one more chart, to show an overview of how salaries were paid by category:

Overview of Salaries

Status	Count	Average $	Average Quad	Totals
Senior Pastor	1	$115,000	Q1	$115,000
Executive Pastor	1	$99,000	Q1	$99,000
Core Team	3	$79,037	Q1 Note 1	$237,111
Pastor	2	$62,000	Q3	$124,000
Assistant Pastor	4	$47,750	Q2	$191,000
Ministry Director	2	$59,933	Q4+ Note 2	$80,933
Director (exempt)	3	$67,413	Q1	$202,238
Director (non-exempt)	5	$42,622	Q2	$213,110
Assistant	8	$36,815	Q2	$294,522
Receptionist, etc.	4	$23,064	Q2	$92,255
Facility Worker	5	$35,000	Q3 Note 3	$175,000
Lead Teacher	30	$17.50	Q3 Note 4	$737,100
Teacher	30	$14.50	Q3	$610,740
Assistant Teacher	30	$12.50	Q3	$526,500
Total	**128**			**$3,698,509**

Notes

1—Ed Baker's low salary skews the Core Team.

2—Irene Steele is twenty hours a week. When annualized ($77,866) at a full-time rate, she is way over Q4.

3—The facility workers all make $35,000—almost Q4. "Danger, Will Robinson!" Rightsize this as new workers are hired in at Q1 and Q2.

4—Better salary comparisons are needed for the teachers. It seems logical to hire in new teachers in Q1 and Q2.

"I'm done. It's noon and I need to get to lunch with Doris. A few more issues to solve next week and I'll be ready for the Compensation Team meeting. Between now and lunch, I should take Doris' advice and pray about these issues!"

Dan ended his work for the second week of the Compensation Study.

Toolbox

Principles

1. Let's review the first five elements of *Smart Money for Church Salaries*:

    1—**Invest** in staff salaries with skill, towards fulfillment of the church's vision statement, so that God will entrust spiritual riches.

    2—**Handle** worldly wealth with excellence and trustworthiness, using money to serve God ... and not the other way around.

    3—**Implement** a fair and generous compensation guide that neither underpays nor overpays.

    4—**Follow** federal or state regulations with integrity.

    5—**Learn** from information channels of those with deep knowledge of church finances, avoiding the "stupid tax."

    The sixth element of *Smart Money for Church Salaries* is:

    Be fruitful lest God gives resources to others who will produce fruit.

2. Scripture is clear. If we are found unfaithful or unfruitful, God will give our resources to others. Your church deserves a clean financial bill of health. If the people of your church suspect that money is being poorly invested, it will affect their giving or attendance. They may choose to go to another church that soundly invests their donations in fruitful ministry.

3. One way to be energetic and fruitful is to fulfill the principle from creation. God Himself rested after the seventh day. You are not Superman or Wonder Woman. Ministry often includes a full day of work on Sunday. Take at least one day off a week. Take two days off as much as possible. Personal productivity rapidly declines after fifty hours of work. Rest so that you can be fruitful in your ministry.

Steps

After you have done the necessary mind-numbing research on the role of each employee, you are ready to work on salary! Without the research, you could implement a faulty compensation guide.

❑ Research Comparable Salaries

Public School Teachers

Research the salaries of public school teachers in your county, as they can make an excellent reference point. People in the congregation generally readily understand if their pastors are paid similarly to teachers. You may gather data on district officials but those salaries tend to be significantly higher than church wages. The following are frequent findings:

- Associate pastors parallel what public school teachers receive.
- Core Team, senior associate pastors and well-experienced pastors are paid similarly to higher paid teachers and elementary school principals.
- Executive pastors receive wages akin to middle school principals or high school principals.
- Senior pastors are compensated in the same level as high school principals.

Police Departments

Continue your research with local police departments. Many times a new officer earns the same wage as a new associate pastor. The scales for other officers often align with pastors, Core Team, executive pastors and senior pastors.

Church Salaries

1. Collect data as possible from local churches and use at least one national salary survey. The data from national surveys can be overwhelming.
2. Consider what key positions in your church need research, such as senior pastor, executive pastor, worship pastor and senior staff. Use data from comparably-sized churches. Record the data from five to ten other churches per position.
3. Use an *In Toto* salary comparison to see all key positions in a church. Understand key salaries and measure the differential between significant tiers of leadership.

Local Cost of Living

There are significant differences in the data of what it costs to live in various cities. Weigh the differentials between the percentages. The bottom line is that you'll better understand what it takes to live in your community.

Summarize Benefits

Compile a complete list of benefits that your church offers. Examples include: Workers' Compensation and FICA for non-ministry staff, health insurance, COBRA, retirement,

and life insurance. Other insurance includes: dental, vision, accidental death and dismemberment and long-term disability. Allowances include automobile and cell phone.

❑ Set Quadrant Salary Levels

Form Your Salary Grid

1. Establish how many segments you desire in your grid. Four is a common number but you can go as high as seven before it becomes burdensome. Consider four grids that denote minimum, low to medium, medium to high and maximum pay.
2. Determine what you hope to be the minimum and maximum for each salary tier.
3. Consider how you will list those employees below the minimum quadrant or above the maximum.
4. Chart the tiers that your church currently has and will need in the near future. Tiers are commonly: senior pastor, executive pastor, Core Team, pastor, assistant pastor ministry director, director, administrative assistant, coordinator, receptionist, intern, and facility worker.

Fill in the Numbers

1. For each salary tier, examine your data on the qualifications for employees. Place the salaries in various quads. For example, if you have an experienced pastor, place their salary in Quad 3. Less experienced pastors should be in Quads 1 and 2. Hopefully, few will fall in Quad 4 so that you can give future raises.
2. Review the range of salaries in the quads. Most often, the salaries in Quad 4 should be below the beginning of Quad 1 of the next higher tier. For example, the maximum that a pastor might earn in Quad 4 is $72,000. The next tier might be the Core Team, where salaries start at $75,000.
3. Smooth out the numbers to even dollar amounts. Remember that the quadrants do not dictate exact salaries but give guidelines for starting salaries and future raises. Rounded numbers are easier to work with.
4. Compare what you hoped the grids might be to the first draft of actual salaries in the grid. Based on your thorough research, there should be a close correlation.
5. Complete your salary quadrants for the senior pastor, executive pastor, Core Team, pastors, ministry directors, directors and all other staff.
6. Compile your notes of any outliers to the quadrants for discussion with your Compensation Team.

❑ Plan for an Audit

The worst possible audit is a state payroll audit. This is often triggered by an unhappy employee who files a complaint about unpaid overtime. By following state and federal regulations, as well as the best practices, a state audit should flag no errors.

Consider a salary audit by a competent professional. This could be a member of your

Compensation Team or Finance Team who has experience in HR. They may volunteer their time for an internal audit. You may want to have an external audit by an outside professional who understands church salary issues. An outsider brings objectivity and a vast knowledge of other churches.

Consider hiring a Certified Public Accountant for an annual financial review or financial audit. A financial review is less expensive and is often sufficient. A review can cost from $4,000 to $8,000. A financial audit may be required by your bank if you have a loan on church property. Audits are time consuming and thorough. If you are considering a building campaign in the near future, the time to do an audit is now! An audit can run from $10,000 to $20,000.

Have your Finance Team conduct internal audits several times a year. These focus on one or two ministry areas and go into greater depth than an external audit. An internal audit focuses on alignment with policy. It performs a great number of random reviews of expenses and reimbursements.

Join the Evangelical Council for Financial Accountability. Align your church with their acclaimed *Seven Standards of Responsible Stewardship*™ which are national standards of church financial health:[94]

1. Doctrinal Issues—affirming a commitment to the evangelical Christian faith.
2. Governance—a responsible board of not less than five individuals.
3. Financial Oversight—complete financial statements with board review.
4. Resources and Compliance—appropriate management and controls.
5. Transparency—provide current financial statements upon written request.
6. Compensation and Related-Party Transactions—with integrity and propriety.
7. Stewardship of Gifts—truthfulness, giver intent, best interests of donors.

Let your church know that you adhere to national standards for your financial policies and practices. Get the ECFA seal to show your alignment with the Seven Standards.

---

[94] Evangelical Council for Financial Accountability, *Seven Standards of Responsible Stewardship*™," (Winchester, Virginia: ECFA) available from www.ecfa.org / Content / Standards.

Questions to Consider

One

Dan did an internet search for the salaries of public school teachers and police. What are the pros and cons of such data? Would you use those numbers for your church compensation study?

_____

_____

_____

_____

_____

_____

_____

Two

There are at least four major national church salary studies: Christianity Today, Leadership Network, MinistryPay and XPastor. Would you use national data? Would you prefer to use data from local churches? How does the church data align with the police and teacher data?

_____

_____

_____

_____

_____

_____

_____

Three

Your church may have different job titles than WheatFields. You may also have a score of different types of positions. For example, some churches separate executive assistants, administrative assistants and coordinators. What are the titles and levels of employees in your church? How would you begin to fill in the compensation grid for your church?

	Quad 1	Quad 2	Quad 3	Quad 4	SECA
Ministerially Exempt					
Senior Pastor					15.3%
Executive Pastor					15.3%
Leadership Team					15.3%
Campus Pastor					15.3%
Pastor					15.3%
Assistant Pastor					15.3%
Ministry Director					15.3%
Assistant Ministry Director					15.3%
Managerially Exempt					
Director					
Assistant Director					
Administratively Exempt					
Executive Assistant					
Non-Exempt					
Directors					
Assistant Director					
Executive Assistant					
Office Manager					
Administrative Assistant					
Coordinator					
Intern					
Receptionist					
Facility Worker					
Security Team					
Cost-Center Areas					
Bookstore					
Café					
Preschool or Daycare					
Other Cost-Center					

Tools

This section provides you with material that was introduced or finalized in this chapter. These items are also available at https://www.xpastor.org/smart. The password for this page is: smart money.

Shown below is the full list of the staff at WheatFields. They are sorted by exempt status and category of employee. Core Team members are in bold.

Department	D#	Title	FLSA	Annual
Leadership	**17**	**Senior Pastor**	**Ministerial**	**$115,000**
Leadership	**17**	**Executive Pastor**	**Ministerial**	**$99,000**
Family	**37**	**Family Pastor**	**Ministerial**	**$93,000**
Mission	**47**	**Mission Pastor**	**Ministerial**	**$59,000**
Worship	**27**	**Worship Pastor**	**Ministerial**	**$85,111**
Preschool	67	Preschool Pastor	Ministerial	$62,000
Family	37	High School Pastor	Ministerial	$62,000
Family	37	High School Assistant Pastor	Ministerial	$43,000
Family	37	Junior High Pastor	Ministerial	$40,000
Family	37	Discipleship Assistant Pastor	Ministerial	$53,000
Family	37	College & Young Adults Pastor	Ministerial	$55,000
Worship	27	Worship Ministry Director	Ministerial	$38,933
Preschool	67	Assistant Ministry Director for Preschool	Ministerial	$42,000
Worship	27	IT Director	Exempt	$75,238
Operations	57	Finance Director	Exempt	$65,000
Operations	57	Facility Director	Exempt	$62,000
Worship	27	Creative Director	Non-Exempt	$38,366
Worship	27	Media Director	Non-Exempt	$48,744
Operations	57	Database Director	Non-Exempt	$42,000
Operations	57	Facility Overseer	Non-Exempt	$42,000
Preschool	67	Assistant Director for Preschool	Non-Exempt	$42,000
Leadership	17	Executive Assistant	Non-Exempt	$40,000
Family	37	Administrative Assistant	Non-Exempt	$40,000
Family	37	Administrative Assistant	Non-Exempt	$40,000
Worship	27	Worship Administrative Assistant	Non-Exempt	$34,522
Family	37	Coordinator	Non-Exempt	$37,000
Family	37	Coordinator	Non-Exempt	$37,000
Operations	57	Secretary	Non-Exempt	$33,000
Mission	47	Secretary	Non-Exempt	$33,000
Operations	57	Receptionist	Non-Exempt	$22,800

Operations	57	Receptionist	Non-Exempt	$22,800
Worship	27	Stage Hand	Non-Exempt	$21,840
Worship	27	Worship Intern	Non-Exempt	$24,815
Operations	57	Facility Worker	Non-Exempt	$35,000
Operations	57	Facility Worker	Non-Exempt	$35,000
Operations	57	Facility Worker	Non-Exempt	$35,000
Operations	57	Facility Worker	Non-Exempt	$35,000
Operations	57	Facility Worker	Non-Exempt	$35,000
Preschool	67	30 Lead Teachers	Non-Exempt	$737,100
Preschool	67	30 Teachers	Non-Exempt	$610,740
Preschool	67	30 Assistant Teachers	Non-Exempt	$526,500
	13	Ministerial—Pastors & Directors		**$3,698,509**
	3	Exempt		
	112	Non-Exempt		
	128			

Criteria for Merit Increases

1. Experience—years in jobs that impact their current role.
2. Education—formal education as seen in a bachelor's degree, master's degree or doctorate. Ongoing education that signifies the person as a life-long learner.
3. Responsibility—the ability to carry out their work in a timely and effective manner. Key staff carry the weight of more ministry responsibility.
4. Team spirit—contributes to the morale of the staff and is excited to be here.
5. Missional alignment—implements the vision of the church in their area.
6. Special considerations—published songs, books, national speaking engagements, teaching that enhances high performance of local ministry.

- 8 -

IMPLEMENTING THE SALARY GRID

Health Insurance Crisis

It was Monday morning of the third week. Sunday had been a wonderful day of worship. Attendance continued to increase, proving that WheatFields was in a growth spurt. "I have three days until the Compensation Team meeting ... three days to bring together all my data and make recommendations," Dan thought.

Up before sunrise, and before getting distracted by emails, Dan plunged into the compensation process. He had an enormous unease about the preschool situation. "Things just don't seem right there but I don't know what it is. Perhaps I'm just uneasy about not offering health insurance to ninety full-time teachers. I can't place my angst ... something just doesn't feel right."

Dan thought back to his conversation with Wade at GuideStone. Wade had said, "Under the Affordable Care Act, and probably before, you need to offer them health insurance. You're going to have to pay a fine of $188.33 per month for 2017." Dan wondered, "I didn't ask about that fine. If it is a fine to the church, that would be 12 months x $188.33. That's close to $2,200 and we could easily pay that every year. But it could be per person."[95]

Dan did the math for a possible medical insurance fine:

Dan's First Estimate of the Penalty

Title	#	Penalty	Total
Lead Teachers	30	$188.33	$5,650
Teachers	30	$188.33	$5,650
Assistant Teachers	30	$188.33	$5,650
Total			$16,950

"Wow, a penalty of $16,950 is too steep. Medical coverage for ninety people could run well over $450k, even for the least expensive plan. But if we broke the law in 2017 and part of 2018, then we have an obligation to pay the fine. And it bugs me that we weren't offering the health care as we were supposed to. That's a bummer for those teachers."

Though he didn't want to get distracted by emails, Dan drafted a quick note to Wade that included his chart. Wade also was working early and responded immediately to Dan.

---

[95] Based on an email dialogue between the author and Wade Wilkerson.

Wade's Email

Hey early riser! Your figures are right and wrong. The fine is not per person per year. The penalty is **per month**!

The rules of the fine are that the first thirty employees are subtracted from the calculation. For you that would be ninety teachers minus thirty. The church would only be penalized on sixty employees.

If you have a penalty on 60 employees, that comes to $11,300 per month.

I checked with our records. The church leaders said, 'The preschool is covered, so don't give us a bid on that.' That is why GuideStone didn't submit a proposal on the preschool.

The penalty for not offering coverage or offering coverage that is not affordable or compliant only comes into play if an employee goes to the Marketplace Exchange for coverage and receives a government subsidy. The way I understand it, receiving the subsidy triggers a check to see if the employer offered the right product to the employee.[96]

Dan couldn't believe what he was reading:

- The church staff said that the preschool was covered and they are not!
- The fine will be $11,300 per month.

Dan double checked the numbers:

Dan's Second Estimate of the Penalty

		Penalty	Monthly	Annual
Basis of the fine	60	$188.33	$11,300	**$135,598**

"GuideStone is rock solid, but maybe there's an error somewhere," Dan hoped. Just to be sure of the fact, he found a webpage from Louise Norris, a healthcare broker.

If an employer with 50 or more FTE employees doesn't offer coverage to at least 95 percent of FTE employees, the potential penalty is $2,320 per full-time employee in 2018 (that amount started at $2,000, but it's indexed for inflation), although the first 30 employees aren't counted in the calculation. So if an employer has 65 FTE employees, doesn't

---

96 Based on an email dialogue between the author and Wade Wilkerson.

offer coverage, and at least one employee gets coverage in the exchange with a premium subsidy, the employer would owe a $74,240 penalty for 2018. The calculation is: (65-30) x $2,320 = $74,240.[97]

"This is worse than I thought. The annual penalty in 2017 was $2,260 and went up to $2,320 in 2018. We're up a creek without a paddle."

Dan was seeing red, mostly in the red ink of the penalty that WheatFields would have to pay. He knew better than to send an email to Janet in Finance when he was this angry. That conversation would have to wait for a face-to-face meeting.

While he was fuming, he saw an email from Janet. "Let's see what other bad news I'm going to get. What a way to begin a Monday morning, and I haven't even gotten to the office yet."

Final Salary Spreadsheet
Janet Williams was diligent and knew the importance of deadlines. Her email said:

> Dan—We had hoped to get you this by EOD Thursday. It was so good of you to lend us Nancy to help with the project. My staff worked with her during the week and we all had to come in on Saturday to finish it—sorry about the overtime for the non-exempt staff.
>
> I promised it to you by Monday and we had so many different places to look for the information that you wanted. We had to look in many accounting and HR files for all the different benefit and insurance data.
>
> After church, I got to my computer and worked straight from 1:00 to 10:30 pm. I barely got time for dinner.
>
> I think that you will be pleased with the salary spreadsheet. It contains all the information that you requested. Let me know how happy you are with it!

The email had arrived at 10:31 pm Sunday night. Dan wasn't pleased, thinking "Great, I have all this happy talk. But through somebody's carelessness, we have to pay close to 200

[97] Louise Norris, *Does Every Business with 50 or More Employees Pay a Penalty if it Doesn't Offer Affordable, Comprehensive Insurance?* (St. Louis Park, Minnesota: HealthInsurance.org, January 9, 2018) available from https://www.healthinsurance.org/faqs/will-every-business-with-more-than-50-employees-pay-a-penalty-if-they-dont-offer-affordable-comprehensive-insurance/.

grand in penalties."

Dan opened the file and saw the columns laid out as he had asked [due to the width of the spreadsheet, this has been split into two tables for print publication]. Dan looked at the first section of the spreadsheet, the Family Department:

Family Department—Part 1

Dept.	D#	Title	FLSA	Last	First	Hours	Hourly	Annual	FICA
Family	**37**	**Family Pastor**	**Ministerial**	**Jackson**	**Liz**	**F/T**		**$93,000**	
Family	37	High School Pastor	Ministerial	Martinez	Will	F/T		$62,000	
Family	37	College & Young Adults Pastor	Ministerial	Manta	Colton	F/T		$55,000	
Family	37	High School Assistant Pastor	Ministerial	Jones	JB	F/T		$43,000	
Family	37	Discipleship Assistant Pastor	Ministerial	Stanley	John	F/T		$53,000	
Family	37	Junior High Pastor	Ministerial	Yang	David	F/T		$40,000	
Family	37	Administrative Assistant	Non-Exempt	Nelson	Brooke	F/T	$19.23	$40,000	$3,060
Family	37	Administrative Assistant	Non-Exempt	Turner	Tasha	F/T	$19.23	$40,000	$3,060
Family	37	Coordinator	Non-Exempt	Beal	Art	F/T	$17.79	$37,000	$2,831
Family	37	Coordinator	Non-Exempt	Dodson	Carly	F/T	$17.79	$37,000	$2,831

Family Department—Part 2

Last	403B %	403B $	Medical Insurance	Employee Medical 21%	Dental	Vision	Life	Auto	Cell	Total Cost
Jackson	**9%**	**$8,370**	**$19,744**	**-$4,146**	**$985**	**$200**	**$885**	**$2,000**	**$918**	**$121,956**
Martinez	8%	$4,960	$16,068	-$3,374	$985	$160	$885	$1,000	$459	$83,142
Manta	2%	$1,100	$8,034	-$1,687	$985	$200	$455	$1,000	$459	$65,546
Jones	2%	$860	$3,005	-$631	$488	$102	$455	$684	$459	$48,422
Stanley	4%	$2,120	$8,034	-$1,687	$985	$200	$455	$684	$459	$64,250
Yang			$3,005	-$631	$985	$200	$455	$1,000	$459	$45,473
Nelson	2%	$800	$19,744	-$4,146	$985	$160	$342			$60,945
Turner	2%	$800	$12,051	-$2,531	$985	$160	$455			$54,980
Beal	4%	$1,480	$12,051	-$2,531	$985	$160	$455			$52,431
Dodson	4%	$1,480	$8,034	-$1,687	$985	$200	$455			$49,297

"Now that's what I'm talking about. Every cost is accounted for. Janet and her team put everything that I asked for on this sheet. Let me check on how the numbers look for someone, perhaps Liz," and Dan thought through each of her benefits:

- The salary is $93,000 and no FICA is taken out. "That's good because she is a pastor and pays SECA."
- The church contributed 9% of Liz's salary into her 403B retirement plan. "I don't know what she puts in but we're doing our part. Because of her many years here,

Liz is at the maximum percentage that the church will contribute."
- The premium on Liz's medical insurance is $19,744. The employee portion of medical insurance is there. She pays $4,146 which is 21% of the premium. The Affordable Care Act says the maximum an employee can contribute is 9.56% of their wages. She is at 4.4%, so that's fine.
- The church pays all the costs for dental, vision and life insurance: $985, $200 and $885. Liz has to pay tax on the life insurance premium over $50,000 but that's only about $150 or so of taxable income.
- Liz received a $2,000 taxable automobile allowance and a tax-free cell phone allowance of $918.

"So, the total cost to the church for Liz's employment is $121,956." Dan continued to reflect on that number.

"Let's see what the ACA maximum of 9.65% looks like for various salary levels. The federal minimum wage is $7.25 or $15,080 a year and California's minimum wage is $11.00 or $20,880 a year." Dan listed:

Maximum Premium Contributions

Annual Pay	ACA Max	Maximum Contribution
$15,080	9.56%	$1,442
$22,880	9.56%	$2,187
$40,000	9.56%	$3,824
$60,000	9.56%	$5,736
$80,000	9.56%	$7,648
$100,000	9.56%	$9,560

"I'd better see if anyone is over the ACA maximum employee contribution of 9.65%. I doubt that we do, but I'd better check." Dan chose a few salaries to do some rough checking across-the-board:

Maximum Premiums

Employee	Salary	Coverage	Age-Based Premium	9.56% ACA Max	21% Contribution	Out of Compliance
JB Jones	$43,000	Employee	$3,005	$4,111	$631	$0
Derek Mayes	$38,366	Employee & Spouse	$6,427	$3,668	$1,350	$0
Helen Getz	$34,522	With 1 Child	$12,051	$3,300	$2,531	$0
Charlie Black	$35,000	With 2 Children	$19,744	$3,346	$4,146	$800
Jeanie Wilson	$22,880	With 4 Children	$25,708	$2,187	$5,399	$3,211

"This can't be! Charlie and Jeanie are out of compliance. They are contributing too much of their salaries toward the health insurance premiums. Another health insurance issue ... this stuff is too complicated."

Dan looked online and found an article from the Society for Human Resource Management which said:

> For plan years beginning in 2018, employer-sponsored coverage will be considered affordable if an employee's required contribution for self-only coverage for the least-expensive plan option that meets ACA requirements does not exceed 9.56 percent of the employee's household income for the year (down from 9.69 percent in 2017).[98]

"And it looks like there is a $3,000 per employee annual penalty if we charge too much. It looks like I'm becoming a mini-professional in health insurance. Ugh. I'd better call Wade at GuideStone and get this settled."

Analyze Benefit Percentages

"I wonder what the benefit percentages are in the Family Department," Dan asked himself. He created a table to look at the compensation for Liz, the highest paid in the Family Department, and Carly Dodson the lowest paid:

Family Department Salary and Benefit Analysis

Last	First	Salary	FICA	Benefits	Total Cost	% FICA & Benefits
Jackson	Liz	$93,000		$28,956	$121,956	31%
Dodson	Carly	$37,000	$2,831	$9,467	$49,297	33%

---

[98] Stephen Miller, *Don't Overlook 2018 Change in 'Affordability' Safe Harbor Percentage,* Alexandria, Virginia: SHRM, June 9, 2007, available from https://www.shrm.org/resourcesand-tools/hr-topics/benefits/pages/2018-aca-affordability-safe-harbor-percentage.aspx.

"For these two staff, our benefits are running between 31-33%. That's a reasonable number."

Dan found the U.S. Department of Labor, Bureau of Labor Statistics page on *Employer 2017 Costs for Employee Compensation*:

> Employer costs for employee compensation averaged $35.87 per hour. Wages and salaries were $24.49 or 68%, and benefits were $11.38 or 32%.[99]

"On the good side, with national benefits at 32% of compensation, when I average Liz and Carly, they exactly fit the national numbers."

"I wonder what those DOL hourly rates roll out to on an annual basis?" and Dan created a table:

National Benefit Averages

Compensation	Hourly	Annually	Percent
Wages	$24.49	$50,939	68.3%
Benefits	$11.38	$23,670	31.7%
Totals	**$35.87**	**$74,610**	**100.0%**

"I really need to remember those numbers when we consider new staff. I doubt that anyone realizes that when we pay someone 50k that it actually costs us almost 75k."

"Let me see what the rest of the staff percentages are." The distraction of working the numbers numbed Dan's irritation over the upcoming health insurance penalty. "I'll create a summary of the benefits paid."

Benefit Percentages

Category	Benefits %
Ministerial	24.52%
Exempt	35.52%
Non-Exempt	44.13%
Teachers	7.65%

---

[99] U.S. Department of Labor, Bureau of Labor Statistics, *Employer Costs for Employee Compensation news release text,* for release 10:00 am (EDT) Tuesday, March 20, 2018, last modified date: March 20, 2018, available from https://www.bls.gov/news.release/ecec.nr0.htm.

"It makes sense that our benefit percentages increase from ministerial to exempt to non-exempt. We have higher paid people in the first and second categories. Medical insurance is the major cost in our benefits, and it's the same for each tier of employee."

"Now let me see who doesn't receive many benefits or none at all."

Low Benefit Percentages

Title	Last	First	Salary	Medical Insurance	Other Benefits	Percent
Worship Ministry Director	Steele	Irene	$38,933		$542	1.39%
Worship Intern	Clark	Erica	$24,815		$1,898	7.65%
High School Assistant Pastor	Jones	JB	$43,000	$3,005	$5,422	12.61%
Junior High Pastor	Yang	David	$40,000	$3,005	$5,473	13.68%
Preschool Lead Teachers	30		$737,100		**$56,388**	**7.65%**
Preschool Teachers	30		$610,740		**$46,722**	**7.65%**
Preschool Assistant Teachers	30		$526,500		**$40,277**	**7.65%**

"There are a few outliers. Irene Steele is at 1.4% and Erica Clark at 7.7%. They both have medical insurance elsewhere. Of course the preschool teachers only received the mandated FICA of 7.65%," and Dan began to fume again at being reminded of that problem.

"How about those employees with high benefit costs? Most of those costs will be in medical insurance. I can't discriminate in the hiring process for people who have large families, but I can know what it costs us."

High Benefit Percentages

Title	Last	First	Salary	Medical Insurance	Other Benefits	Percent
Secretary	Farley	Donna	$33,000	$12,051	**$17,045**	**51.7%**
Administrative Assistant	Nelson	Brooke	$40,000	$19,744	**$20,945**	**52.4%**
Assist. Min. Dir. for Preschool	White	Tamika	$42,000	$25,708	**$26,515**	**63.1%**
Receptionist	Smithey	Janet	$22,800	$12,051	**$14,662**	**64.3%**
Facility Worker	Black	Charlie	$35,000	$19,744	**$24,077**	**68.8%**
Facility Worker	Franco	Linda	$35,000	$25,708	**$25,446**	**72.7%**
Stage Hand	Wilson	Jeanie	$21,840	$25,708	**$26,255**	**120.2%**

"Oh my, I never realized that some people receive more than 50% of their salary in benefits. Those are some whopping medical insurance numbers and humongous percentages of salary. Jeanie Wilson's is the highest ... 120% of her salary goes to benefits. Her medical insurance premium is $25,708 ... incredible. Jeanie would donate her time to the church if she could. She only takes minimum wage so she can get medical insurance for her family."

Dan had to remind himself that, "It's unethical for me to fire someone because their benefits cost us too much. There have been a number of lawsuits over that. Those with the highest medical insurance premiums tend to have kids from age 20 to 26. If we wait a few years, those costs will go down as the kids get their own policies."

Preschool Salary Detail

Dan scrolled down Janet's file and found the preschool area. "Good, now in one area of the sheet we have all the preschool salaries—pastor, ministry director, assistant to the director and the teachers. I can get a sense of the total employee costs for the preschool." Dan now had a cost center for preschool salary data:

Preschool Salary Detail

Title	FLSA	Last	First	Hours	Hourly	Annual
Preschool Pastor	Ministerial	Stairs	Julie	F/T		$62,000
Assist. Min. Dir. for Preschool	Ministerial	White	Tamika	F/T		$42,000
Assistant Director for Preschool	Non-Exempt	Peterson	Grace	F/T	$20.19	$42,000
30 Lead Teachers	Non-Exempt	30		27	$17.50	$737,100
30 Teachers	Non-Exempt	30		27	$14.50	$610,740
30 Assistant Teachers	Non-Exempt	30		27	$12.50	$526,500
						$2,020,340

"So, the salaries, not counting benefits, run to $2.02 million. Adding in all the benefits, preschool compensation is $2.22 million. Let me think about this as a cost center." Dan did the math:

Preschool Profit

Income	
Tuition	$3,175,000
Restricted Donations	$325,000
Total Income	**$3,500,000**
Expenses	
Pastor	$80,589
Assistant Ministry Director	$68,515
Assistant to the Director	$58,746
Lead Teachers	$793,488
Teachers	$657,462
Assistant Teachers	$566,777
Fair Value Rent & Maintenance 30 Classrooms, Offices & Playground	$285,000
Supplies for Children	$127,500
Utilities	$55,000
Umbrella Insurance	$23,000
Accounting	$34,000
Total Expense	**$2,750,077**
Net Profit to Church	**$749,923**

"The school is a money maker! For running a family business, Pastor Wilson was shrewd. I can't believe that it brings in almost 750k in net profit. I like it. And, I'm going to need that surplus to pay for the medical insurance for the teachers."

As Dan looked more at the preschool section of the table, he couldn't believe what he saw.

Teacher Section of the Preschool Salaries

Department	D#	Title	FLSA	Hours	Hourly	Annual
Preschool	67	30 Lead Teachers	Non-Exempt	27	$17.50	$737,100
Preschool	67	30 Teachers	Non-Exempt	27	$14.50	$610,740
Preschool	67	30 Assistant Teachers	Non-Exempt	27	$12.50	$526,500

It was Christmas coming in springtime. It was almost too good to be true. The numbers were there and he quickly checked the math. This was a gift and wonderful surprise, if true.

Though it was 7:30 in the morning, he called Janet to confirm his bliss:

Dan: "Janet, you and your team did fantastic work on the salary spreadsheet. I was just reviewing it."

Janet: "I'm really not very awake yet. I was up working on that blasted spreadsheet of yours until late last night ... and then couldn't fall asleep with all those numbers floating in my head. With triple confirmation, I hope that we got everything right."

Dan: "That's what I'm calling about."

Janet: "Oh, great. Share a mistake and make my morning before I've even had a cup of coffee?"

Dan: "I saw that the spreadsheet has the hours of the preschool teachers at 27 hours a week. It seems to me that I see the teachers on campus full time. Pastor Wilson always called them full-time staff. Isn't the school open from 7:00 am to 5:00 pm?"

Janet: "Yeah, that's right. Pastor Wilson kinda exaggerated. They stagger the hours of the teachers. Some come in early and some stay late. No teacher works more than 27 hours a week. That's written in stone."

Dan: "None of them work overtime?"

Janet: "No, they have to stay at 27 hours a week. Another church with a school required the teachers to do home visits with each student. They had to do lots of back pay when the church learned that those visits were on the clock. So, we're pretty tough on monitoring the teachers at 27 hours a week."

Dan: "I didn't know that."

Janet: "Somewhere or other the Department of Labor said that with the Affordable Care Act, that 27 hours a week was a 'safe harbor level.' If staff average more than thirty hours a week, then we have to offer them medical insurance for a year. We do offer full benefits to Julie, Tamika and Grace, as they're all full-time."

Dan: "So that's why we don't offer any of the teachers medical insurance?"

Janet: "That's what I just said. Would you like me to repeat it?"

Dan: "Sorry, I'm kinda giddy because I thought that we were going to have to pay a huge penalty for not offering insurance."

Janet: "Oh no. I went through all of that with the people at GuideStone when ACA was first announced. Pastor Wilson thought we'd have to raise tuition by 20% if medical insurance was required for the teachers."

Dan: "So, what do the teachers do for medical insurance?"

Janet: "The assistant teachers are mostly young enough that they can be on their parent's plan, until they turn 26. Most of the others are covered by spouses; some work another job."

Dan: "You are utterly fantastic. You have covered the bases so well. Thanks for your partnership in ministry. I owe you an extra hot, extra big latte the next time I see you."

Janet: "And I hope that won't be for a few more hours, Mr. Early Bird."

Dan was relieved. "We just escaped a fine that probably would have been over $200k. Janet and GuideStone did an amazing job when ACA was enacted. One part of the compensation crisis was solved before it even began ... but I would have known that earlier if the salary spreadsheet had shown complete information! Without full and complete data, I'm a dead duck."

Inflation and Raises

With a lighter heart, Dan returned to his main job at hand—setting compensation levels. He began by reviewing the 2014-17 inflation numbers from the Department of Labor.[100] He created a table that included estimated inflation for 2018:

Recent Inflation Figures

2014	2015	2016	2017	2018
1.8%	1.7%	2.2%	2.0%	2.4%

[100] U.S. Department of Labor, Bureau of Labor Statistics, *Databases, Tables & Calculators by Subject*, data extracted on April 20, 2018, available from https://data.bls.gov/timeseries/CUUR0000SA0L1E?output_view=pct_12mths.

Dan created another table to see the loss of buying power if the church had not given cost of living increases for those years:

Loss of Buying Power

	2014	2015	2016	2017	2018
Inflation	1.8%	1.7%	2.2%	2.0%	2.4%
Buying Power	$50,000	$49,150	$48,069	$47,107	$45,977

"If no raises were given for five years, the $50,000 salary would drop in buying power to $45,977. That's a 9.2% decrease. For many folks that equates to three to five months of housing expenses."

Dan read on a Social Security webpage that "monthly Social Security benefits for more than 66 million Americans will increase 2% in January, 2018."[101]

"So, two government sources say inflation was 2% last year. That jives with other internet sources, at least by a few tenths of a percent. It seems reasonable to create a 2% Cost of Living Adjustment (COLA) raise pool for all employees. I'll call it a raise pool, in case some salaries are already too high. For those people, we will keep their salary the same but give a bonus to them. The bonus is cash in their pocket but won't increase their base salary."

Possible Total Cost of a 2% COLA

Area	#	Salary	FICA	Total	2.0% COLA
Church Salaries	35 Staff	$1,678,169	$71,537	$1,749,706	$34,994
Preschool Salaries	93 Staff	$2,020,340	$146,600	$2,166,940	$43,339
Totals	**128 Staff**	**$3,698,509**	**$218,137**	$3,916,646	$78,333

"Giving $78,333 in inflation increases to our staff seems fair," Dan reasoned. "But, now I need to think about merit increases on top of inflation increases."

Dan reviewed the criteria for merit increases. "I'm going to use my draft from last week as a working model for raises." Dan looked at his six criteria:

1. Experience—years in jobs that impact their current role.
2. Education—formal education as seen in a bachelor's degree, master's degree or doctorate. Ongoing education that signifies the person as a life-long learner.
3. Responsibility—the ability to carry out their work in a timely and effective manner. Key staff carry the weight of more ministry responsibility.
4. Team spirit—contributes to the morale of the staff and is excited to be here.

---

[101] U.S. Social Security Administration, *Cost-of-Living Adjustment (COLA) Information for 2018*, available from https://www.ssa.gov/news/cola/.

5. Missional alignment—implements the vision of the church in their area.
6. Special considerations—published songs, books, national speaking engagements, teaching that enhances high performance of local ministry.

"The Compensation Team needs to approve these concepts, but until then I'll use them."

Core Team

Dan began the slow process of reviewing each employee and considering a raise, bonus or inflation adjustment.

Senior Pastor

"The Elder Board will determine Steve's raise but I can make some recommendations. He should move from Quad 1 to Quad 2. That will take him from $115,000 to $126,000. That's a 10% raise."

"He has the education and responsibility of a Quad 2 leader. As the church has grown, and with comparable salaries being paid elsewhere, he merits an increase. An early bump would give him plenty of encouragement to continue on strong."

"I may get some pushback since Steve is so new, but this church is rapidly growing. The Compensation Team will need to make this recommendation to the elders for a decision. The timing may need to wait for Steve's six-month review by the elders."

Executive Pastor

"I'll have to pass on this one. I can't make recommendations on my own salary!"

Core Team

"My hunch is to make all three pastors on the Core Team have the same salary. My rationale is that they have huge areas of responsibility. They're leaders in team spirit and missional alignment."

"Ed in Missions needs an increase of $34,000. He'll go from $59,000 to 93,000. That's a whopping 58% raise. We've been underpaying him for so long! The other day Ed told me that when he was being interviewed, he told us his overseas salary ... and we matched it. That wasn't a deal, but a steal. Ed is a national leader in missional thinking, speaking all over the place. He probably brings more great ideas on improving his area than anyone else on staff."

"If we're going to have all the pastors on the Core Team earn the same, Mark in Worship should get an increase of 9.3%. That is $7,889 and would take him from $85,111 to $93,000. Mark is writing songs that are used around the country. We can't let some other church steal him away by paying him better than we do. Of course, if someone offers him 50% more, we couldn't match that. But we can offer him a salary that keeps his family happy and doesn't give an inducement to move."

"Liz in Family Ministry is already the top earner at $93,000 but we'll give her a COLA. Her experience and responsibility earn that. For years, she and Pastor Wilson just about ran the entire church. I could give her an inflation adjustment … but if I do that, then her salary will bump to $94,860 and still be above the other two. So just a bonus for her, perhaps double what others receive. If we did a 4% bonus, that would be $3,720."

Pastors and Ministry Directors
Pastors

"I think we need to keep Junior High Pastor David Yang with the title of *pastor*. His pay grade is that of an assistant pastor. We can live with a problem in titles for five to seven years, until he reaches the pastor pay grade. He's a terrific team player. David has brought more alignment of the junior high ministry to our church goals than anyone before him. Let's give him a 5% raise, from $40,000 to $42,000. He's young but doing amazing work for a newbie."

"Will Martinez over high school is doing great and already receives a good salary at $62,000. A 2% COLA of $1,240 and a 2% bonus of another $1,240 should be fine for him."

"Julie Stairs, Preschool Pastor, deserves a 6% raise, from $62,000 to $66,000. That puts her right in the middle of Quad 3. She is a super star with 600 kids in her weekday program. I couldn't dream of being responsible for ninety teachers and all those kids. I don't know how she does it."

Assistant Pastors

"Change the title of John Stanley from *Assistant Discipleship Pastor* to *Discipleship Pastor*. Give a raise of 8%, taking him from $53,000 to $57,500. We've been underpaying him with his eleven years of experience. Since he's been here, John has finished his master's degree and is just about done with his doctorate in *Spiritual Formation*. He deserves a move from Quad 1 into Quad 2 this year and probably into Quad 3 in a year or two."

"I need to talk to Will Martinez, High School Pastor, and Liz over all of Family about JB Jones, High School Assistant Pastor. Some think he is terrific and others are mixed. Will has been coaching him. I need input on this one."

Ministry Directors

"I need to add the word *ministry* to the titles for Irene and Tamika. That will signify and help me remember that their roles are ministerial in nature."

"Irene needs a new title as *Worship Ministry Director*. No COLA for her but let's do a 2% bonus of $779. She is paid well at $38,933 for twenty hours a week. That would be the equivalent of $77,866 for forty hours. That's a sweet deal."

"Tamika gets a new title as *Assistant Ministry Director for Preschool*. That's a mouthful. She is currently at $42,000 in Quad 1. I'll move her inside of Quad 2 at $48,500. Her years on the job and vast responsibilities deserve merit increases. She just finished her master's degree in *Early Childhood Development and Spiritual Life*. That degree is money in the bank. $6,500 is a 15% raise ... mighty significant but we can't lose her. If another preschool in the area poached her, we would be in big trouble."

Directors

"My conversations with the directors were productive. Those that are losing their housing allowances are fine with that, as long as I compensate them for it. The first folks that I need to determine are the managerially exempt directors."

"José in facilities will be managerially exempt due to his wage and role. He earns $62,000 and should get a $57 increase for losing his housing allowance—unless he can make a case for a bigger amount. For him it's not the amount but the principle that we made adjustments for all who will be affected. Let's do a 2% COLA and 2% bonus, each will be $1,240."

"Hank in IT becomes managerially exempt based on salary and job function. He earns $75,238 and deserves every penny of it. No overpay there! He will probably realize a $506 gain by going to FICA and losing his housing allowance. No housing adjustment for him, unless he can show me otherwise. 2% COLA and 2% bonus: $1,505 each."

"Janet Williams in Finance goes to managerially exempt, again based on compensation and job description. She earns a nice salary of $65,000. By losing the housing allowance and SECA, she should see a gain of $473. If not, I will work with her on an adjustment. 2% COLA and 2% bonus: $1,300 each."

Non-Exempt Directors

"I would like to see Charlie, Derek, Todd and Grace be managerially exempt. But either their roles or salaries prohibit that. They'll have to get used to filling out a time card and we'll pay for any overtime. I better make a note to remind them that all overtime must be approved in advance! I don't like paying time and a half, or, even worse, the dreaded double time."

"Charlie in media will become a non-exempt director. By job function, he qualifies as managerially exempt but being exempt would mandate pay increases as California raises minimum wage each year. He earns $48,744 now. Just because his salary qualifies, the rules say that I'm not obligated to make him non-exempt. With double minimum wage, if Charlie were managerially non-exempt, he would move to $62,400 on January 1, 2022. Ouch! That position in media is not of that salary level. He should also net $129 more by not having to pay SECA, unless he tells me otherwise. Charlie requested a raise and now is between Quad 3 ($45,000) and Quad 4 ($50,000). He could be given a 5% raise and be taken to $51,000. Oh no! I'm already seeing a problem with my salary grid for non-exempt directors—Charlie is maxing out. Bummer. I'll have to work on that."

Derek in the Creative Department will become a non-exempt director. He is at $38,366 and requested a raise. I'll first give him $365 for losing his housing allowance—unless he tells me it's more. Derek is between Quad 1 ($35,000) and Quad 2 ($40,000). Derek's salary is low and could be given a 5% increase to $40,284. I like it that with a 5% raise, Derek would be above $40k. I don't like paying people something like $39,500. It's demoralizing to pay people just below a major break like that. Derek's creative designs really bring pop to our print pieces, emails and website."

"Todd with the database moves to a non-exempt director. He'll get a $537 adjustment for losing his housing allowance. I doubt that he can show me that it will be more than that. Todd earns $42,000 and is doing entry level work for a database director. I want to see him improve by taking some tech classes and teaching the staff on more effective use of the database. He has resisted that so far. 2% COLA and 2% bonus: $840 each."

"Grace, Assistant to Preschool Director, needs a $987 adjustment for losing her housing allowance. Like Todd, I doubt it will be more. She does good work but not exceptional. 2% COLA and 2% bonus: $840 each."

Support Staff

"I'm stumped at what to do with our facility workers. I love them all, but at $35,000, I can't justify giving them a raise. Perhaps a 2% bonus would work, that would be $700 each. I need to remember to tell the Compensation Team that a bonus is from this year's cash and doesn't impact next year's budget. I'd better get some input on doing just a bonus for those five workers."

"We blew it by not giving three staff raises implementing the new California minimum wage on January 1, 2018. The receptionists, Janet and Carolyn, need back pay of 4 cents an hour. Jeanie, our Stage Hand, needs back pay of 50 cents an hour."

"I need to plan for the increase in California minimum wage on January 1, 2019. It goes from $11.00 to $12.00. Janet, Carolyn and Jeanie will each need an increase of $2,080. That's a lot of money! Nice for them! Also, I see conflicting salary numbers for Jeanie. One sheet says $7.25 an hour and another says $10.50. She needs to be at $11.00."

"All the other staff, including all ninety preschool teachers should receive a 2% COLA and 2% bonus. That would run $54,987."

"Those staff who are getting raises have their inflation adjustment in their raise. So my number for just the inflation adjustment drops from my initial projection of $78,333 to $54,987."

"The great thing about the $62,986 in bonuses is that we have the cash on hand. It will be a great encouragement to them. And the bonuses have no impact on next year's budget."

"Of course, sooner or later people will talk about their salaries. Some will slip and mention a raise and some may have side conversations. I'll just have to live with that. These are fair numbers and we're rewarding each person in some degree."

Cash and Budget Impact

Area	Amount
Ministerial Housing Changes	$1,946
COLA 2% Inflation	$54,987
Bonus	$62,986
Raise	$74,063
Total	**$193,982**
Original 4% across the board	$159,795
Delta Increase	**$34,188**

Dan realized that, "The total dollar impact is $193,983 and that is $34,188 more than a 4% across-the-board raise. Of course, 99.4% of that $34,188 delta is in one raise, that of Ed Baker's $34,000."

"There is another way to look at it. We'll be giving bonuses of $62,986 and that comes from this year's cash. Those dollars have no impact on next year's budget. Let's see how the raises impact our salary budget."

Impact on Salary Budget

Area	Budget
2017 Salaries	$3,747,253
2018 Salaries	$3,880,140
	$132,887
Salary Increase	3.5%

"The real change to our salary budget is only 3.5%. That's .5% lower than the original 4% across-the-board proposal. That's a $17,003 savings."

As Dan finished his compensation work, Monday was coming to a close. "That was a long day of thinking through and implementing COLA, bonuses and merit increases."

Toolbox

Principles

1. We have seen the first six elements of *Smart Money for Church Salaries*:

   1—**Invest** in staff salaries with skill, towards fulfillment of the church's vision statement, so that God will entrust spiritual riches.

   2—**Handle** worldly wealth with excellence and trustworthiness, using money to serve God ... and not the other way around.

   3—**Implement** a fair and generous compensation guide that neither underpays nor overpays.

   4—**Follow** federal or state regulations with integrity.

   5—**Learn** from information channels of those with deep knowledge of church finances, avoiding the "stupid tax."

   6—**Be fruitful** lest God gives resources to others who will produce fruit.

   The seventh and final element of *Smart Money for Church Salaries* is:

   Find success in the wise use of the finances that God provided as measured by changed lives.

2. The definition of success sets the bar for measuring our work. *Smart Money for Church Salaries* begins that definition with "the wise use of finances." This takes planning, hard word and the counsel of others. Both the financial newbie and the old hand do best when surrounded by excellent counselors.

3. The measurement of that success is ultimately in the changed lives of the people of your church and community. That is seen through the implementation of your church's vision statement. The immediate success is in the changed lives of your staff—good morale, people fairly compensated for their hard work and strong families that have the money to survive and thrive.

Steps

❏ Analyze Benefits

Health Insurance

1. Create a table based on the Affordable Care Act maximum allowable employee contribution. For 2018 the number is 9.56% of annual wages.
2. Ensure that employees contribute no more than the maximum. If you have employees over the maximum, adjust their contribution to meet the ACA standards.
3. Create a table that shows the percentage of each person's benefits to their salaries. Look at the low and high outlying percentages, such as those below 10% and others above 50%. The largest factor in erroneous data is inaccurate or missing medical premiums.

All Other Benefits

1. Examples of benefit areas include: Workers' Compensation and FICA for non-ministers, COBRA, retirement, life insurance, dental insurance, vision insurance, accidental death and dismemberment insurance and long-term disability insurance, automobile allowance, cell phone allowance.
2. Consider the tax-free cell phone allowance as a good perk for key staff. Ethically, you should pay for any employee that uses their personal cell phone in the course of their work. You can have different levels of cell phone allowance based on the amount of usage or category of employee. Remember to consider facility workers for a cell allowance if they use a personal cell phone while on the job.
3. Consider a taxable auto allowance. Many pastors prefer an allowance over a reimbursement system where they have to log miles for every use of their car.
4. Consider a SECA equivalency bonus for pastors. This can be instituted over several years at 2% or 3% a year.

Controlling Benefit Costs

1. The national norm is that 32% of compensation goes to benefits. You cannot ethically terminate an employee based on the cost of benefits.
2. Set a plan for reducing areas of high benefit cost. You can require employees to contribute a percentage of their medical insurance premiums. If you are not doing this, set a reasonable starting point such as 2% or 3% of the premium amount. Each year, increase the employee contribution by a reasonable amount until you reach your desired goal. Many businesses require a 25% contribution for the employee's premium and a 50% contribution for covered family members. As a church you can have a non-ERISA health insurance plan that has different categories of employees with distinct levels of coverage and premium costs.
3. Summarize a list of recommended changes to your benefit offerings.

❑ Review Cost Centers

The worth and value of each cost center should be measured by your mission statement. Dan found a church that ran an assistance shop of clothing and furniture for the needy. The net cost to the church was $29,000 and a highly-valued piece of implementing vision.

Determine the true net profit or loss from a cost center. Often forgotten items include fair rent value, utilities, umbrella insurance coverage, maintenance and accounting costs. If a staff member devotes part of their time to the cost center, prorate that portion of their salary to it.

Examples of cost centers: assistance shop, bookstore, café, daycare center, elementary-high school, preschool, sports clinic and summer camp. Compare the purpose and results from the cost center to your vision statement.

❑ Draft Raises or Bonuses

Review the Big Burrito Salary Spreadsheet

1. Ensure that all employees are accounted for on the spreadsheet.
2. Review all wages and benefits. Check all formulas used in the sheet. It is easy to paste a fixed number into the cell for a formula.
3. Copy the file and rename the new copy, something like "Proposed Raises and Bonuses."
4. If you are having difficulty with creating or working with the spreadsheet, you should consider a class in Microsoft Excel, Apple Numbers or Google docs.

Understand Inflation

1. Inflation amounts for the preceding calendar year will vary depending on your source. Local issues can cause a regional spike in the cost of living, such as a surge in real estate values.
2. Determine a base amount of inflation. Consider that if this amount is not given, then your employees will lose that amount of buying power in the current year.
3. Use your inflation percentage to do a rough calculation on how that will affect your salaries.

Review Metrics for Merit Increases

The metrics give you a sane rationale basis for giving or not giving increases. Suggested metrics include: experience, education, responsibility, team spirit, missional alignment and special considerations.

Review Your Salary Grid

Certify that you have included categories for each tier of staff person. Ensure that the salary levels make sense. Have room to take salaries to Quads 3 and 4.

Work the Numbers to Create

1. Work through one category at a time.
2. Apply your metrics to each person. Keep notes on your rationale for a raise, bonus, cost of living increase or no change. You may need those notes when explaining the change to the Compensation Team.
3. You cannot make a recommendation about your own salary.

Questions to Consider

One

If inflation was 2% last year, what would be your rationale to give or not give a 2% cost of living adjustment?

_____
_____
_____
_____
_____
_____
_____

Two

Churches often have one or more staff that are highly compensated for their work. Irene Steele is one of those people. What advice would you give Dan about her $38,933 salary for twenty hours of weekly work? What would you advise for the facility workers who each make $35,000?

_____
_____
_____
_____
_____
_____
_____

Three

Your church may not have a history of giving bonuses. What are the pros and cons of instituting bonuses? What red flags might your leaders have about a bonus? Why might they want one?

_____
_____
_____
_____
_____
_____

Tools

This section provides you with material that was introduced or finalized in this chapter. These items are also available at https://www.xpastor.org/smart. The password for this page is: smart money.

Federal minimum wage is $7.25 or $15,080 a year. California minimum wage is $11.00 or $20,880 a year. ACA requires that no more than 9.56% of an employee's salary be paid for their own medical insurance premiums. The chart below shows the maximum contribution that can be made by salary level:

Maximum Insurance Premium Contributions

Sample Wage	Annual Pay	9.56%	Maximum Contribution
Federal minimum	$15,080	9.56%	$1,442
California minimum	$22,880	9.56%	$2,187
Coordinator	$40,000	9.56%	$3,824
Pastor	$60,000	9.56%	$5,736
Executive Pastor	$80,000	9.56%	$7,648
Senior Pastor	$100,000	9.56%	$9,560

Health Insurance at WheatFields

Maximum Premiums

Employee	Salary	Coverage	Age-Based Premium	9.56% ACA Max	21% Contribution	Out of Compliance
JB Jones	$43,000	Employee	$3,005	$4,150	$631	$0
Derek Mayes	$38,366	Employee & Spouse	$6,427	$3,702	$1,350	$0
Helen Getz	$34,522	With 1 Child	$12,051	$3,331	$2,531	$0
Charlie Black	$35,000	With 2 Children	$19,744	$3,378	$4,146	**$769**
Jeanie Wilson	$22,880	With 4 Children	$25,708	$2,208	$5,399	**$3,191**

Use the following table as a starting point to determine the maximum premium amounts allowable under the Affordable Care Act.

Your Church Maximum Premiums

Employee	Salary	Coverage	Age-Based Premium	9.56% ACA Max	Percent Contribution	Out of Compliance

- 9 -

COMPENSATION DISCUSSIONS

Final Week

Tuesday morning came but did not see Dan rise before dawn. The pace of work had taken its toll and he slept in. At 10:00 am, Dan drug himself to the office. Janet Williams was the first to see him.

Janet: "You look like you need that extra hot, extra large latte. Up late partying?"

Dan: "I wish. That would have been more fun. The workload is immense. Not only do I have to do all my regular work but this compensation crisis has to be solved."

Janet: "You took the job, boss. Now you get all the perks of responsibility that come with it."

Dan: "My business career was easier than this but I'm about done with the salary work. I just have the Compensation Team meeting tomorrow night."

Janet: "And you think that your crisis is over? I've heard stories for years from Pastor Wilson about that group. Buena suerte, that's good luck in Spanish."

Dan: "Sí, hablo un poco Español también. Do pray for that meeting, your COLA and bonus will depend on it."

Janet: "I have some motivated self-interest for that prayer. Will do."

Dan: "By the way, that's über insider information."

Janet: "Roger that."

Nancy had scheduled a 10:00 am appointment for Dan and Steve to discuss the compensation issues.

Core Team Discussion
Without going into his recommendation for an increase for Steve, Dan laid out

the compensation grid, 2% COLA increase, bonuses and raises. The meeting lasted a full hour as they discussed each item. Steve took it all in and considered the issues. At the end of the time, there was agreement on the items.

A lunch meeting with the Core Team was from 11:00 am to 1:00 pm. Steve had given Dan a full hour to present the principles of the compensation guide.

> Dan: "Soon, each of you will receive a spreadsheet listing every employee in your department. It will contain the employee's salary, benefits and total compensation. Here's a sample of Tasha Turner." Dan put Tasha's information on the video monitor.

Tasha Turner Salary Item, Part 1

Department	D#	Title	FLSA	Last	First	Hours	Hourly	Annual	FICA
Family	37	Administrative Assistant	Non-Exempt	Turner	Tasha	F/T	$19.23	$40,000	$3,060

Tasha Turner Salary Item, Part 2

Last	403B %	403B $	Medical Insurance	Medical CoPay 21%	Dental	Vision	Life	Auto	Cell	Total Cost
Turner	2%	$800	$12,051	-$2,531	$985	$160	$455			$54,980

> Liz: "That's so cool. I can know how much it takes to have someone like Tasha on our staff."

> Dan: "You're getting ahead of me ... "

> Liz: "No wait, I'm just getting my arms around a whole, new thought. I thought that it cost us $40,000 to have Tasha on staff. Now I'm seeing that it costs us $54,980. That's a big difference. That's like 30% or so."

> Dan: "It's 37.5% and yes, the benefits piece of compensation is a large number. That's why we need to be careful in adding staff who work more than thirty hours a week."

> Ed: "How do we know that Tasha's $40,000 is a fair wage?"

> Dan: "I researched comparative salaries in local and national school districts, police departments and churches. Here's a compressed salary

grid for the Chicago Police Department." Dan knew what the response would be but put it on the screen anyway.[102]

Chicago Police

	Start	Step 4	Step 8	Max
Officer	$48,078	$76,266	$90,024	$99,414
Detective	$70,980	$82,614	$97,440	$107,550
Sergeant	$76,932	$89,171	$101,422	$114,828
Lieutenant	$87,402	$100,668	$117,894	$128,346
Captain	$95,844	$111,018	$129,282	$138,138
Superintendent	—	—	—	$260,004

Ed: "Frank Sinatra, I hear you now, 'Chicago is my kind of town.' Those are some nice salaries! Mark, can you lead us in singing ..."

Mark: "Let's skip the song and get hired there. Dan, are you a recruiter for the Chicago police? I'll sign on just as a captain ... I don't have to be the superintendent. I would even come on at Step 4 and wouldn't complain."

Dan: "What you are seeing is the graduated steps of compensation. You see the minimums and maximums for each pay grade or category of staff. The Chicago data helps us see what our full-time pastors could be making. And I kept in the superintendent just for eye candy."

Mark: "So back to Ed's question. How do we determine if Tasha is being paid fairly? I have seven people in my department."

Liz: "And I have twelve in the Family Department and ninety preschool teachers."

Dan: "Believe it or not, comparative salaries for support staff are fairly easy to get. For many of our support staff, like Tasha, we can get salary information from local businesses. We can find how much an administrative assistant earns in our community. The challenge is fair salaries for pastors."

Ed: "So ... did you use a crystal ball, or what?"

---

[102] Chicago Police Department, *2017 Position & Salary Schedule*.

Dan: "As I said before, I researched local and national churches, police departments and teachers. In looking at all that data, I think that we'll have fair salaries for everyone."

Mark: "While the Chicago police info is fun, why police and school teachers?"

Dan: "If we only look at other churches, we obviously only see church salaries. What if church salaries are out of line with local standards of living?"

Mark: "So you have comps from police and teachers in our area?"

Dan: "Yes. I could show those to you sometime."

Liz: "I bet that people in our church would respond favorably if we said, 'Our salaries are in line with what a high school teacher makes.' It sounds a lot better than 'we pay similarly to other churches.' They can't relate to that."

Dan: "That's exactly the point. Most people feel that police and teachers are paid fairly by local standards. Plus, all that salary data is online. Anyone can take a look at what we based our salaries on."

Ed: "Could we see one of those?"

Dan: "Okay, if you're game, let me put one on the screen."

2017 Teachers, Newport-Mesa, California[103]

Years/ Step	BA +30 or Credential	BA +60 or Master's	BA +75 Master's or Doctorate	BA +75, Master's or Doctorate & Certification
1	$54,043	$60,420	$65,350	$66,608
5	$58,538	$70,683	$76,451	$77,921
10	$58,539	$85,996	$93,014	$94,802
15	$58,539	$93,014	$100,604	$102,538
28	$58,539	$104,628	$117,692	$119,955

---

[103] School Loop, *2016-2017 Teacher Salary Schedule 188 days, Newport-Mesa Unified School District.*

Ed: "When I returned from the mission field, I should have gone into the public school system. Work nine months for $94,802. I'd take that. Ha! Just kidding. I wouldn't trade my ministry role for any pile of cash."

Dan: "We do have some adjustments to make for selected staff. By creating a compensation grid based on solid data, we have a rational basis for salary decisions."

Dan tried to introduce issues of the ministerial exemption, managerial exemption and California minimum wage. It was too much information for the Core Team to take in.

He did present his solutions for directors who should not be considered ministerially exempt and will lose their housing allowance.

Dan concluded with a few principles of merit increases and COLA for inflation.

Dan: "Inflation was about 2% last year. So if someone earned $50,000 last year, that would only buy $48,000 in goods this year."

Mark: "That's a great way of illustrating it. If we don't give raises of any kind, our people will lose 2%."

Dan: "That's right. To be fair to our people, we ought to give most staff members a 2% COLA, a raise for inflation."

Ed: "You said, 'most staff.' Why not all?"

Dan: "Well ... this is between us, in this group. I trust you with what I'm about to say. I love our facility workers, but each and every one of them earn $35,000. There are no entry level positions, none at even close to minimum wage. It's a sweet job if you can get it."

Ed: "I've never heard of anything like that. I mean, I want our folks to be paid well, but that doesn't seem to be reasonable ... or fair to the rest of us."

Dan: "Those folks will get a bonus but not a raise. A raise is compounded annually, which is why they probably got to such a high salary level."

Steve: "This is outstanding information. We've learned so much from Dan today. We're out of time for this part of our agenda, but if you want to learn more, get some time with Dan."

The presentation and discussion lasted exactly an hour. "There's so much more to cover but that will have to wait for another day," Dan thought.

Compensation Summary Sheets

Dan had a major project to do on Tuesday afternoon. He needed to create two sample sheets of salary and benefits—one version to give to a pastor and another version for a support staff member.

"I'm going to begin with the one for pastors. I need to list every item of compensation and benefits." He created his draft:

John Stanley—Salary Overview

Name	John Stanley
Department	Family
Status	Full-Time
Current Title	Discipleship Assistant Pastor
New Title	Discipleship Pastor
Exemption Status	Ministerial
Housing Allowance as a part of Salary	$28,000
Housing Allowance Approval Date	April 6, 2018
Current Salary	$53,000
Raise	$4,500
Percent	8%

John Stanley—Total Compensation

	Church Cost	Your Cost	Total Compensation
New Annualized Wages			**$57,500**
Medical Insurance 21% Employee Participation	$8,034	$1,687	$6,347
Retirement: 403B Plan	4%	$0	$2,120
Dental Insurance	$985	$0	$985
Auto Allowance (taxable)	$684	$0	$684
Workers' Compensation Insurance	$490	$0	$490
Cell Phone Allowance (non-taxable)	$459	$0	$459

Life Insurance, 2x salary Taxable on premium over $50,000	$455	$0	$455
Vision Insurance	$200	$0	$200
Accidental Death & Dismemberment Insurance	$50	$0	$50
COBRA, if used on exit, you pay 102% of the health premium	$12	$0	$12
Long-Term Disability	$60	$0	$60
Total			**$69,362**
Percent Benefits			**20%**

"This is a good start and I don't think that I left anything out. Those numbers for accidental death, COBRA and long-term disability are estimates, but close enough for government work. They are so minor that they don't belong on the salary spreadsheet, but the staff needs to know that those items are a part of the salary package."

"I was thinking of putting vacation and sick time on this spreadsheet. We could list the rate of accrual and totals. To be complete, we should also list family leave time and conference time allowed. I don't know about that for now … perhaps another year."

"Now I need to create a slightly different one for other staff. Let me do one for Tasha. I had better delete or change things that don't apply to her. So the new title and ministerial housing allowance lines need to go. Plus, I should show that Tasha is hourly without implying that she is getting a salary, so I'll call that 'annualized wages.' I also want to show the total effect of the COLA, which I will call a raise, and the bonus. I'm going to label that *Percent Raise and Bonus*."

Tasha Turner—Salary Overview

Name	Tasha Turner
Department	Family
Status	Full-Time
Title	Administrative Assistant
Exemption Status	Non-Exempt
Current Hourly	$19.23
Proposed Hourly	$19.62
Cash Bonus	$800
Percent Raise & Bonus	4%

Tasha Turner—Total Compensation

	Church Cost	Your Cost	Total Compensation
New Annualized Wages			**$40,800**
FICA	$3,121	$0	$121
Medical Insurance 21% Employee Participation	$12,051	$2,531	$9,520
Retirement: 403B Plan	2%	$0	$800
Dental Insurance	$985	$0	$985
Workers' Compensation Insurance	$490	$0	$490
Life Insurance, 2x salary Taxable on premium over $50,000	$455	$0	$455
Vision Insurance	$160	$0	$160
Accidental Death & Dismemberment Insurance	$40	$0	$40
COBRA, if used on exit, you pay 102% of the health premium	$12	$0	$12
Long-Term Disability	$50	$0	$50
Total		**Total**	**$56,433**
Percent Benefits			**38%**

Creating those sample sheets took longer than Dan had hoped. "It's going to take HR a fair amount of time to prepare the final sheets for each employee, but it will be worth it."

Dan's work for Tuesday was complete. The next day passed quickly and the meeting was that night.

Compensation Team Discussion

As the Compensation Team entered the room, people greeted each other warmly. However, there was an air of uncertainty. Dan thought, "It's as if they're hoping that I finished the compensation work but fearing that I haven't."

Dan decided to have some fun. "Instead of presenting all the facts and then the conclusion, I'm going to give them the price tag first." Dan began the meeting:

> Dan: "When we met three weeks ago, we had talked about 4% across-the-board raises. That would have cost $159,795. That number was incorrect. We should give $195,239 in raises." Dan stopped and let the number sink in.

Attorney: "Well, of course, if you have the data to support such a figure, we would consider it."

CPA: "That's a lot of cash. Your ledger better prove it."

Entrepreneur: "So you did the 'big ask' right out of the gate. That's an effective sales technique. You have our attention, so go on with the show."

Over the next ninety minutes, Dan walked through the major issues from the last three weeks:

Required Items Leading to a Compensation Review
- Review of board minutes and the need to commission several pastors.
- Finding a mixed bag of job descriptions.
- Housing allowances were not approved by the board.
- Compliance issues with FICA, SECA, opting out of Social Security, FLSA exemption standards and non-exempt issues.

Staff Issues
- Discussions with the pastors and directors about compensation issues and whether some directors are really ministry directors.
- Sorting of existing salaries by levels of staff.
- Proposals to change some directors to non-ministerial status.

Data Sources and Grid Creation
- School Districts
- Police Departments
- National church compensation reviews
- Compensation Grid at WheatFields

Compensation
- Back pay for unpaid minimum wage
- Inflation adjustments and/or bonuses for many staff
- Raises for selected staff

There wasn't much discussion during Dan's presentation. The team absorbed all the new information, then they commented:

Staff Who Are Overpaid

CPA: "Dan, you know how to fish, don't you? You set the hook and we bit. But you delivered too. That was a first rate presentation."

Attorney: "Getting into some specifics, what can we do about the 'sweetheart deal' that Irene has? She earns a lot of money."

Entrepreneur: "Dan is beginning to address her issue and the facility workers being overpaid. The 'no raise but bonuses' will keep up morale and not increase future budgets. I don't think this is the year to reduce anyone's salary."

Pastor not Paying SECA and SECA bonus

CPA: "Client confidentiality prohibits me from giving the name, but one of our pastors has not paid SECA this year. He's young and thought the church was taking it out."

Dan: "I'm sorry to hear about that. I'll look at our offer letter to ensure that it's clear on that."

CPA: "As self-employed for tax purposes, it's the pastor's responsibility, not the church's ... but he will pay a penalty, unless I can get a first-year waiver on the penalty part."

Entrepreneur: "I'd like to make a motion that over the next four years, we pay a bonus to offset the SECA contribution that pastors make. I move that we do a continuing bonus of 2% of salary, increasing it to 8% in four years."

Dan: "Leadership Network did show that 38% of churches around the nation gave a bonus to offset the SECA taxes. Here is their chart."[104]

---

[104] Warren Bird, *12 Salary Trends Every Church Leader Should Know*, chart used by permission: *38% of Surveyed Churches Offer FICA Reimbursement.*

Leadership Network's Large Church Salary Survey

38% of Surveyed Churches Offer FICA Reimbursement for Pastors Who File Taxes as "Self-Employed"

Church Size	Amount of Raise	Church Size	Amount of Raise
10,000-30,000+	41%	4,000s	44%
8,000s-9,000s	50%	3,000s	41%
7,000s	Insufficient data	2,000s	42%
6,000s	50%	1,000s	38%
5,000s	42%	500-999	35%

CPA: "But the employer's equivalency in the SECA contribution is 7.65% ..."

Entrepreneur: "If we got to the 8% level in four years, we would be giving an extra .35% to help with the taxes on the SECA equivalency bonus."

Approving Housing Allowances

Attorney: "As you were talking, I did a search on my laptop. I have some scribbled notes from past meetings. Once a year, Pastor Wilson would bring a cryptic list of housing allowance information to us. We all agreed to it."

Entrepreneur: "Can we take that as the church approving the allowances?"

Attorney: "The church's constitution does mandate our role as a committee of the Elder Board. After each of those meetings, I did convey to the Finance Team that we looked at the housing allowances."

Dan: "So those minutes would work!"

Attorney: "They're really not minutes but a bunch of chicken scratches. The computer has the date of each note so I could write up some brief, formal minutes."

CPA: "Please do that. They may be brief but they can be the official minutes of the meetings when the housing allowances were approved."

Opting Out of Social Security

CPA: "I have another pastor who is a client. He said that his former church forced him to opt out of Social Security."

Dan: "A church can't force someone to do that."

CPA: "They said, 'Opt out or we won't hire you.' They also filed Form 8274 and didn't pay the employer's portion of social security for support staff.[105] It's a rare church that files that.[106] The employees, though, had to pay 15.3% SECA tax."[107]

Attorney: "That's way too technical for today. As to the first issue, why force a pastor to opt out? It doesn't cost the church anything. Why force someone to involuntarily sign that IRS form? They're forcing the pastor to lie."

Dan: "I can't address that church's actions. I can say that we will uphold the law and ethical issues in the IRS rules and regulations."

Raises

CPA: "Dan, I'm not trying to nit-pick but you know I'm a numbers guy. On the raises, you said that you wanted to give JB Jones, the high school assistant pastor, a raise. But on the raise sheet, he got a COLA and a bonus, no raise."

Dan: "Mea culpa. That's my mistake. I'll do a raise for JB. I was trying to juggle too many balls in the air and one dropped."

Attorney: "We'll have to recommend your and Steve's raise to the elders for consideration. I noted you didn't put in anything for you ... good job on that. We'll take care of you."

---

[105] IRS *Form 8274.*

[106] U.S. Department of Treasury, Internal Revenue Service, *Elective FICA Exemption - Churches and Church-Controlled Organizations,* last reviewed or updated August, 4, 2017, available from https://www.irs.gov/charities-non-profits/churches-religious-organizations/elective-fica-exemption-churches-and-church-controlled-organizations.

[107] Richard R. Hammar, *Exemption from Social Security: Many Churches Mistakenly Assume that They Are Exempt* (Wheaton: Christianity Today, Church Law & Tax, July-August 1992) available from https://www.churchlawandtax.com/cltr/1992/july-august/exemption-from-social-security.html.

CEO to Worker Pay Ratio

Entrepreneur: "In my businesses, I like to know the salary ratio between the worker and the CEO. That is, between the lowest and highest paid people in an organization."

Dan: "On the fly, let's take some of those tables and show what those ratios are. I can put the spreadsheets on the video screen and add some columns. Here are nine salaries from a church with 2,100 in worship."

2,100 in Worship

	2018 Data	Percent	Factor
Senior Pastor	$126,815	100%	1.0
Executive Pastor	$83,951	66%	1.5
Education Pastor	$77,553	61%	1.6
Business Administrator	$74,567	59%	1.7
Worship Pastor	$63,783	50%	2.0
Facility Director	$49,622	39%	2.6
Youth Staff	$47,763	38%	2.7
Administrative Assistant	$35,855	28%	3.5
California Minimum Wage	$22,880	18%	5.5

Dan: "The top pay is 3.5 times their lowest reported full-time salary and 8 times federal minimum wage. Now let's look at a church of 3,100 in worship."

3,100 in Worship

	2018 Data	Percent	Factor
Senior Pastor	$243,969	100%	1.0
Executive Pastor	$104,873	43%	2.3
Worship Pastor	$81,691	33%	3.0
Student Pastor	$63,366	26%	3.9
Facility Director	$60,716	25%	4.0
Worship Director	$44,157	18%	5.5
Executive Assistant	$39,741	16%	6.1
Administrative Assistant	$26,494	11%	9.2
Federal Minimum Wage	$15,080	6%	16.2

Dan: "The salary ratios are quite different. The top pay is nine times that of their lowest reported full-time salary and sixteen times the federal minimum wage. One final chart, that of local school administrators and teachers."

Newport-Mesa Unified School District

	2017 Data	Percent	Factor
Principal High School	$162,676	100%	1.0
Principal Elementary	$139,556	86%	1.2
Coordinator III	$118,503	73%	1.4
Teacher BA +75	$100,604	62%	1.6
Teacher BA +60	$70,683	43%	2.3
Teacher BA +30	$54,043	33%	3.0
California Minimum Wage	$22,880	14%	7.1

Entrepreneur: "Let's see the Chicago Police and then our church's ratios:"

Dan: "I didn't want to kill you with numbers, but you asked for it."

Chicago Police

	2017 Data	Percent	Factor
Superintendent	$260,004	100%	1.0
Chief	$185,364	71%	1.4
Commander	$162,684	63%	1.6
Captain	$138,138	53%	1.9
Lieutenant	$128,346	49%	2.0
Sergeant	$101,422	39%	2.6
Detective	$70,980	27%	3.7
Officer	$48,078	18%	5.4
Chicago Minimum Wage	$22,880	9%	11.4

Ratios at WheatFields

	Current	Percent	Factor
Senior Pastor	$115,000	100%	1.0
Executive Pastor	$100,000	87%	1.2
Core Team	$95,000	83%	1.2
Directors—exempt	$67,500	59%	1.7
Pastors	$62,000	54%	1.9
Assistant Pastors	$50,000	43%	2.3
Directors—nonexempt	$45,000	39%	2.6
Assistants & Coordinators	$35,000	30%	3.3
California Minimum Wage	$21,632	19%	5.3

Dan: "Our ratios are lower than most. This means that we have room for raises without being a top-heavy organization."

CPA: "I'm loving all these numbers. I'm in dog heaven."

Attorney: "Enough already. You made your point. Great work on all this!"

Entrepreneur: "Let's make some motions, get all this approved and go home. I've already missed most of the game but could get home for the final fifteen minutes."

CPA: "Go ahead ..."

Entrepreneur: "I move that we:

• Recommend the compensation grid to the Elder Board for approval.
• Empower Dan to make salary adjustments for inflation and give bonuses and raises according to the principles, direction and amounts that he outlined at tonight's meeting.
• Begin a 2% SECA equivalency bonus on top of any other bonuses that we give to pastors, going up to 8% over 4 years.
• Certify the actions of past Compensation Teams, as indicated in their minutes, for approvals of prior ministerial housing allowances.
• Recommend that the Elder Board consider merit increases for our senior pastor and executive pastor."

Dan: "Is there a second to the motion? Any discussion? Seeing that there is no further discussion, let me call for the vote."

The motion was unanimously approved.

Crisis Resolved

As Dan drove home from the meeting, he felt good. "It seems that my compensation crisis is solved. Three hard weeks of work produced something of value for the church."

He got home and talked with Doris:

Dan: "Of all the things that happened tonight, one really surprised me."

Doris: "Are you going to tell me or do I have to guess."

Dan: "The Compensation Team approved the 2% SECA equivalency bonus. Someone recommended it, virtually no discussion on it, and boom. It was approved."

Doris: "I don't know what a FEMA equivalency bonus is, but it's nice that it was approved."

Dan: "That's SECA and stands for ..."

Doris: "Really, let's stay out of the weeds of details and acronyms. Just enjoy tonight's rousing success. I have the day off tomorrow and I suggest that you take one too."

Dan: "I suppose that they can live without me for a day. The work of implementing those raises has to wait until after the board approves the recommendations of the Compensation Team anyway."

The compensation crisis at WheatFields required the principles of *Smart Money for Church Salaries*. Dan needed to invest in staff salaries with skill. He needed to focus the budget and salary spreadsheets to show the fulfillment of the church's vision statement. If he was faithful with the budget, God would entrust spiritual riches to the church.

Dan needed to handle worldly wealth with excellence and trustworthiness. That money needed to serve God—and not the other way around. God gave the money through the people of the church.

The Compensation Team approved a fair and generous compensation guide that neither underpaid nor overpaid. There were a few outliers and these would be solved over time. The team was generous in approving the SECA equivalency bonus for the pastors.

The church needed to follow federal or state regulations with integrity. There were some places where the church had skirted the law and amends needed to be made. Back pay for missing the new California minimum wage increase needed to happen immediately. The records of the Compensation Team and Elder Board needed to be improved. These steps were taken.

Dan had learned from information channels of those with deep knowledge of church finances, avoiding the "stupid tax." The online resources provided a wealth of material. His coach and emails to various professionals certified that Dan was on the right track.

WheatFields needed to be fruitful with the money that God had provided. Otherwise, Scripture indicated that God would give those resources to others who would produce fruit. The church was in a wonderful season of growth. Excellent handling of church finances could help continue that growth. Poor handling of salaries, and resulting demoralization of staff, could end that growth.

Dan had found success in the wise use of church finances. At appropriate times and levels, he brought Steve, the Core Team and all pastors and directors into the discussion. The Compensation Team was the constitutionally appointed group to make many salary decisions and recommend a few others to the Elder Board. The right teams had been involved in the process.

Most important for Dan was that success could be measured in changed lives. The staff would be empowered and encouraged through their salaries. The ministry could move forward to bring the love of Jesus to their community. The scorecard wasn't how much money WheatFields had or the number of people in worship, but in lives that were being changed.

Dan Black had lived out the principles of *Smart Money for Church Salaries*. As his favorite Rabbi said, "Good measure, pressed down, shaken together, is overflowing."

As Dan was falling asleep that night, he wondered:

> "I worked through my first crisis in ministry. I'm going to hope that most of church life will be less crazy than that."

> "Yet, I wonder if this crisis is a sign of things to come ..."

Toolbox

Principles

1. The elements of *Smart Money for Church Salaries* are:

> 1—**Invest** in staff salaries with skill, towards fulfillment of the church's vision statement, so that God will entrust spiritual riches.
>
> 2—**Handle** worldly wealth with excellence and trustworthiness, using money to serve God ... and not the other way around.
>
> 3—**Implement** a fair and generous compensation guide that neither underpays nor overpays.
>
> 4—**Follow** federal or state regulations with integrity.
>
> 5—**Learn** from information channels of those with deep knowledge of church finances, avoiding the "stupid tax."
>
> 6—**Be fruitful** lest God gives resources to others who will produce fruit.
>
> 7—**Find success** in the wise use of the finances that God provided as measured by changed lives.

2. These biblical principles bring God's wisdom and generosity to your church finances. When the biblical value of generosity is included, the church can take care of the financial needs of the employee, spouse and family. People do not feel used or like a cog in the machine. They know they are valued as a part of the mission of the church.

3. Living without biblical principles makes every financial decision a murky one. Salaries are a prime example. Without solid principles, compensation becomes a chore at best, and a nightmare at worst. Inequity prevails.

Steps

❑ Consult with Senior Staff

1. Share the core concepts, titles of categories and formation of your compensation grid. Present the findings from one or two of the sources of your compensation comparisons. Define inflation for the preceding year.
2. Share your criteria for merit increases. Walk through each item and get consensus on the list.
3. Give a high level overview of the dollar totals of your proposed inflation adjustment—bonuses or raises. Present an example of one support staff member's line in the *Big Burrito* spreadsheet. Walk through the salary and each of the benefits. Show the total cost to the church for that person. Highlight that person's percentage of salary to benefits.

❑ Prepare for Employee Presentations

1. Draft an initial compensation summary sheet for a pastor and a support staff member. For pastors, include the date of their housing allowance approval.
2. If the person is getting a raise or bonus, list the dollar amount and percentage.
3. Itemize each of the benefits and the cost to the church and employee. Highlight items that have no cost to the employee.
4. Present the total cost to the church for the employee. Highlight the percentage of benefits in their total compensation.

❑ Meet with the Compensation Team

1. Collect all your notes, lists and ideas. Think through how you will present the trove of data and recommendations. Do not come unprepared to this meeting. Create a PowerPoint or Keynote presentation of your findings.
2. Walk through the positive aspects of the church's existing compensation structure and your lessons learned. Do not sugar-coat anything. Show the profit or loss of the cost centers and how they relate to your church's mission statement.
3. Share all sources of data for salary comparisons. This may include local churches, national church salary surveys, public school teachers, police departments and local non-profits. Have print copies available for inspection. Consider adopting one salary comparison for discussing compensation with the congregation, such as "We based our salaries on local public school teachers." Also seek a recommendation for national financial standards, such as through the Evangelical Council for Financial Accountability. Aligning with national standards is beneficial to mention to the congregation.
4. Present your recommendations for all staff, except yourself. Have print copies available. Consider collecting the print copies at the end of the meeting.
5. Allow sufficient time for discussion. Discuss challenging issues and items that need continued improvement. Be ready for new ideas, such as the SECA equivalency bonus that Dan heard about. Be prepared for anything and everything. Take notes on their recommendations.

Questions to Consider

One

Who are the key staff in your church who need to receive an overview of your compensation system? These are generally heads of departments and managers who conduct reviews and give input on raises. Do they understand the metrics of raises and quads of the compensation grid?

_____

_____

_____

_____

_____

_____

_____

Two

What items should be included or omitted on your compensation summary sheet?

_____

_____

_____

_____

_____

_____

_____

Three

When you are getting ready to share your recommendations for raises, how can you best prepare for a Compensation Team meeting? What information will you give them to take home and what should be returned at the end of the meeting?

_____

_____

_____

_____

_____

_____

Tools

This section provides you with material that was introduced or finalized in this chapter. These items are also available at https://www.xpastor.org/smart. The password for this page is: smart money.

Inflation

U.S. Inflation 2014-18

2014	2015	2016	2017	2018
1.8%	1.7%	2.2%	2.0%	2.4%

Examples from WheatFields

Final Cash and Budget Impact

Area	Amount
Ministerial Housing Changes	$1,946
COLA 2% Inflation	$54,146
Bonuses	$62,145
Raises	$89,063
Total	**$207,301**
Original 4% across the board	$159,795
Delta Increase	**$47,506**

Final Impact on Salary Budget

Area	Budget
2017 Salaries	$3,699,469
2018 Salaries	$3,844,260
	$144,791
Percent	3.9%

Final Raise List

Title	Last	First	Salary	House Adj.	Raise	New Salary	Raise %
Creative Director	Mays	Derek	$38,366	$365	$1,918	$40,284	5%
Junior High Pastor	Yang	David	$40,000		$2,000	$42,000	5%
High School Assistant Pastor	Jones	JB	$43,000		$3,000	$46,000	7%
Media Director	Ethelridge	Charlie	$48,744		$2,256	$51,000	5%
Preschool Pastor	Stairs	Julie	$62,000		$4,000	$66,000	6%
Discipleship Pastor	Stanley	John	$53,000		$4,500	$57,500	8%
Assist. Ministry Director for Preschool	White	Tamika	$42,000		$6,500	$48,500	15%
Worship Pastor	Houdini	Mark	$85,111		$7,889	$93,000	9%
Executive Pastor	Black	Dan	$99,000		$12,000	$111,000	12%
Senior Pastor	Borneo	Steve	$115,000		$11,000	$126,000	10%
Mission Pastor	Baker	Ed	$59,000		$34,000	$93,000	58%
		Totals	**$685,221**	**$365**	**$89,063**	**$774,284**	

Final Bonus and COLA List

Title	Last	First	Salary	House Adj.	COLA 2%	Bonus %	Bonus	New Salary
Receptionist	Smithey	Janet	$22,800		$456	2.0%	$456	$23,256
Receptionist	Morrison	Carolyn	$22,800		$456	2.0%	$456	$23,256
Stage Hand	Wilson	Jeanie	$22,800		$456	2.0%	$456	$23,256
Worship Intern	Clark	Erica	$24,815		$496	2.0%	$496	$25,311
Secretary	Farley	Donna	$33,000		$660	2.0%	$660	$33,660
Secretary	Vance	DeDe	$33,000		$660	2.0%	$660	$33,660
Worship Admin. Assist.	Getz	Helen	$34,522		$690	2.0%	$690	$35,212
Facility Worker	Cruse	Joe	$35,000			2.0%	$700	$35,000
Facility Worker	Franco	Linda	$35,000			2.0%	$700	$35,000
Facility Worker	Haines	Trudy	$35,000			2.0%	$700	$35,000
Facility Worker	Snead	Jon	$35,000			2.0%	$700	$35,000
Facility Worker	Black	Charlie	$35,000			2.0%	$700	$35,000
Coordinator	Beal	Art	$37,000		$740	2.0%	$740	$37,740
Coordinator	Dodson	Carly	$37,000		$740	2.0%	$740	$37,740

Title	Last	First	Salary	House Adj.	COLA 2%	Bonus %	Bonus	New Salary
Worship Ministry Director	Steele	Irene	$38,933			2.0%	$779	$38,933
Administrative Assistant	Nelson	Brooke	$40,000		$800	2.0%	$800	$40,800
Administrative Assistant	Turner	Tasha	$40,000		$800	2.0%	$800	$40,800
Executive Assistant	Rearson	Nancy	$40,000		$800	2.0%	$800	$40,800
Database Director	Petrey	Todd	$42,000	$537	$840	2.0%	$840	$43,377
Facility Overseer	McDean	Dean	$42,000		$840	2.0%	$840	$42,840
College & Young Adults Pastor	Manta	Colton	$55,000		$1,100	2.0%	$1,100	$56,100
High School Pastor	Martinez	Will	$62,000		$1,240	2.0%	$1,240	$63,240
Facility Director	Mendoza	José	$62,000	$57	$1,240	2.0%	$1,240	$63,297
Finance Director	Williams	Janet	$65,000		$1,300	2.0%	$1,300	$66,300
IT Director	Fogarty	Hank	$75,238		$1,505	2.0%	$1,505	$76,743
Family Pastor	Jackson	Liz	$93,000			4.0%	$3,720	$93,000
		Total	**$1,097,908**	**$594**	**$15,820**		**$23,819**	**$1,114,322**
Assistant Director for Preschool	Peterson	Grace	$42,000	$987	$840	2.0%	$840	$43,827
30 Lead Teachers			$737,100		$14,742	2.0%	$14,742	$751,842
30 Teachers			$610,740		$12,215	2.0%	$12,215	$622,955
30 Assistant Teachers			$526,500		$10,530	2.0%	$10,530	$537,030
		Total	**$1,916,340**	**$987**	**$38,327**		**$38,327**	**$1,955,654**
		Total	**$3,014,248**	**$1,581**	**$54,146**		**$62,145**	**$3,069,975**

The Big Burrito Salary Spreadsheet

Department	D#	Title	FLSA	Last	First	Hours	Hourly	Annual	FICA
Family	**37**	**Family Pastor**	**Ministerial**	**Jackson**	**Liz**	**F/T**		**$93,000**	
Family	37	High School Pastor	Ministerial	Martinez	Will	F/T		$63,240	
Family	37	College & YA Pastor	Ministerial	Manta	Colton	F/T		$56,100	
Family	37	HS Assist. Pastor	Ministerial	Jones	JB	F/T		$46,000	
Family	37	Discipleship Pastor	Ministerial	Stanley	John	F/T		$57,500	
Family	37	Junior High Pastor	Ministerial	Yang	David	F/T		$42,000	
Family	37	Administrative Assist.	Non-Exempt	Nelson	Brooke	F/T	$19.62	$40,800	$3,121
Family	37	Administrative Assist.	Non-Exempt	Turner	Tasha	F/T	$19.62	$40,800	$3,121
Family	37	Coordinator	Non-Exempt	Beal	Art	F/T	$18.14	$37,740	$2,887
Family	37	Coordinator	Non-Exempt	Dodson	Carly	F/T	$18.14	$37,740	$2,887
Mission	**47**	**Mission Pastor**	**Ministerial**	**Baker**	**Ed**	**F/T**		**$93,000**	
Mission	47	Administrative Assist.	Non-Exempt	Farley	Donna	F/T	$16.18	$33,660	$2,575
Worship	**27**	**Worship Pastor**	**Ministerial**	**Houdini**	**Mark**	**F/T**		**$93,000**	
Worship	27	Worship Ministry Dir.	Ministerial	Steele	Irene	20		$38,933	
Worship	27	IT Director	Exempt	Fogarty	Hank	F/T		$76,743	$5,871
Worship	27	Creative Director	Non-Exempt	Mays	Derek	F/T	$19.37	$40,284	$3,082
Worship	27	Media Director	Non-Exempt	Ethelridge	Charlie	F/T	$24.52	$51,000	$3,902
Worship	27	Worship Intern	Non-Exempt	Clark	Erica	24	$20.28	$25,311	$1,936
Worship	27	Administrative Assist.	Non-Exempt	Getz	Helen	F/T	$16.93	$35,212	$2,694
Worship	27	Stage Hand	Non-Exempt	Wilson	Jeanie	F/T	$11.18	$23,256	$1,779
Leadership	**17**	**Senior Pastor**	**Ministerial**	**Borneo**	**Steve**	**F/T**		**$126,000**	
Leadership	**17**	**Executive Pastor**	**Ministerial**	**Black**	**Dan**	**F/T**		**$111,000**	
Leadership	17	Executive Assistant	Non-Exempt	Rearson	Nancy	F/T	$19.62	$40,800	$3,121
Operations	57	Finance Director	Exempt	Williams	Janet	F/T		$66,300	$5,072
Operations	57	Database Director	Non-Exempt	Petrey	Todd	F/T	$20.85	$43,377	$3,318
Operations	57	Facility Director	Exempt	Mendoza	José	F/T		$63,297	$4,842
Operations	57	Facility Overseer	Non-Exempt	McDean	Dean	F/T	$20.60	$42,840	$3,277
Operations	57	Administrative Assist.	Non-Exempt	Vance	DeDe	F/T	$16.18	$33,660	$2,575
Operations	57	Facility Worker	Non-Exempt	Cruse	Joe	F/T	$16.83	$35,000	$2,678
Operations	57	Facility Worker	Non-Exempt	Franco	Linda	F/T	$16.83	$35,000	$2,678
Operations	57	Facility Worker	Non-Exempt	Haines	Trudy	F/T	$16.83	$35,000	$2,678
Operations	57	Facility Worker	Non-Exempt	Snead	Jon	F/T	$16.83	$35,000	$2,678
Operations	57	Facility Worker	Non-Exempt	Black	Charlie	F/T	$16.83	$35,000	$2,678
Operations	57	Receptionist	Non-Exempt	Smithey	Janet	F/T	$11.18	$23,256	$1,779
Operations	57	Receptionist	Non-Exempt	Morrison	Carolyn	F/T	$11.18	$23,256	$1,779
Preschool	67	Preschool Pastor	Ministerial	Stairs	Julie	F/T		$66,000	
Preschool	67	Assist. Ministry Director	Ministerial	White	Tamika	F/T		$48,500	
Preschool	67	Assistant to Director	Non-Exempt	Peterson	Grace	F/T	$21.07	$43,827	$3,353
Preschool	67	30 Lead Teachers	Non-Exempt	30		27	$17.85	$751,842	$57,516
Preschool	67	30 Teachers	Non-Exempt	30		27	$14.79	$622,955	$47,656
Preschool	67	30 Assistant Teachers	Non-Exempt	30		27	$12.75	$537,030	$41,083

Last	403B %	403B $	Medical Insurance	Medical CoPay 21%	Dental	Vision	Life	Auto	Cell	Total Cost
Jackson	9%	$8,370	**$19,744**	**-$4,146**	**$985**	**$200**	**$885**	**$2,000**	**$918**	**$121,956**
Martinez	8%	$5,059	$16,068	-$3,374	$985	$160	$885	$1,000	$459	$84,482
Manta	2%	$1,122	$8,034	-$1,687	$985	$200	$455	$1,000	$459	$66,668
Jones	2%	$920	$3,005	-$631	$488	$102	$455	$684	$459	$51,482
Stanley	4%	$2,300	$8,034	-$1,687	$985	$200	$455	$684	$459	$68,930
Yang			$3,005	-$631	$985	$200	$455	$1,000	$459	$47,473
Nelson	2%	$816	$19,744	-$4,146	$985	$160	$342			$61,822
Turner	2%	$816	$12,051	-$2,531	$985	$160	$455			$55,857
Beal	4%	$1,510	$12,051	-$2,531	$985	$160	$455			$53,257
Dodson	4%	$1,510	$8,034	-$1,687	$985	$200	$455			$50,124
Baker	8%	$7,440	**$8,034**	**-$1,687**	**$985**	**$200**	**$885**	**$2,000**	**$918**	**$111,775**
Farley	9%	$3,029	$12,051	-$2,531	$985	$160	$885			$50,815
Houdini	9%	$8,370	**$16,068**	**-$3,374**	**$1,231**	**$160**	**$885**	**$2,000**	**$918**	**$119,257**
Steele							$342		$200	$39,475
Fogarty	4%	$3,070	$16,068	-$3,374	$1,231	$160	$455	$684	$459	$101,366
Mays			$6,427	-$1,350	$985	$102	$342		$450	$50,322
Ethelridge	2%	$1,020	$8,034	-$1,687	$1,231	$128	$248		$450	$64,325
Clark										$27,248
Getz	9%	$3,169	$12,051	-$2,531	$985	$200	$329		$200	$52,310
Wilson	9%	$2,093	$25,708	-$5,399	$1,458	$200	$451		$200	$49,746
Borneo			**$16,068**	**-$3,374**	**$985**	**$160**	**$455**	**$3,200**	**$1,200**	**$144,693**
Black			**$16,068**	**-$3,374**	**$985**	**$160**	**$455**	**$3,200**	**$1,200**	**$129,693**
Rearson	4%	$1,632	$12,051	-$2,531	$985	$160	$342			$56,560
Williams	6%	$3,978	$12,051	-$2,531	$985	$160	$342		$459	$86,816
Petrey			$3,005	-$631	$488	$102	$342			$50,001
Mendoza	6%	$3,798	$19,744	-$4,146	$1,458	$200	$342		$459	$89,994
McDean	6%	$2,570	$8,034	-$1,687	$985	$200	$342	$684	$459	$57,705
Vance	9%	$3,029	$8,034	-$1,687	$985	$200	$885			$47,681
Cruse	4%	$1,400	$12,051	-$2,531	$985	$160	$455		$459	$50,657
Franco			$25,708	-$5,399	$1,458	$200	$342		$459	$60,446
Haines	2%	$700	$8,034	-$1,687	$985	$200	$455		$459	$46,823
Snead	4%	$1,400	$12,051	-$2,531	$985	$160	$342		$459	$50,544
Black	8%	$2,800	$19,744	-$4,146	$1,458	$200	$885		$459	$59,077
Smithey	6%	$1,395	$12,051	-$2,531	$985	$160	$885			$37,981
Morrison	2%	$465	$3,005	-$631	$488	$102	$342			$28,806
Preschool										
Stairs	9%	$5,940	$12,051	-$2,531	$985	$160	$885	$1,000	$459	$84,949
White	6%	$2,910	$25,708	-$5,399	$1,458	$200	$885	$684	$459	$75,405
Peterson	2%	$877	$12,051	-$2,531	$985	$160	$885	$684	$459	$60,750
30 Lead										$809,358
30 Teacher										$670,611
30 Assist.										$578,113

SMART MONEY FOR CHURCH SALARIES

Summary of Salaries and Income at WheatFields

Summary of Compensation

Area	Church	Preschool
Salaries	$1,774,106	$2,070,154
FICA	$73,006	$149,608
403B	$73,782	$9,727
Health Insurance	$401,907	$49,810
CoPay	-$84,401	-$10,460
Dental	$33,645	$3,428
Vision	$5,576	$520
Life	$16,988	$2,655
Auto	$18,478	$2,368
Cell	$13,080	$1,377
Total	**$2,326,167**	**$2,279,186**
Benefits	**31%**	**10%**

Fiscal Year 2017-18 Donations and Income

	Midweek Deposit	Sunday Deposit	Weekly Total	Weekly Target	Weekly Delta	Annual Target	Annual Actual	Annual Delta
June	$45,831	$116,721	$162,552	$163,462	-$910	$163,462	$162,552	-$910
June	$66,662	$100,293	$166,955	$163,462	$3,493	$326,923	$329,507	$2,584
June	$90,030	$99,331	$189,361	$163,462	$25,899	$490,385	$518,868	$28,483
June	$66,576	$74,875	$141,451	$163,462	-$22,011	$653,846	$660,319	$6,473
July	$39,037	$72,058	$111,095	$119,143	-$8,048	$772,989	$771,414	-$1,575
July	$94,273	$39,481	$133,754	$119,143	$14,611	$892,132	$905,168	$13,036
July	$89,510	$41,951	$131,461	$119,143	$12,318	$1,011,275	$1,036,629	$25,354
July	$85,481	$31,490	$116,971	$119,143	-$2,172	$1,130,418	$1,153,600	$23,182
July	$90,470	$29,009	$119,479	$119,143	$336	$1,249,561	$1,273,079	$23,518
August	$61,051	$87,481	$148,532	$163,462	-$14,930	$1,413,023	$1,421,611	$8,588
August	$59,281	$101,928	$161,209	$163,462	-$2,253	$1,576,484	$1,582,820	$6,336
August	$45,555	$106,669	$152,224	$163,462	-$11,238	$1,739,946	$1,735,044	-$4,902
August	$51,078	$110,999	$162,077	$163,462	-$1,385	$1,903,407	$1,897,121	-$6,286
September	$32,698	$128,477	$161,175	$143,006	$18,169	$2,046,413	$2,058,296	$11,883
September	$48,442	$98,655	$147,097	$143,006	$4,091	$2,189,418	$2,205,393	$15,974
September	$42,957	$108,831	$151,788	$143,006	$8,782	$2,332,425	$2,357,181	$24,756
September	$97,436	$44,439	$141,875	$143,006	-$1,131	$2,475,431	$2,499,056	$23,625
October	$15,098	$92,378	$107,476	$115,735	-$8,259	$2,591,166	$2,606,532	$15,366
October	$88,448	$47,795	$136,243	$115,735	$20,508	$2,706,901	$2,742,775	$35,874
October	$50,275	$62,851	$113,126	$115,735	-$2,609	$2,822,636	$2,855,901	$33,265

October	$47,387	$70,008	$117,395	$115,735	$1,660	$2,938,371	$2,973,296	$34,925
October	$63,306	$52,272	$115,578	$115,735	-$157	$3,054,106	$3,088,874	$34,768
November	$22,743	$132,894	$155,637	$165,408	-$9,771	$3,219,514	$3,244,511	$24,997
November	$101,893	$110,384	$212,277	$165,408	$46,869	$3,384,922	$3,456,788	$71,866
November	$52,789	$108,440	$161,229	$165,408	-$4,179	$3,550,330	$3,618,017	$67,687
November	$89,089	$100,038	$189,127	$165,408	$23,719	$3,715,738	$3,807,144	$91,406
December	$41,691	$145,890	$187,581	$264,108	-$76,527	$3,979,846	$3,994,725	$14,879
December	$117,964	$144,469	$262,433	$264,108	-$1,675	$4,243,954	$4,257,158	$13,204
December	$140,418	$129,889	$270,307	$264,108	$6,199	$4,508,062	$4,527,465	$19,403
December	$123,575	$168,903	$292,478	$264,108	$28,370	$4,772,170	$4,819,943	$47,773
December	$500,381	$100,403	$600,784	$264,108	$336,676	$5,036,278	$5,420,727	$384,449
January	$30,044	$152,946	$182,990	$163,462	$19,528	$5,199,740	$5,603,717	$403,977
January	$42,663	$91,078	$133,741	$163,462	-$29,721	$5,363,201	$5,737,458	$374,257
January	$31,874	$92,884	$124,758	$163,462	-$38,704	$5,526,663	$5,862,216	$335,553
January	$39,932	$98,007	$137,939	$163,462	-$25,523	$5,690,124	$6,000,155	$310,031
February	$52,005	$91,234	$143,239	$163,462	-$20,223	$5,853,586	$6,143,394	$289,808
February	$38,759	$122,224	$160,983	$163,462	-$2,479	$6,017,048	$6,304,377	$287,329
February	$54,622	$149,873	$204,495	$163,462	$41,033	$6,180,509	$6,508,872	$328,363
February	$39,113	$141,059	$180,172	$163,462	$16,710	$6,343,971	$6,689,044	$345,073
March	$40,004	$162,925	$202,929	$163,462	$39,467	$6,507,432	$6,891,973	$384,541
March	$62,491	$208,482	$270,973	$163,462	$107,511	$6,670,894	$7,162,946	$492,052
March	$49,877	$139,500	$189,377	$163,462	$25,915	$6,834,355	$7,352,323	$517,968
March	$35,005	$162,586	$197,591	$163,462	$34,129	$6,997,817	$7,549,914	$552,097
April	$46,079	$139,001	$185,080	$163,462	$21,618	$7,161,278	$7,734,994	$573,716
April	$51,117	$125,724	$176,841	$163,462	$13,379	$7,324,740	$7,911,835	$587,095
April	$71,127	$132,058	$203,185	$163,462	$39,723	$7,488,201	$8,115,020	$626,819
April	$38,057	$142,999	$181,056	$163,462	$17,594	$7,651,663	$8,296,076	$644,413
April	$39,743	$150,924	$190,667	$163,462	$27,205	$7,815,124	$8,486,743	$671,619
May	$53,853	$149,004	$202,857	$163,462	$39,395	$7,978,586	$8,689,600	$711,014
May	$74,580	$152,494	$227,074	$163,462	$63,612	$8,142,048	$8,916,674	$774,626
May	$49,338	$151,033	$200,371	$163,462	$36,909	$8,305,509	$9,117,045	$811,536
May	$52,093	$142,824	$194,917	$194,491	$426	$8,500,000	$9,311,962	$811,962
Total	$3,553,801	$5,758,161	$9,311,962	$8,500,000	$811,962			
Surplus					9.6%			$811,962

BIBLIOGRAPHY

Bibliography

Augenblick, Palaich and Associates with Chris Stoddard. *Study of Hawaii's Compensation System*. Honolulu: Hawaii State Teacher's Association, November, 2014. Available from www.hsta.org/images/uploads/Comprehensive_Salary_Study_ Hawaii_1.27.15_Web.pdf.

Barnes, Louis B., C. Roland Christensen and Abby J. Hansen. *Teaching and the Case Method: Text, Cases, and Readings*. Boston: Harvard Business Review Press, 3rd edition, 1994.

Bird, Warren. *Leadership Network Large Church Salary, Staffing, and Benefits Survey*. Dallas: Leadership Network, 2018. Available from http://leadnet.org/salary/.

_____. *12 Salary Trends Every Church Leader Should Know: 2016 Large Church Salary Study, Complete Report*. Dallas: Leadership Network and Vanderbloemen Search Group, 2016.

Buford, Bob. *Halftime: Changing Your Game Plan from Success to Significance*, Grand Rapids: Zondervan. Revised and updated edition, 2011.

Busby, Dan. *Qualifications for Ministerial Tax Status*. Excerpted from *Zondervan Church & Nonprofit Tax & Financial Guide* and *Zondervan Minister's Tax & Financial Guide* by Dan Busby. Winchester, Virginia: ECFA. Available from www. ecfa.org/Content/Qualifications-for-Ministerial-Tax-Status.

Busby, Dan, Michael Martin and John Van Drunnen. *Zondervan 2018 Church and Nonprofit Tax and Financial Guide: For 2017 Tax Returns*. Grand Rapids: Zondervan, 2018.

_____. *Zondervan 2018 Minister's Tax and Financial Guide: For 2017 Tax Returns*. Grand Rapids: Zondervan, 2018.

Chamberlain, Kaufman and Jones, Attorneys at Law (Albany: FLSA Home Page), *Coverage under the FLSA*, available at https://www.flsa.com/coverage.html.

Chand, Samuel R. *Cracking Your Church's Culture Code*. San Francisco: Jossey-Bass, 2011.

_____. *Culture Trumps Vision*. Dallas: Leadership Network. June 23, 2015. Available from leadnet.org/culture-trumps-vision/.

Chicago Police Department. *2017 Position & Salary Schedule, Chicago Police Department, Sworn & Civilian Personnel, July-December, 2017*. Revised July 14, 2017. Available from directives.chicagopolice.org/forms/CPD-61.400.pdf.

Christianity Today. Church Law & Tax Report. *Church Salary*. Carol Stream, Illinois: Christianity Today. Available from ChurchSalary.com.

The Church Network. *The Church Salary Survey of the Church Network*. Richardson, Texas: The Church Network and the National Association of Church Business Administration. Available from https://www.ministrypay.com.

City of Orlando. *Compensation*. Available from www.cityoforlando.net/police/recruiting/compensation/.

_____. *Police Pension Fund Participants' Retirement Options*. Available from http://www.cityoforlando.net/pension/police-pension-fund-participants-retirement-options/.

City of Seattle. *Salary and Benefits*. Available from https://www.seattle.gov/police/police-jobs/salary-and-benefits.

Cohen, Patricia. *Where Did Your Pay Raise Go? It May Have Become a Bonus*. The New York Times, February 10, 2018. Available from https://www.nytimes.com/2018/02/10/business/economy/bonus-pay.html.

Evangelical Council for Financial Accountability. *About ECFA*. Available from http://www.ecfa.org/Content/About.

_____. *Pastoral Ordination, Licensure, or Commissioning Procedure*. Winchester, Virginia: ECFA. Available from www.ecfa.org/Content/Pastoral-Ordination-Licensure-or-Commissioning-Procedure.

_____. *Seven Standards of Responsible Stewardship^{TM}*. Winchester, Virginia: ECFA. Available from www.ecfa.org/Content/Standards.

Fletcher, David R. *Exit of a Founding Pastor*. Austin, Texas: XPastor. Available from https://www.xpastor.org/strategy/10-year-planning/exit-of-a-founding-pastor-jeff-jones-slated-to-replace-gene-getz/.

_____. *Four-Wall Discussions*. Austin, Texas: XPastor. Available from https://www.xpastor.org/hey-fletch/four-wall-discussions/.

Franczek Redelete. Attorneys and Counselors. *Lesser Known Exemptions: The 'Ministerial' Exception to the FLSA*. Chicago: Wage Hour Insights, April 7, 2015. Available from https://www.wagehourinsights.com/2015/04/lesser-known-exemptions-the-ministerial-exception-to-the-flsa/.

Glasmeier, Amy K. *The MIT Living Wage Calculation for Orange County, California*. Boston: Massachusetts Institute of Technology, 2018. Available from livingwage.mit.edu/counties/06059.

_____. *The MIT Living Wage Calculation for Orlando-Kissimmee-Sanford, Florida*. Boston: Massachusetts Institute of Technology, 2018. Available from livingwage.mit.edu/metros/36740.

Hammar, Richard R. *Exemption from Social Security: Many Churches Mistakenly Assume that They Are Exempt*. Church Law & Tax Report: July/August, 1992. Carol Stream, Illinois: Christianity Today. Available from https://www.churchlawandtax.com/cltr/1992/july-august/exemption-from-social-security.html.

_____. *Pastor, Church & Law: Church Legal Issues for Pastors*. 4 volumes. Carol Stream, Illinois: Your Church Resources. 4th edition. 2008. Also available from https://www.churchlawandtax.com/library/legal-issues-for-pastors/.

Hawaiʻi Police Department. *Police Officers, County of Hawaiʻi Jobs*. Available from www.hawaiipolice.com/recruitment/police-officers.

Investopedia. *About Investopedia*. New York: Investopedia. Available from https://www.investopedia.com/corp/about.aspx.

_____. *Smart Money*. New York: Investopedia. Available from https://www.investopedia.com/terms/s/smart-money.asp.

Jones, Jeff. *Succession Thoughts*. Austin, Texas: XPastor. Available from https://www.xpastor.org/strategy/10-year-planning/succession-thoughts/.

Merriam-Webster. *Integrity*. Springfield, Massachusetts: Merriam-Webster, updated on April 17, 2018. Available from https://www.merriam-webster.com/dictionary/integrity.

Miller, Stephen. *Don't Overlook 2018 Change in 'Affordability' Safe Harbor Percentage.* Alexandria, Virginia: SHRM, June 9, 2007. Available from https://www.shrm.org/resourcesandtools/hr-topics/benefits/pages/2018-aca-affordability-safe-harbor-percentage.aspx.

Nadeau, Carey Anne. *Massachusetts Institute of Technology Living Wage Calculator, User's Guide, Technical Notes for Amy K. Glasmeier, 2017 Update."* Boston: Department of Urban Studies and Planning, Massachusetts Institute of Technology. Available from http://livingwage.mit.edu/resources/Living-Wage-User-Guide-and-Technical-Notes-2017.pdf.

Norris, Louise. *Does Every Business with 50 or More Employees Pay a Penalty if it Doesn't Offer Affordable, Comprehensive Insurance?* St. Louis Park, Minnesota: HealthInsurance.org, January 9, 2018. Available from https://www.healthinsurance.org/faqs/will-every-business-with-more-than-50-employees-pay-a-penalty-if-they-dont-offer-affordable-comprehensive-insurance/.

Orange County [Florida] Public School System. *Orange County Public Schools 2016-2017 Instructional Grandfathered/Performance Salary Schedule.* Board approved June, 14, 2016. Available from https://www.ocps.net/UserFiles/Servers/Server_54619/File/Departments/Human%20Resources/Compensation/Salary%20Schedules/Salary%20Schedule%20docs%20WP/Open%20Range%20Schedule%202016-17.pdf.

_____. *Orange County Public Schools 2017-18 School Based Administrator Performance Salary Schedule.* Board approved July 25, 2017. Available from https://www.ocps.net/UserFiles/Servers/Server_54619/File/Departments/Human%20Resources/Compensation/Admin-School%20Based%202017-18%20Salary%20Schedule%20FINAL.pdf.

PayScale. *Cost of Living Calculator - Orange County, California.* Seattle: PayScale, 2018. Available from https://www.payscale.com/cost-of-living-calculator/California-Orange-County.

_____. *Cost of Living Calculator - Orlando, Florida.* Seattle: PayScale, 2018. Available from https://www.payscale.com/cost-of-living-calculator/Florida-Orlando.

Pensions and Benefits USA, The Church of the Nazarene. *Church Employees as Independent Contractors*, posted with permission. Winchester, Virginia: ECFA. Available from www.ecfa.org/Documents/ChurchEmployees_IndependentContractors.pdf.

Ramsey, Dave. *How It Started*. Brentwood, Tennessee: Ramsey Solutions. Available from https://www.daveramsey.com/careers/about-dave?snid=footer.company.about.

_____. *Smart Money Tour*. Brentwood, Tennessee: Ramsey Solutions. Available from https://www.daveramsey.com/store/smart-money-tour/cSmartMoney.html.

Shapiro, T. Rees. *Garza Receives Four-Year Contract Extension as Fairfax Schools Superintendent*. The Washington Post, July 1, 2016. Available from https://www.washingtonpost.com/local/education/garza-receives-four-year-contract-extension-as-fairfax-schools-superintendent/2016/07/01/fc7f1c18-3fb9-11e6-80bc-d06711fd2125_story.html.

School Loop. *2016-2017 Teacher Salary Schedule 188 days, Newport-Mesa Unified School District, Salary Schedule #44*. Approved January 31, 2017. San Francisco: School Loop. Available from nmusd-ca.schoolloop.com/file/1281197594254/1246559508790/561603266115719012.pdf.

_____. *Management Salary Schedule 2016-2017, Newport-Mesa Unified School District*. Approved January 31, 2017. San Francisco: School Loop. Available from nmusd-ca.schoolloop.com/file/1281197594254/1246559508790/8305085910870398259.pdf.

_____. *Management Transportation Allowance, Newport-Mesa Unified School District*. San Francisco: School Loop. Available from nmusd-ca.schoolloop.com/file/1281197594254/1246559508790/8156724607258361966.pdf.

Society for Human Resource Management. *What Is the Difference Between California Overtime Exemption Requirements and Federal Overtime Exemption Requirements?* December 26, 2017. Alexandria, Virginia: SHRM. Available from https://www.shrm.org/resourcesandtools/tools-and-samples/hr-qa/pages/californiaexemptionrequirements.aspx.

State of California, Department of Industrial Relations. *Meal Periods*. Revised July 11, 2012. Available from https://www.dir.ca.gov/dlse/faq_mealperiods.htm.

State of California. Department of Industrial Relations. Labor Commissioner's Office. *Minimum Wage*. December 2016. Available from https://www.dir.ca.gov/dlse/faq_minimumwage.htm.

Thieme, Daniel L. and Sebastian Chilco. *Exempt Employee Pay Minimums Will Increase in 2018 in Various States*. San Francisco: Littler Mendelson, December 11, 2017.

Available from https://www.littler.com/publication-press/publication/exempt-employee-pay-minimums-will-increase-2018-various-states.

Transparent California. *2013-2016 Salaries for Newport-Mesa Unified.* Las Vegas: Nevada Policy Research Institute. Available from https://transparentcalifornia. com/salaries/school-districts/orange/newport-mesa-unified/.

United States Centers for Medicare & Medicaid Services. *Affordable Care Act (ACA).* Available from https://www.healthcare.gov/glossary/affordable-care-act/.

United States Department of Labor. *Health Plans & Benefits: ERISA.* Available from https://www.dol.gov/general/topic/health-plans/erisa.

_____. *Our Mission.* Available from https://www.dol.gov/general/aboutdol/mission.

United States Department of Labor. Bureau of Labor Statistics. *Databases, Tables & Calculators by Subject.* Data extracted on: April 20, 2018. Available from https:// data.bls.gov/timeseries/CUUR0000SA0L1E?output_view=pct_12mths.

_____. *Employer Costs for Employee Compensation news release text.* For release 10:00 am (EDT) Tuesday, March 20, 2018. Last modified date: March 20, 2018. Available from https://www.bls.gov/news.release/ecec.nr0.htm.

United States Department of Labor. Employee Benefits Security Administration. *COBRA Continuation Health Coverage FAQs.* Available from https://www.dol. gov/agencies/ebsa/about-ebsa/our-activities/resource-center/faqs/cobra-continuation-health-coverage-compliance.

United States Department of Labor. Employment Standards Administration. Wage and Hour Division. *Opinion Letter FLSA2006-23NA.* October 26, 2006. Available from https://www.dol.gov/whd/opinion/FLSANA/2006/2006_10_26_23NA_ FLSA.pdf

United States Department of Labor. Wage and Hour Division. *Defining and Delimiting the Exemptions for Executive, Administrative, Professional, Outside Sales and Computer Employees; Final Rule.* April 23, 2004. Available from https://www. dol.gov/whd/overtime/regulations.pdf.

_____. *Fact Sheet #17A: Exemption for Executive, Administrative, Professional, Computer & Outside Sales Employees Under the Fair Labor Standards Act (FLSA).* Revised July 2008. Available from https://www.dol.gov/whd/overtime/ fs17a_overview.pdf.

_____. *Handy Reference Guide to the Fair Labor Standards Act*. Revised September, 2017. Available from https://www.dol.gov/whd/regs/compliance/hrg.htm.

_____. *Opinion Letter FLSA2005-12NA*. September 23, 2005 Available from https://www.dol.gov/whd/opinion/FLSANA/2005/2005_09_23_12NA_FLSA.htm.

_____. *Overtime*. Revised January, 2018. Available from https://www.dol.gov/whd/overtime/final2016/.

_____. *Overtime Pay*. Available from https://www.dol.gov/whd/overtime_pay.htm.

_____. *Questions and Answers from the General Information Overtime Webinars*. Revised January, 2018. Available from https://www.dol.gov/whd/overtime/final2016/webinarfaq.htm.

United States Department of the Treasury. Internal Revenue Service. *Elective FICA Exemption - Churches and Church-Controlled Organizations*. Last reviewed or updated, August 4, 2017. Available from https://www.irs.gov/charities-non-profits/churches-religious-organizations/elective-fica-exemption-churches-and-church-controlled-organizations.

_____. *Form 4361: Application for Exemption From Self-Employment Tax for Use by Ministers, Members of Religious Orders and Christian Science Practitioners*. Revised January 2011. Available from https://www.irs.gov/pub/irs-pdf/f4361.pdf.

_____. *Form 8274: Certification by Churches and Qualified Church-Controlled Organizations Electing Exemption From Employer Social Security and Medicare Taxes*. Revised August, 2014. Available from https://www.irs.gov/pub/irs-pdf/f8274.pdf.

_____. *IRS Issues Guidance on Tax Treatment of Cell Phones; Provides Small Business Recordkeeping Relief*. September 14, 2011. Available from https://www.irs.gov/newsroom/irs-issues-guidance-on-tax-treatment-of-cell-phones-provides-small-business-recordkeeping-relief.

_____. *Publication 517, Social Security and Other Information for Members of the Clergy and Religious Workers*. December 29, 2017. Available from https://www.irs.gov/pub/irs-pdf/p517.pdf.

_____. *Unrelated Business Income Tax*. Last reviewed or updated, April 3, 2018. Available from https://www.irs.gov/charities-non-profits/unrelated-business-income-tax.

United States Equal Employment Opportunity Commission. *Questions and Answers: Religious Discrimination in the Workplace*. Revised January 31, 2011. Available from https://www.eeoc.gov/policy/docs/qanda_religion.html.

United States Social Security Administration. *Cost-of-Living Adjustment (COLA) Information for 2018*. Available from https://www.ssa.gov/news/cola/.

_____. *What is FICA?* March, 2017. Available from https://www.ssa.gov/thirdparty/materials/pdfs/educators/What-is-FICA-Infographic-EN-05-10297.pdf.

Vega, Priscella. *Newport-Mesa Schools Superintendent Gets $34,450 Bonus for 'Exceptional' Performance*. The Los Angeles Times, December 13, 2017. Available from www.latimes.com/socal/daily-pilot/news/tn-dpt-me-nmusd-supt-20171213-story.html.

Wikipedia. *Dave Ramsey*. Page last edited on April 21, 2018. San Francisco: Wikimedia Foundation. Available from https://en.wikipedia.org/wiki/Dave_Ramsey.

_____. *Hosanna Tabor Evangelical Lutheran Church & School vs. the Equal Opportunity Employment Commission*. Page last edited on April 13, 2018. San Francisco: Wikimedia Foundation. Available from https://en.wikipedia.org/wiki/Hosanna-Tabor_Evangelical_Lutheran_Church_&_School_v._Equal_Employment_Opportunity_Commission.

XPastor. *Operations 101*. Austin, Texas: XPastor. Available from https://www.xpastor.org/courses/ops-101-staffing/.

_____. *Compensation Survey*. Austin, Texas: XPastor. Available from https://www.xpastor.org/courses/church-compensation/.

Zenefits. *Compliance Checklist: Federal Employment Laws You Need to Know at Every Stage of Your Company's Growth*. June 12, 2017. San Francisco: YourPeople. Available from https://www.zenefits.com/blog/compliance-checklist-each-company-size-threshold/.